EDUCATION, POLITICS, AND PUBLIC LIFE

Series Editors:
Henry A. Giroux, McMaster University
Susan Searls Giroux, McMaster University

Within the last three decades, education as a political, moral, and ideological practice has become central to rethinking not only the role of public and higher education, but also the emergence of pedagogical sites outside of the schools—which include, but are not limited to, the Internet, television, film, magazines, and the media of print culture. Education as both a form of schooling and public pedagogy reaches into every aspect of political, economic, and social life. What is particularly important in this highly interdisciplinary and politically nuanced view of education are a number of issues that now connect learning to social change, the operations of democratic public life, and the formation of critically engaged individual and social agents. At the center of this series are questions regarding what young people, adults, academics, artists, and cultural workers need to know to be able to live in an inclusive and just democracy and what it would mean to develop institutional capacities to reintroduce politics and public commitment into everyday life. The books in this series aim to play a vital role in rethinking the entire project of the related themes of politics, democratic struggles, and critical education within the global public sphere.

SERIES EDITORS

HENRY A. GIROUX holds the Global TV Network Chair in English and Cultural Studies at McMaster University in Canada. He is on the editorial and advisory boards of numerous national and international scholarly journals. Professor Giroux was selected as a Kappa Delta Pi Laureate in 1998 and was the recipient of a Getty Research Institute Visiting Scholar Award in 1999. He was the recipient of the Hooker Distinguished Professor Award for 2001. He received an Honorary Doctorate of Letters from Memorial University of Newfoundland in 2005. His most recent books include *Take Back Higher Education* (co-authored with Susan Searls Giroux, 2006); *America on the Edge* (2006); *Beyond the Spectacle of Terrorism* (2006); *Stormy Weather: Katrina and the Politics of Disposability* (2006); *The University in Chains: Confronting the Military-Industrial-Academic Complex* (2007), and *Against the Terror of Neoliberalism: Politics Beyond the Age of Greed* (2008).

SUSAN SEARLS GIROUX is Associate Professor of English and Cultural Studies at McMaster University. Her most recent books include *The Theory Toolbox* (co-authored with Jeff Nealon, 2004) and *Take Back Higher Education* (co-authored with Henry A. Giroux, 2006) and *Between Race and Reason: Violence, Intellectual Responsibility, and the University to Come* (2010). Professor Giroux is also the Managing Editor of *The Review of Education, Pedagogy, and Cultural Studies*.

Critical Pedagogy in Uncertain Times: Hope and Possibilities
Edited by Sheila L. Macrine

The Gift of Education: Public Education and Venture Philanthropy
Kenneth J. Saltman

*Feminist Theory in Pursuit of the Public: Women and
the "Re-Privatization" of Labor*
Robin Truth Goodman

*Hollywood's Exploited: Public Pedagogy, Corporate Movies, and
Cultural Crisis*
Edited by Benjamin Frymer, Tony Kashani, Anthony J. Nocella, II, and
Richard Van Heertum; with a Foreword by Lawrence Grossberg

*Education out of Bounds: Reimagining Cultural Studies for
a Posthuman Age*
Tyson E. Lewis and Richard Kahn

Academic Freedom in the Post-9/11 Era
Edited by Edward J. Carvalho and David B. Downing

Educating Youth for a World beyond Violence
H. Svi Shapiro

*Rituals and Student Identity in Education: Ritual Critique for
a New Pedagogy*
Richard A. Quantz with Terry O'Connor and Peter Magolda (forthcoming)

America According to Colbert: Satire as Public Pedagogy post-9/11
Sophia A. McClennen (forthcoming)

Citizen Youth: Culture, Activism, and Agency in a Neoliberal Era
Jacqueline Joan Kennelly (forthcoming)

Educating Youth for a World beyond Violence

A Pedagogy for Peace

H. Svi Shapiro

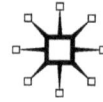

EDUCATING YOUTH FOR A WORLD BEYOND VIOLENCE
Copyright © H. Svi Shapiro, 2010.
All rights reserved.
First published in 2010 by
PALGRAVE MACMILLAN®
in the United States—a division of St. Martin's Press LLC,
175 Fifth Avenue, New York, NY 10010.

Where this book is distributed in the UK, Europe and the rest of the world, this is by Palgrave Macmillan, a division of Macmillan Publishers Limited, registered in England, company number 785998, of Houndmills, Basingstoke, Hampshire RG21 6XS.

Palgrave Macmillan is the global academic imprint of the above companies and has companies and representatives throughout the world.

Palgrave® and Macmillan® are registered trademarks in the United States, the United Kingdom, Europe and other countries.

ISBN: 978–0–230–10933–9

Library of Congress Cataloging-in-Publication Data

Shapiro, H. Svi.
    Educating youth for a world beyond violence : a pedagogy for peace / H. Svi Shapiro.
        p. cm.—(Educations, politics, and public life series)
        ISBN 978–0–230–10933–9 (alk. paper)
        1. Peace—Study and teaching. 2. Moral education. I. Title.

JZ5534.S54 2010
303.6'6071—dc22   2010023975

A catalogue record of the book is available from the British Library.

Design by Newgen Imaging Systems (P) Ltd., Chennai, India.

First edition: December 2010

For
Sherry, who made possible our six extraordinary months in South Africa and David Purpel, friend, mentor and comrade for 30 years

Books by H. Svi Shapiro

Education and Hope in Troubled Times: Visions of Change for Our Children's World (2009)

Losing Heart: The Moral and Spiritual Crisis of America's Children (2005)

Critical Social Issues in American Education: Democracy and Meaning in a Globalizing World, co-edited with David E. Purpel (2004)

Body Movements: Pedagogy, Politics and Social Change, co-edited with Sherry Shapiro (2002)

Strangers in the Land: Pedagogy, Modernity, and Jewish Experience (1999)

Critical Social Issues in American Education: Transformation in a Postmodern World, co-edited with David E. Purpel (1998)

Beyond Liberation and Excellence: Reconstructing the Public Discourse on Education, with David E. Purpel (1995)

Critical Social Issues in American Education: Towards the 21st Century, co-edited with David E. Purpel (1992)

Between Capitalism and Democracy: Educational Policy and the Crisis of the Welfare State (1990)

Schools and Meaning: Essays on the Moral Nature of Schooling, co-edited with David E. Purpel (1985)

The world we have created is a product of our thinking; it cannot be changed without changing our thinking.
—Albert Einstein

No one is born hating another person because of the colour of his skin, or his background, or his religion. People must learn to hate, and if they can learn to hate, they can be taught to love, for love comes more naturally to the human heart than its opposite.
—Nelson Mandela

Punishment and fear have replaced compassion and social responsibility as the most important modality mediating the relationship of youth to the larger social order.
—Henry Giroux

Imagine there's no countries
It isn't hard to do
Nothing to kill or die for
And no religion too
Imagine all the people
Living life in peace
    —John Lennon

Peace is possible. We are not talking vaguely, we mean concrete action. That action is directed to ourselves and to the world at the same time.
—Thich Nhat Hanh

Nation shall not lift up sword against nation,
Neither shall they learn war anymore
        —Isaiah

War is a drug.
    —Christopher Hedges

Contents

Acknowledgments	xi
1 Giving Peace a Chance	1
2 Truth and Violence	25
3 Undoing the Narrative of Competition	49
4 Justice Then Peace	75
5 The Violence of Invisibility	103
6 Violence and the Crisis of Meaning	129
7 Critical Citizenship	153
8 A Pedagogy of Peace	179
Appendix: Peace Organizations	207
Notes	219
Index	227

Acknowledgments

I wish to express my appreciation to the University of North Carolina at Greensboro for granting me a research leave that made possible the writing of much of this manuscript. My thanks to Tema Okun who worked diligently to compile the list of peace organizations found in the appendix of this volume. I am very grateful for the support of Henry Giroux in my quest to publish this work. I am appreciative of the suggestions and supportive words of my dear friend and colleague David Purpel in respect to this manuscript. While in Cape Town I was privileged to spend some time in conversation about the politics of peace and reconciliation with Archbishop Emeritus Desmond Tutu. This was a moving and inspiring experience that I remember with deep appreciation. The *baristas* at "Gloria Jean's" coffee shop in Cape Town provided me with a friendly and hospitable environment where some of my best conversations and moments of reflection took place. And, finally, to Sherry, my partner and comrade in life, my deep gratitude for your love, support, and patience. In my moments of caution or panic you remind me of the joys of change and possibility.

Chapter One

Giving Peace a Chance

> Peace and democracy go hand in hand.
> It is not easy to talk about peace to people who are mourning every day.
> I will go down on my knees to beg those who want to drag our country into bloodshed and persuade them not to do so.
> Peace and prosperity, tranquility and security are only possible if these are enjoyed by all without discrimination.
> From *In the Words of Nelson Mandela*,
> edited by Jennifer Crwys-Williams

> If you could read the secret history of your enemies, you should find in each man's life sorrow and suffering enough to disarm all hostilities.
> —From *The Native Commissioner*, by Shaun Johnson

Violence Names Our World

I am writing the first chapter of this book while sitting in my comfortable apartment in Cape Town, South Africa, enjoying the privilege of a research leave from my university in the United States. The apartment is set in the beautiful leafy suburb of Newlands. As I write I hear the sweet chirping of birds in the trees and the gurgling of an outside fountain. And from my window I see the magnificent peaks of Table Mountain. It is hard to believe, sitting here, that nothing but peace and beauty surrounds me. Unfortunately, what I describe represents only a part of the present truth here. For our apartment complex, like every other residence in the vicinity, is surrounded by electrified wire. We have a 24-hour security guard at the front gate. And, like almost every other residence in this part of the city, attached to the wall at the entrance is a warning stating that this place is protected by "armed response." The ubiquity of these security measures is a reflection that South Africa is in the throws of a crime epidemic.

The crime is often more than the merely instrumental forms of burglary and street muggings. It is often accompanied by deliberate and sadistic violence against victims. There is an intentional wish to hurt, maim, rape, and kill victims. Alongside the beauty and vibrancy of this wonderful city there are the constant danger warnings about being out at night, about locking one's car doors at all times, about being alert to who is around you when entering your house. Fear of violence stalks people's lives.

Here in South Africa it is certainly possible to understand some of the motivation for crime. Fifteen years after this country's liberation from apartheid, its society remains deeply unequal. A short distance from the affluent neighborhoods, with their gleaming, high-priced stores, chic restaurants and bars, and Mercedes dealerships, are impoverished shanty towns and rough townships with their poverty, unemployment, drugs, and violence. It is not difficult to understand why the unmet expectations of democracy in the new South Africa are so quickly transformed into forms of rage and a brutal, depoliticized form of class warfare. If the official and state organized mechanisms for producing a better life fail, then other, more violent forms of redistribution emerge. The latter do not, however, follow a rational path of reallocating wealth. The fury and frustration are often directed not just at the wealthy minority, but at those very individuals who share the same economic struggles. The quest for social justice becomes social pathology. Illegal acts and crime are equally about venting one's fury and frustration at the hopelessness of one's situation. Most violence here takes place *within* the impoverished townships themselves. Sadly, much of it is directed at those with whom one is intimate, and who are most vulnerable. Violence against women is frequent and brutal, licensed by a machismo that diminishes and demeans women. It is not merely democracy that raises expectations of a better life, but capitalism, too. Whether or not one has a job or an income, the images of a life filled with every satisfaction and pleasure surrounds us. The propaganda of consumption blasts from every billboard and TV. This is what you must have to make yourself happy, secure, sexy, beautiful, and exciting. Don't wait! Get it now! Everyone is entitled to have more, and to have it immediately. Certainly South Africa is not alone in the phenomenon of violent crime. Everywhere the confluence of poverty, unemployment, hopelessness, and the insistent seductions of a materialist culture and consumerist pleasure goad individuals towards an angry and often violent retaliation towards a society that promises everything and provides very little.

Unmet Promises: Global Rage

Perhaps what I have described in South Africa is a metaphor for our world—comfortable and attractive neighborhoods, with their spacious and well-stocked homes and their educated and healthy children and adults, secured by high walls and fences to protect them from the majority, who live in a world that offers them little prospect of a decent, comfortable, or dignified life. And we are all subjected to the same relentless and seductive messages about the joy and excitement that comes with owning and buying more. The inequities and frustrations of a city or a country have now gone global. Is it any wonder that violence and the fear of violence now name our world? We find ourselves living in a world in which promise and reality meet and clash with greater intensity. Countries conspire, wheedle, and sometimes attack others in order to maintain or expand their hold on raw materials or to keep their advantages in trading, and elites kill and destroy their opponents in order to ensure that they can continue to enjoy their grotesque lifestyles and the privileges of uncontested power. It is a world in which corporations lie, cheat, and buy influence so as to expand their profits, and men harass, threaten, and assault women so as to keep the material and psychological benefits of masculinity. In which minorities, whether racial, ethnic, sexual, or religious, become the foil for social and economic grievances with which they may have little to do, but for which they are convenient scapegoats for populist anxiety about loss of status, jobs, or security. And in which individuals increasingly learn to behave with distance and caution towards others whom they suspect will use and manipulate them to gain some advantage.

This is a world in which violence takes many forms. In which children are enlisted as soldiers to serve the interests of corrupt dictators, and in which tens of thousands of girls and young women are kidnapped, traded, and violently sexually exploited. In which the most sophisticated and deadly weapons the world has ever seen are unleashed with devastating effect on poor and undeveloped countries. It is a world in which greedy political and business elites appropriate the land and natural resources of indigenous peoples who have resided on them for countless generations. And in which nature itself is contaminated and made uninhabitable because of the callous irresponsibility of corporations that increasingly rule our planet. It is a world in which there is the unseen, though massive, theft of money and resources that might be used to feed, house, and provide medical care for millions, but is spent instead on new and more lethal weapons systems. A world in which hatred is stirred up among neighboring groups who are willing to maim, mutilate, and murder one another in the name of righting an injustice. And in which, in many places, migrants or members of minority groups walk in fear that they will be assaulted, harassed, or summarily deprived of their homes and livelihoods. Beyond this there is the insidious and pervasive violence of human relationships in which children are frequently abused; in which women are commonly assaulted, injured, and sometimes murdered; and in which there continues to be a culture of violence directed towards gays and lesbians.

The Insidious Culture of Violence

Violence is much more than individual or even collective acts of terror or brutality. It is insinuated into the very texture of culture, invading our thoughts and sensibilities and warping the nature of everyday life. Globalization sweeps away the bonds of community and ways of living and working developed over generations. It disrupts and destroys the fabric of trust, interdependence, and sociability upon which ordered and viable human life depends. Alongside the wonders and extraordinary powers of technological change is a darker reality—one that makes masses of human beings expendable and replaceable by machines, and that is making our environment increasingly inhospitable to continued life on earth. Consumer capitalism invades every aspect of our waking lives (as well as our dreams) with its message of materialism and money. Under its influence, every aspect of our humanity becomes a salable commodity. Human beings learn to view themselves and others as performers vying to make the right impression and present themselves in the most alluring, successful, or compelling way. Sociability becomes a matter of gaming and strategies. A capitalist ethic defines our lives more and more around egoist self-interests. In every social arena, children and adults are urged to see themselves and their needs as the sole focus of their concerns. Other people become viewed as obstacles to our own selfish pursuits, whether on the roads, in workplaces, in schools, and even in our intimate personal relationships. And the pervasive presence of competitive individualism in our lives makes human interaction increasingly characterized by aggression and invidious comparison. Our world becomes a place in which we quickly become the objects of others' envy, resentment, or even murderous intent. Not surprisingly, in this moral climate, as Jonathan Sacks points out,[1]

Codes of civility, self-restraint and politeness have broken down, giving rise to new forms of verbal and physical abuse. A doctor, appearing as part of a television discussion of an illness, is howled down by the audience who disagrees with his suggestion that it may be of psychosomatic origin. Politicians confronted by a hostile interviewer storm out of the studio. Motorists break off arguments and engage in direct violence in a new syndrome described as "road rage"... Increasingly street attacks are justified in terms of the affront given by "staring" or "dissing"... There is no comparison between linguistic and physical violence, but they are ends of a common spectrum, part of a general fraying of the civic bond which allows strangers to meet and differ without either assaulting the integrity or the person of the other.

Although Sacks writes this from the viewpoint of someone living in Britain, it is not difficult to see the similarities with the American experience, in which Jerry Springer and others have helped make TV entertainment of people verbally and physically assaulting one another over personal and intimate matters and disagreements. And in which cable news networks and radio call-in shows have reduced the culture of reasoned conversation to slanderous *ad hominem* attacks and shouting matches between polarized antagonists. And, on a more lethal level, in which those who disagree with the right of women to choose to abort an unwanted pregnancy take it into their hands to kill doctors who perform such procedures.

We must, as a result, see violence as something that is present in more than the visible acts of physical harm. Violence is present in the very way we treat one another—in our work situations, schools, families, sports, and social lives. It is present wherever we see or treat others as beings to be exploited, made invisible, jettisoned, manipulated, objectified, connived against, outmaneuvered, ridiculed, bullied, or cheated.

Education for What?

How strange it is that when we talk about educating our children, so little of all this seems to enter into our private or public discourse. I argue in this book that nothing is more important to human beings now than our need for a more peaceful, less violent world (and violence is understood here in all of its manifestations). Yet when parents, politicians, or educators talk about the educational needs of our children, questions about peace are almost never on the agenda. Given the fear of guns and shootings in schools, security is a concern and plans for

6   EDUCATING YOUTH FOR A WORLD BEYOND VIOLENCE

how to detect and search for weapons, as well as the need for adequate psychological monitoring and counseling of students, are a priority. Yet the issue of violence is considered only in the most limited and palliative form. It rarely extends beyond the immediate concern to seek out the potential perpetrators and to secure buildings. Where, we may ask, are the demands for a more intensive engagement with our students about violence in our society and in our world? Where is the curriculum that seeks to explore the pervasiveness of violent behavior among human beings, and where are the possibilities for creating more peaceful and non-antagonistic cultures? Where are the opportunities for young people to question the degree to which societies like ours invest such huge resources in the development of weapons of war and why there are so many people in our world engaged in military activities?

On one level it is certainly not difficult to see the way that schools, to a great degree, play shy at engaging young people around matters that directly bear on their lives as future citizens. Such "relevant" matters necessarily raise social, moral, and political concerns that almost certainly generate passionately held views and touch on beliefs that are rooted in family, community, and religious convictions. Yet if we are, again, to take seriously the role of education in democratic society, classrooms must indeed become places where potentially contentious matters that reveal conflicting values and perspectives can be debated and critically interrogated. A visit to just about any high school class quickly reveals the boredom and detachment that most learning now produces as students find little in their day-to-day education that speaks to matters of compelling interest or passionate engagement. Most of the emotion generated in classrooms today is the result of students' fears and anxieties about test scores or grades rather than the kind that is produced when students are asked to reflect upon, and struggle with, the really crucial issues that confront human beings in today's world. Even when social or moral issues are raised, they are invariably approached with the same purely instrumental attitude that students bring to solving an algebraic equation or parsing a sentence of language.

Constraints on schools to become places of serious democratic intent also come from the political and religious right. These forces have worked to ensure that the classroom is a place that values ideological conformity and intellectual timidity.[2] Their goal is to resist any attempt to make education a process that allows and encourages students to reflect and consider, and, where appropriate, challenge a culture's prevailing beliefs, attitudes, ideas, and assumptions. With great success they have ensured that American textbooks are reduced to a bland mush that erases and eliminates anything that might be a catalyst for serious intellectual and moral engagement with issues that determine the quality and character of life in the twenty-first century. Among these, things that might lead to reflection on issues of violence, war, militarism, and a culture of dehumanization are quickly removed from the curriculum under the guise of being unpatriotic and anti-American. For teachers, to refuse these constraints is to put their future employment at risk. Although the right has quite aptly asserted that education is always a moral matter in which values and beliefs are transmitted, it has usually equated morality with a narrow and unquestioning blend of religious conservatism, free-market capitalism, and American triumphalism. It excludes from this process the deep and courageous questioning that comes from our democratic and religious commitments, that calls us to reflect upon, and challenge, those institutions, practices, and ways of living that violate the humanity, dignity, and worth of all human beings.

Factories of Conformity

The ideology of moral and social conformity is by no means the only force that shapes education in ways that exclude a serious concern with questions of war, violence, and dehumanization. Teaching is increasingly gripped by the mania of measurable outcomes, objectively assessed performance, and standardized testing. Fueled by the panic of falling standards and inadequate accountability, politicians, business leaders, and others have driven our schools toward becoming testing factories in which only those things that are quantifiable have any real curricular value. And a regime that stresses the constant measurement of student achievement shapes life for our children. The grim consequences of all this are now well documented. Students face ever-mounting pressure to succeed in a hothouse competitive environment. It is no surprise that we see increasing signs of stress and anxiety among young people. (In the United Kingdom this mounting level of anxiety has led to well-publicized calls for a change in direction away from the emphasis on high-stakes testing.) Teachers are increasingly forced to make the classroom a place in which test performance is the central activity. Preparation and rehearsal for the test occupies much of classroom time. The relentlessness of this process drives away some of the best and most creative teachers who are looking for something more stimulating and humane in their work. And most sadly, this regime of demonstrable accountability empties education of anything that cannot be measured and tested in a standardized form.[3] The result is a curriculum that becomes increasingly narrow and constrained, eliminating anything that might demand more complex, interpretive, or imaginative responses from students. The arts and other forms of creative activity become marginalized or left out entirely. Or they, too, are transformed into more rigidly structured and "objective" forms of learning. There is less time in the classroom for things that depend on dialogue, discussion, and the development of respectful and tolerant social relationships. In other words, the skills and dispositions that are necessary to an engaged and reflective civic life. The classroom becomes a place less and less concerned with students as holistic beings and educating individuals in the totality of their lives as moral, intellectual, imaginative, and spiritual persons. In this sense the goal of peace education, which (and as I argue in this book) demands educating students in the fullness of their humanity, is negated by the limited and narrowly defined focus that subsumes our schools today. The call to focus on peace in education is necessarily a call to re-envision the very way we educate young people, away from the deadening and confined forms that currently dominate our classrooms.

Much of educational reform in recent years has been driven by the demands of business for an adequately trained and prepared workforce. We are frequently informed that our economic future as a state and a nation depends on schools producing individuals with the skills needed by corporate employers. In many ways business executives working with politicians have driven the "train" of educational reform in the United States and helped to shape and define the goals and purposes of education. Whether the White House or State House is occupied by Democrats or Republicans, there is wide agreement that the first priority of schooling is to ensure increasing productivity and economic competitiveness. In the light of this, it is easy to see why, for example, math and science are given far greater emphasis than other areas of the curriculum. Or why, in higher education, general or liberal education is increasingly supplanted by a focus on job skills and knowledge. As argued by a number of commentators, universities have increasingly become adjuncts of business in their funding, research aims, and curricular focus.[4] It is not difficult to see why the notion that education is primarily about work and vocational or professional opportunities finds support more widely within the community. Certainly it is understandable that parents would be concerned about the future employment prospects for their children. For most of us, adult security depends on the acquisition of skills and qualifications that can promise future jobs and a decent income. The instability and rapidity of change in the global economic situation makes parents' concerns even greater. Yet in defining education in this limited way, something very important is being lost—a larger vision of education that speaks to us as citizens of a democratic society. When education is reduced to the process of simply preparing us for work, it denies our role as beings that have a moral responsibility for helping to shape and determine the world in which we live. Education that is all about jobs and work represents a truncated view of what it means to be human. It ignores the fact that human beings must learn to live with, and care for, one another in our families, communities, nation, and globally. It says nothing about our responsibility for sustaining the earth. And it offers nothing that teaches us how we, collectively and with respect for our differences, are able to determine and manage our shared world. In short, an educational vision that is all about job preparation and training is based in an impoverished understanding of the meaning of being human.[5]

A Holistic Vision

Educating for peace is always a holistic process. It means recognizing that for human beings to move towards a less violent and more cooperative and caring mode of existence, the broad development of all our potentialities will be required. It will demand change and development in our social consciousness and our capacity to reason, in our sentient life as feeling and embodied creatures, in our moral sensitivity and conscience, and in an awakening or enlargement of our spiritual awareness. The kind of education that schools are now focused upon is hardly capable of bringing about such change. The emphasis on performance and measurable outcomes leads to a denial of the relevance of anything that cannot be immediately turned into quantifiable data. An empirically driven education can have little relevance to the quest for moral and spiritual change with its more intangible, but nonetheless crucial, nature. Nor can it speak to an education that is about our emotional lives with its far more complex and interior qualities. The attempt to reduce human experience to a series of test bubbles rests on a simplistic, cartoon-like version of individual complexity. And can there be any doubt as to the conflict between a standardized education with its "one right answer" and an education that seeks to encourage the questioning and challenging of a single truth and an appreciation for multiple ways of understanding the world and our lives?

Finding our way to a more peaceful world will mean constructing a world that is more just, more compassionate, more democratic, and more reverential of all life. Education can and should be an important component in pursuing this goal. What and how we teach our children is surely a critical dimension in the social and moral changes that we so urgently need. But it will mean a bold and radical re-visioning of both the purpose of education and the way we seek to teach. In my own state of North Carolina, the State Board of Education recently decided that teacher training needs to be re-oriented to (and here I quote) "preparing students for twenty-first century life." On the surface this would appear to be a positive step forward. Yet after attending several day-long retreats for university faculty concerned with teaching licensure I discovered to my disappointment that only about 20 minutes were actually allocated to a discussion of what human beings in the twenty-first century may actually *need* by way of preparation. There was virtually no time for serious conversation about the kind of social, ethical, environmental, economic, and technological challenges that human beings will need to be able to confront and address in this new century. Certainly there was no discussion about how we might help teachers shape a world that is less violent, inequitable, or militaristic (the latter being not so surprising given the centrality of military bases to the economy and employment in North Carolina). Instead, most of our time was spent arguing about how we would organize and assess the new state plan. It also became pretty clear that those who were pushing the plan probably had in mind getting schools to be more focused on job preparation and training rather than anything more fundamental was what those who were pushing the plan probably had in mind. So it goes. The rhetoric of twenty-first century education represented little more than old wine in new bottles.

Defining Peace Education

Several years ago I was fortunate enough to attend a workshop at the University of Haifa in Israel devoted to "peace education research." This workshop brought together both academic scholars and those directly engaged in various forms of peace education.[6] Many of the participants were from places that had experienced severe episodes of communal violence. In addition to those from

Israel—both Palestinians and Jews—there were people from South Africa, Ireland, Bosnia, Rwanda, Spain, Norway, as well as other countries. Naively, I'd hoped that I would learn from these experienced researchers and practitioners exactly how one went about educating for peace. My social science training led me to expect that there would be some kind of scientifically foolproof method of achieving peaceful relationships between hitherto warring groups. I learned that nothing could be further from the truth. Even the commonly practiced "contact hypothesis," which assumes that bringing individuals together in a supportive social and educational setting in order to get to know each other as real human beings undoes prejudices and hostilities, was found to have only limited effect. After a while, if no other political or institutional changes took place, and under the cultural pressures at home, old patterns of animosity reemerged. What I did find at this workshop, however, was not a single method or approach to peace education, but a variety of experiments that used different modalities and media. These approaches had varying degrees of success, though their long-term consequences were difficult to assess. Some of these approaches provided shared social and educational experiences for children from hostile communities in order to "deconstruct the otherness" of the protagonists; others had developed textbooks that helped students understand and discover the world from the experience of others. Some engaged in travel to places that evoked the painful history and suffering of the "enemy" community. There were projects that brought groups of children together around shared art, music, and dance projects. Some placed young people in the homes and families of the other community. Some involved joint political projects to create more socially just situations and contexts. Some simply attempted to have children experience others' holiday festivals and celebrations. And there were many other thoughtful and creative ventures and efforts.

SIX ROOTS OF VIOLENCE

By the end of all this I concluded that any approach to peace education would be far messier. It would involve a multiplicity of approaches, interventions, and educational initiatives. There would be no "one size fits all" method. (I should add that I write this book *not* as a scholar within the important and growing field of peace studies, but as an educator whose focus has been on the moral and civic dimensions of education and the possibilities offered by critical forms of pedagogy. Certainly the former offer rich insights and evidence around issues that I can only touch upon in a limited way in this work, and I offer my apologies to those in peace studies who might see me as an interloper in another field.) Yet out of this mélange of possible directions for affecting change among young people, away from violence, hate, prejudice, and misunderstanding, I also saw that there were certain shared principles and concepts that ran through all of the experiments. And, several years after this life-changing event, it is these that I have attempted to bring together and elucidate in this short volume. Let me try to briefly enumerate them here, though I shall devote greater space to them in subsequent chapters:

1. I believe that violent conflict often follows when people view their understanding of the world as the only correct and acceptable one and all others as heretical or dangerous and to be fought and rejected. What follows is a Manichean worldview that divides the world up between those who have the right beliefs and all others who threaten them. With this view there is no acknowledgment that one's "truth" might be partial and others might have some understanding, knowledge, or beliefs that are worthy of respect. Nor is there recognition that truth and knowledge evolve and change. Instead, there is only an intransigent and authoritarian fixation on what this group believes at this place and at this point in time. Built into such a view is an intolerance and disrespect for any other culture and way of life, which sooner or later is sure to inflame anger and conflict.
2. I have come to believe, too, that the invisibility of human beings is a certain recipe for frustration and resentment that will inevitably break out into open conflict and rage. By invisibility I mean the failure to fully appreciate and validate the presence of other human beings. They are ignored or remain unnoticed, except in the most limited and exploitative ways, in the eyes of others. At the extreme end of this phenomenon the very humanity of a group is withdrawn or denied. In these situations human beings have frequently been taught to see and believe that their own worth and value is much less than that of others. Invisibility represents an often quiet, but no less traumatic, form of violence perpetrated by one group of human beings on another. Beyond our material needs is a deep imperative to be recognized in the fullness of our humanity, to be seen and recognized by others as beings of unconditional value. The urge to have one's own humanity confirmed

in the face of an often violent refusal is, I believe, at the root of so many struggles and conflicts in history.
3. The problem of invisibility is, I believe, a dimension of the larger process of social injustice and the domination of human beings by those with more power. This domination is always, in some way, a violent process. Whether through the overt use of might to maintain control over others' lives or through the less direct form of economic deprivation, social injustice always disfigures and undermines human worth and limits the capacity of humans to live full lives. There is no more powerful driver of anger and conflict than social inequality. History teaches us that social injustice is always accompanied by some form of violence that seeks to suppress the human desire for respect and dignity and undermines or destroys the possibility of a decent life for oneself and others who are part of one's family and community. We often witness violence used against those who struggle to demand fulfillment of their human and democratic rights. A violence that often, in turn, produces a counter-rage and a violent response by those who will no longer accept continued deprivation, humiliation, or denial of their humanity. We live in a world deeply scarred by social injustice and profound inequalities in the conditions of our lives. There can be no lasting global peace while such disparities continue and so many people must barely survive because of poverty, starvation, sickness, and malnutrition.
4. Social injustice, domination, and invisibility are linked to another phenomenon that is inevitably connected to violent behavior—the culture of competition. This competition is typically sustained by a "narrative" of scarcity that tells us life is a race, and that in order to get what we believe we should have we must compete aggressively against others who are after the same thing. As a result, invidious comparison rules all of our lives. Envy for what others have controls much of how we think and feel. We consider ourselves to be in a state of constant lack or inadequacy and are always threatened by what others have or are. The relentless propaganda of competition (found in every part of our lives, but nowhere with greater influence than in our schools) is a catalyst for always seeing other people as our enemies. "They" are people who want to harm us, exploit or manipulate us, deprive us of what is ours, demean us. And always for their benefit. In a world permeated by this competitive worldview it is very difficult to see or imagine a planet in which compassion and connection, rather than fear and suspicion, shape human relationships.

5. Human beings are impelled by needs that go beyond material desires. And the suffering that turns into anger involves not just a lack of those resources that can guarantee us a comfortable and dignified life, but also the possibility of a life with meaning. We know that meaning is as essential to human well-being and the sense that life is worth living and sustaining as material resources. Pain and anguish can certainly come from material deprivation, but they are also the product of spiritual emptiness. Bereft of deep purpose and meaning, life quickly becomes a journey of despair. And despair provides fertile soil for both the anger that is turned inward as depression and self-destruction and the rage that is focused outward on a world that seems to offer only endless frustration. We live in a world in which there are powerful forces that undermine and corrode authentic sources of meaning; the globalization of capitalism, consumerism, and an ethic of hyper-individualism all contribute to a deep crisis of meaning. In such a world militant assertions of religious beliefs or aggressive expressions of ethnic and national identity offer the consolation of compelling identification for those who feel adrift in a sea of purposelessness.
6. Finally, we are confronted by structures and institutions that thrive on the machinery of war. Political and economic interests benefit greatly when people are taught to believe that they are always under threat and must give their uncritical support to those interests. The result in the United States is a military-industrial-political complex that engineers military budgets that massively distort our nation's priorities and investments. More than this, our citizenry is educated to believe that in situation after situation, war and military force is the necessary solution to global problems. And, as recent events have made clear, we are subject to the deception, deceit, and manipulation of those who lead the "national security state," often abetted by an acquiescent media that will ensure mass support for policies of death and destruction, foreign interventions, and imperial coercion. We are often taught to accept a narrative of an implacable enemy that will understand and respond only to the language of bloody force. Added to this is the way that national purpose—at a time when all else seems to be a matter of individual self-interest—is found in the glory and sacrifice of a nation's military.

This book is not intended to be a how-to manual for peace educators (I certainly take nothing away from the importance of such projects). What I wish to do in this short volume is to define the conceptual landscape for a pedagogy concerned with peace in current times—to offer a "map" that points to and highlights some of the key concerns and issues for such a pedagogy. My focus is on the phenomena that may be recognized as crucial to the task of educating for peace: the authoritarian view of truth; the anguish of human invisibility, social injustice, and domination; the relentlessness of competitive relationships; the crisis of meaning in global capitalism; and the construction of enemies and the propaganda that urges military solutions to all our global problems. My intent is not only to describe the problems in our contemporary world, though that is certainly an important part of what I wish to do. More than this is my intention to point, throughout this volume, to the social, cultural, psychological, moral, and spiritual changes that we must work towards in all the spaces that impact the awareness and attitudes of those we teach. I believe that I approach this task with my feet planted firmly on the ground. The struggle for a less violent, more peaceful and loving world is most assuredly part of a "long revolution" and not a moment of utopian transformation. Even if only a few ideas from this book enter into and shape our work with young people, this effort would have been worthwhile. For, as the Talmud notes, to save the life of even one person is to save a whole world.

Frames of Mind and Heart

My thoughts in this book are shaped by three powerful impulses that together form its overarching framework. These impulses are pedagogic, moral, and spiritual.

First is my belief that the pervasiveness of violence in our society, and in our world, is not the result of some genetic dysfunction in human beings or an ineradicable evil inclination. It is primarily the result of the way human cultures function and the consequences of how particular societies are constructed. In this sense, violence is not some kind of inevitable given that we must forever endure. Societies are the creation of human beings and they can be changed—in ways that ensure more peaceful, loving, compassionate, and just relationships. And in ways that address the pathologies I have identified above—authoritarianism, human invisibility, social injustice, relentless competition, the crisis of meaning, and the war-directed state. This means that the way we typically think about education must change radically. In contrast to how we understand the purpose of education today, as the means of individual recognition, achievement, social mobility, or as the vehicle for job training, the role of education needs to become that of re-visioning a culture. In this sense, education's purpose is a *collective* rather than an *individual* one. It is approached in the spirit of what John Dewey called "the making of a world" and what others like Paulo Freire or Henry Giroux have referred to as education's role in the reconstruction of our social and civic life. Rabbi Jonathan Sacks points out that such a change means turning away from what he calls a libertarian view of human beings in which "the self is prior to its ends" and "persons are imagined as unencumbered consumers freely shopping between alternatives."[7] Instead, education is about the "the obligation to belong" and actively caring about the "moral tone of the whole society." Similarly, the philosopher Michael Sandel contrasts the pursuit of freedom as being the right of individuals to non-interference in their choices with "being a member of a political community that controls its own fate, and a participant in the decisions that govern its affairs."[8] The latter version of freedom to participate and govern necessitates an education that is, first and foremost, about a civic literacy that will enable each of us to become engaged and concerned moral agents who see the purpose and quality of our own individual lives as inseparable from our lives as members of our shared society.

My own belief is that our lives become worthwhile and purposeful precisely when we see them as having a meaning beyond the pursuit of purely personal ends—when we are able to connect who we are and what we do to the larger ends of a shared human existence. Sandel expresses it this way[9]:

To imagine a person incapable of constitutive attachments such as these is not to conceive an ideally free and rational agent, but to imagine a person wholly without character, without moral depth.

The struggle for a world that is less violent and more just and caring is not just about making our world a better place for us to live. It is about us learning to see that lives lived with shared purpose and collective goals offer greater fulfillment, depth, and joy.

It will be not too difficult to see that an important impulse in my view of education is a moral one. As has been said, before there is an "I" there must be a "Thou." Cornel West notes that our identity "is who we are in relationship." My belief here (as in all my writing and in my teaching) is that education is, or should be, first and foremost a moral endeavor concerned with what it means to be a human being and how we live with others who share our world—both human and non-human. This in no sense is meant to suggest that education is not concerned with intellectual development or the enhancement of creative or other aspects of human potential. It simply means that our goals in education must be rooted in an overarching vision of the good society and valued human behavior. Our failure to do this leaves education as little more than a laundry list of curricular objectives without reference to any particular human purpose or aim. Worse than this, however, is that the failure to consciously situate the work of educators in this larger purpose usually means that education and schooling do little more than re-inscribe and perpetuate the unexamined values, beliefs, and assumptions of the world that surrounds us. At this time when so much unnecessary suffering exists and when the very fate of the earth itself is in the balance, to not place what we do in education in a larger context that considers what kind of social world we are contributing to, or perpetuating, is an act of ethical irresponsibility. Whose ends are we serving as teachers? For what purpose do we encourage young people to develop their minds? How will their creative talents be employed and used? What moral values frame the hopes and expectations of young people, and what role does school play in this?

My own moral concerns as an educator are shaped by what is sometimes referred to as the prophetic tradition, after the role of the ancient Hebrew prophets. As brilliantly described by the theologian and Rabbi Abraham Heschel,[10] these individuals provided voices that called the people to attend to the dissonance between their pious pronouncements and lofty invocations and the real world around them with all its suffering, injustice, violence, and neglect. They were the relentless voices of conscience that spoke truth to power, even in the face of their own isolation or the hostility of their audience. In this sense the moral dimension of teaching today should, I believe, not be about mouthing soothing or triumphalist platitudes. It certainly cannot be about re-inscribing a moral universe that leaves so many in pain. It must instead be about calling into question the dissonance between our words and our deeds—a task that we must encourage our students to do relentlessly and fearlessly. When it comes to matters of preferring peace to war and violence, it is difficult to find a naysayer. Words here come easily. Yet a preference for peace involves much more than sentimental gestures. It means learning to confront the ways in which we demean and exploit human beings through how our economy works; the trade policies that ensure a supply of cheap resources to maintain our way of life; the extraordinary proportion of our national wealth that is used to build weapons and our frequent use of them to ensure our political hegemony; our preference for competitive rather cooperative social relations; and all the ways we marginalize and dehumanize others because of our fear of difference. The prophetic voice of morality is always one that questions, disturbs, and unsettles those who maintain that this is the way things are—and there is no alternative.

Finally, this work was inspired by the Jewish concept of *Tikkun Olam*—a vision of the universe that speaks of the spiritual oneness of all being. It asserts that the world is in a state of fragmentation or brokenness and that the human task is to repair and bring about its healing. Two ontological principles undergird the vision of *Tikkun Olam*. The first is that human life is a sacred entity—something that is of precious and indeed of unconditional value. This is envisaged in the biblical book of Genesis through the idea that human beings are made in God's image. This extraordinary assertion about the infinite value of human life has influenced humane thinking through the ages, even if it is formulated in more secular language. Without this concept the notion of universal human rights or the vision of social justice is impossible to contemplate. The preciousness of a single life is precisely why the Talmud states that to destroy one life is to destroy a whole world.

The second principle is that human beings need, for their fulfillment, to live as part of a community. The need to live lives of connection and care is not because it facilitates some advantage to the individual in the way of a social transaction, but because the completion of our very humanity depends on us being with others in loving and reciprocal relationships. Without this connection human life is stunted and empty. The feminist theologian Beverley Harrison noted simply that we love one another into the fullness of being. Jonathan Sacks notes the distinction between relationships founded as a social contract and those that he refers to as embodying the Jewish concept of *brit* or "covenant." Although in the former, relationships are entered into for instrumental and selfish purposes—for what you can get out of your connection to another (in professional circles referred to today as "networking")—covenantal relationships are built around "an internalized sense of identity" or the belief that one is connected to another through a sense of shared responsibility, reciprocity, compassion, and obligation.[11] It is easy to see the degree to which contractual relationships shape our world with their manipulative, strategizing, money, and status-maximizing character. However, we also see, perhaps more clearly than ever, how the sacred value of a single life depends for its nurturance and development on our being part of an interdependent and interconnected world. And the nurturance of human life is not only part of our interdependence and connection with the human world. We are increasingly aware of how much the well-being of human life is inseparable from the well-being of *all* life on our planet. It was not for nothing that Mahatma Gandhi stated that the greatness of a nation and its moral progress can be judged by the way its animals are treated. It is increasingly clear that all life is bound together in a covenant that demands respect, care, and stewardship of all that constitutes our precious world. This is a covenant of being that recognizes that the material and emotional well-being of each of us depends on the well-being of the whole. More than this, the very sense of separation and fragmentation that pervades our world is a denial or obfuscation of the common nature of what we are. We are, in fact, all constituted from those same recycled elemental building blocks of life out of which our individual presence in the world is given but temporary and transitory form.

There is an inspired wisdom in the meaning found in the Hebrew word for peace: *shalom*. The word shares a common etymological root with the Hebrew word for wholeness: *shalem*. I have often asked my classes to suggest how these two meanings are connected. Usually, and with great speed, students see how peace is related to the notion of connection and relatedness that is implicit in the idea of wholeness. Young children who have asked the same question typically, and with amazing insight, have pictured wholeness as a circle in which all parts are linked in ways that give no part greater value than another, but in which each part is needed to complete the circle. Here is a powerful image of peace—one that depicts it as a space of connection, inclusion, and equality.

Shadows of Fear in Our Lives

One of the questions I ask my students to think about is how our lives are shadowed by violence of one kind or another. I start by talking about my own life. I refer to members of my family (distant cousins) murdered by the Nazis for the simple fact of being Jews. I talk about my family in Israel who have endured round after round of war, as well as suicide bombings and the constant experience of violent conflict. I tell them about dealing with anti-Semitic bullies as a kid in England and the nightmares that followed hearing about the Holocaust for the first time during the Eichmann trial in 1961. Revealing some of my or my family's encounters with violence is a catalyst for the students in my class to talk about their fears and anxieties. African-American students have many stories about the violence suffered by their parents and grandparents at the hands of racism: threats and intimidation during the process of breaking down the barriers of segregation; the taunts and actual violence inflicted against loved ones; the tacit knowledge, even now, about where one can safely travel in our state. Women share the universal condition of wariness about where they can walk or go at night without fear of physical violence. Gay students share the ever-present anxiety of being publically identified in terms of their sexuality and the homophobic hostility that continues to permeate society. Students of Latino background reveal the prejudiced assumptions that confront them because of their appearance, name, or accent. Students acknowledge the presence of guns and alcoholism in their homes when they were growing up and the dangers of this mixture to family members. There are those in the class who have been touched by criminal violence—having been robbed, mugged, or threatened on the street or in their homes. In a state that contributes disproportionately to the military, students talk about family members returning from war traumatized by the experience of killing. Before long, some students introduce the less visible forms of violence that are implicit in our way of life: the sweat shops that produce our clothing, electronic items, and home furnishings in which people work in life-damaging situations; the poultry plants in our state in which mainly foreign workers toil in oppressive and dangerous conditions; farm workers who pick fruit and vegetables while exposed to carcinogenic pesticides. And other students remind the class about the pain and suffering inflicted on animals who are reared in inhumane conditions of gross overcrowding, the inability to move around, the lack of exposure to natural conditions of sunlight and pasture, and finally terrifying forms of slaughter.

Soon it becomes apparent that violence and suffering shadow all of our lives, though perhaps we are so inured to it that we have lost the capacity to see it as a problem or a pathology that demands a cure. It is just part of life—something we don't challenge or question. It is merely the water we must swim in. In raising the phenomenon to awareness, what was once taken for granted becomes something to reflect on and perhaps challenge. It suggests the possibility that another world could be created. I stir the pot and add to this realization additional information I have collected. In its annual report, the Stockholm International Peace Research Institute states that world governments spent a record sum of $1.46 trillion on upgrading their armed forces in 2009 (despite the economic downturn). Global military spending according to this report was up 45 percent from the late 1990s. U.S. military spending was $607 billion in 2008, rising to about $800 billion in 2010, and accounted for about 42 percent of global arms spending. A recent United Nations High Commissioner for Refugees (UNHCR) report noted that 42 million people in the world are now displaced refugees because of conflicts and wars. In the United States, 85 people are killed with guns each day, and 30,000 people are shot to death each year. Every three hours, gun violence takes a child's life. Approximately 300,000 children are believed to be combatants in conflicts around the world, nearly a half-million children serve in armies.[12] According to the Family Violence Prevention Fund, one in three women around the world has experienced sexual, physical, or emotional abuse in her lifetime; 40–70 percent of all female murder victims are killed by those with whom they are intimate.[13] And one estimate of "lives deliberately extinguished by politically motivated carnage" in the twentieth century puts the figure at between 167 and 175 million people![14]

These figures represent actual deaths or direct involvement in violence. They do not speak to the "shadow" of violence—the fear, anxiety, apprehension, and nightmares that are present in our psyches and that envelopes so many of us. The blight of violence disfigures our lives and turns our existence into a wary and fearful journey.

Is Change Possible?

The short answer to this question is yes, and even if it were not, it would surely still be worth trying. The longer answer might begin with the story of the biblical Exodus—at least in the way that the eminent political scientist Michael Walzer tells it.[15] Walzer argues that the bible offers two very different visions of social and human change, and each have their echoes in contemporary discourse and theories of societal change. One springs from the bible's apocalyptic imagery: a final battle between the forces of good and evil, the sudden revelation of God's power, the division of the world between those who are transformed and are to be saved and the rest who must vanish from the earth. It is not difficult to see the resonance of this tale in revolutionary political movements with their intent to overthrow the existing evil and oppressive regimes and replace them with a "new world" of transformed men and women liberated from the mentality and behaviors of the previous epoch. In contrast to this is Walzer's depiction of the Exodus from Egypt. Here the end of bondage is not the result of a single apocalyptic happening. Nor is it an episode that occurs in one moment in time. For Walzer, liberation from enslavement is a long, slow process full of trial and error, moments of disillusionment and despair, and hope and possibility. Liberation here involves both internal and external aspects. It certainly involves change from the economic and political regime that held the victims in its grip. It also means liberation from the internalized beliefs that no world was possible other than the one in which they had grown up. The latter is a much slower process of emotional and psychological change. The two kinds of change are not entirely separate events—a dialectic of cause and effect links them. As external events change, so can beliefs, feelings, and outlooks. And changes in the latter can also deepen the conviction about the need for different kinds of social relationships and structures.

Walzer's Exodus metaphor is, I believe, a good one for how we can approach the possibility for moving towards a world that is less violent and is shaped less by war and militarism. We cannot expect change of this magnitude to happen in a single moment. More realistically, it is something that happens as part of what the English social critic Raymond Williams once called "a long revolution"—a revolution that takes place in the practices and policies of our institutions, in our social relationships, and not least in the hearts of individuals. As educators we cannot regard our work as the sole catalyst of such change (this is too often the case when we expect education alone to solve our social problems). But, by the same token, educators can certainly make an important contribution to this revolution—through what we choose to teach and the methods we employ, the kind of relationships we create in our schools and classrooms, and the kind of role models we offer to our students.

In this book I do not seek to offer any kind of blueprint, plan, or recipe for the work of educators committed to this kind of transformation. Such curricular planning is something with which I have long felt uneasy, given the increasing tendency to "de-skill" the work of teachers, thus reducing them to technicians who need do no more than follow the detailed plans and prescriptions of others. My interest in humanizing our society prohibits me from adding to the way we extract from the noble work of education teachers' creativity, imagination, and serious intellectual and moral engagement with pedagogy. Tragically, this tendency is increasingly present in teachers' work. In this book I am seeking to offer some broad parameters for those who would like their work as teachers to contribute to the making of a more peaceful, harmonious, and cooperative world. I try to provide some of the main avenues, as I see them, down which we need to travel with our students to encourage what John Berger famously called "another way of seeing." My view of peace education makes no absolute distinction between changes of consciousness and changes of conscience. Peace education, I believe, is at once a task that demands a critical intellect, an ethic of justice and compassion, and a spiritual recognition of the precious and inviolable nature of human life, as well as the web of being that connects all life. For this reason I have also avoided references to students' ages. Although teachers will certainly recognize that discussions about, for example, the U.S. military budget and numerous foreign adventures is appropriate for older, more mature students, the importance of creating classroom spaces in which all individuals are treated with respect and care should be part of peace education for all youngsters. Clearly there are moral themes that would appropriately be part of the education of children both young and old, though obviously engaged with different degrees of sophistication and complexity—just as there are matters for critical debate and discussion that fit a more mature group of students. I leave how the themes and issues raised in this book might be engaged, discussed, and encountered with students of different age groups and backgrounds to the knowledge and experience of teachers. In the current climate, I do not expect schools to allocate whole blocks of time to something called "Peace Education." That is certainly unlikely—especially if teachers and principals wish to hold onto their jobs! My hope is that teachers or educational leaders will be able to see ways and opportunities in which some of the concerns, foci, and questions raised in this book might be adapted to the ongoing curriculum—both explicit and informal—of their school and classrooms.

A final note. This book was written in the hope and belief that human beings might treat one another with greater care, compassion, and respect, and the belief that education might contribute to a change in human attitudes and behavior. At the same time the difficulty of achieving such change is clear. It is impossible to ignore how much we are motivated by impulses that are completely contrary to the making of a more humane and just world. We see behavior motivated by greed and self-interest. We see an apathy and indifference to human suffering and pain. We also see acts of brutality in which the perpetrators behave with a grisly pleasure, and even delight, in their sadistic violence. No one who follows events around us can ignore the dark reality of human behavior. Nor do I dispute that there are times when one may be justified in having to fight in order to save and protect lives—though I believe these are few (and certainly much fewer than governments would like us to believe). I write this book not as a pacifist, because I believe that there are times when there is a need for armed interventions to stop or end more deaths, brutality, or suffering. The most obvious example of this is the war against Nazism and fascism, which, like most people, I believe to have been unavoidable and absolutely necessary. Nor is it likely that all struggles against colonialism could have been resolved through Gandhian-like nonviolent means. Yet we cannot succumb to this as part of an inevitable and unchangeable reality. As is said often enough, where there is life there is the hope and possibility of a better world. We may believe that our actions are worthwhile and make a difference even if their results are less than what we would want and hope for. Rabbi Tarfon asserted that "it is not your duty to complete the work, but neither are you excused from participating in it." It is in this spirit that this book was written.

Chapter Two

TRUTH AND VIOLENCE

Second night, same group was there. I felt a little more easy because I got some things. The third night, after they elected all the committees, they want to elect a chairman. Howard Clements stood up and said: "I suggest we elect two co-chairpersons." Joe Beckton, executive director of the Human Relations Commission, just as black as he can be, he nominated me. There was a reaction from some blacks. And,. of all things, they nominated Ann Atwater, that big old fat black gal that I had just hated with a purple passion, as co-chairman. I thought to myself: Hey ain't no way I can work with that gal. Finally, I agreed to accept it, 'cause at this point, I was tired of fightin', either for survival or against black people or against Jews or against Catholics.

A Klansman and a militant black woman, co-chairmen of the school committee. It was impossible. How could I work with her? But after two or three days, it was in our hands. We had to make it a success. This gave me another sense of belongin', a sense of pride. This helped this inferiority feelin' I had. A man who has stood up publically and said he despised black people, all of a sudden he was willin' to work with 'em. Here's a chance for a low income white man to be somethin'. In spite of all my hatred for blacks and Jews and liberals, I accepted the job. Her and I began to reluctantly work together. (Laughs.) She had as many problems workin' with me as I had workin' with her.

One day, Ann and I went back to the school and we sat down. We began to talk and just reflect. Ann said: "My daughter came home cryin' every day. She said her teacher was makin' fun of me right in front of the other kids." I said: "Boy, the same thing happened to my kid. White liberal teacher was makin' fun of Tim Ellis's father, the Klansman, in front of other people. He came home cryin'." At this point (he pauses, swallows hard, stifles a sob) I begin to see, here we are, two people from the far ends of the fence, havin' identical problems, except hers bein' black and me bein' white. From that moment on, I tell ya, that gal and I worked together good. I begin to love the girl, really. (He weeps.)

> The amazing thing about it, her and I, up to that point, had cussed each other, bawled each other, we hated each other. Up to that point, we didn't know each other. We didn't know we had things in common.
> —From Studs Terkel, *American Dreams Lost and Found*

My Enemy Is Someone Whose Story I Have Not Yet Heard

There is a direct connection between violent conflict and intransigent, uncompromising worldviews. We can readily see how people who view their own understanding of the world as the only correct, meaningful, and morally acceptable view inevitably come into violent, often hateful conflict with others who do not share their view. This certainty about one's truth rests on the psychological rock of authoritarianism and dogmatism. Others cannot be seen as fellow humans who simply do not share a particular set of meanings about how we might make sense of our lives or the values that guide our day-to-day decision making. They become instead heretics, infidels, or traitors who pose, by their mere existence, a deadly threat to the way of meaningful existence. They appear as obstacles to the unfolding of what is believed to be God's plan or the prophetically revealed truth. In secular terms they are renegades, reactionaries, or insurgents who stand in the way of historical destiny. Either through their own selfish interests or because of their ignorance, the latter refuse to acknowledge the other's truth. Instead they proffer deceit or obfuscations that hide or subvert what they believe to be the one and only path to true knowledge.

For those who follow this road, there is only the certainty of what one believes and the obstinate refusal of other people to accept the right moral, cultural, religious, or political view. Here is a Manichean view of the world, divided up neatly and surely between those who have the right beliefs and those benighted others who refuse them. Of course, for those who "have" the "truth" it is no longer a matter of simply belief, but of revelation or inspired insight. There is certainly, among these groups, no evolving understanding of what is right or true. There is no sense that human knowledge might change with historical context or social situation. Nor is there a sense that people might see things differently according to their position or role in the social order, the nation in which they live, or their gender. Neither is people's truth understood as being dependent on the cosmology supplied by their religious faith. In other words, truth is not something that might vary, change, evolve, or be transformed. And there is no sense that what humans know is always a matter of interpretation.

The Manichean view is not something that belongs only to others in the world. It is equally at home in our country as it is among other cultures. A recent piece in a local newspaper made this point in a startling manner by comparing two quotes.[1] The first is from Adolph Hitler and the second is from President Harry Truman. Although adversaries in the Second World War, these men each claimed God's approval for their killing.

> **Hitler:** By defending myself against the Jew, *I am fighting for the work of the Lord.*
> **Truman:** Having found the atomic bomb, we have used it. We shall continue to use it.... It is an awful responsibility which has come to us. *We thank God that the atomic bomb has come to us instead of to our enemies,* and we pray that God may guide us to use it in his ways and for his purposes.

Sadly, the language of our politics and national debate is still saturated with images of demonic forces, "axes of evil," that must be overcome by the forces of righteousness. Whether it is "godless communism" or fanatical Islam, the same impulses are nurtured and stirred. The world is divided in absolute and categorical ways between good and evil, right and wrong—those of us who claim to represent wisdom and those who are regarded as malevolent. Such a view of the world brings a great sense of comfort to its believers. There is no need to see shades of grey in this black and white world. Good and bad, truth and falsity—each represents a neat and easily understood grid within which the world and our actions in it may be gauged. In the words of one recent U.S. president, there is no need ever to apologize for this country. In his belief we are always on the side of the angels, never intervening in others' affairs out of self-interested or ethically questionable motives. And where our actions lead to the deaths of thousands of innocent people, whether in Hiroshima, Nicaragua, Chile, Iraq, or, perhaps in the future, in Iran, we can rest assured that we are right in our actions, and those we destroy are clearly in the wrong. We have the mental ease of a world that seems to demand no complexity of thinking, no ambiguity in terms of motives, and no reason to try to understand how our adversaries' beliefs, experiences, and history shape the way they make sense of their world.

Such psychology banishes the need for dialogue between people so that differences might give way to compromise and mutual understanding. It also minimizes the importance of an education that might help us understand how our adversaries see their world and how their experience and history has brought them to make sense of things in the way they do. Of course, such understanding won't necessarily lead us to embrace the worldview of the other. The other's values might seem to contradict our cherished beliefs in human rights or our commitment to a society in which women are fully empowered and respected as equal human beings. Nonetheless, it would enable us to proceed with a greater sense of humility in regard to our own beliefs and values. It would puncture the comfortable and often unexamined assumptions about the superiority of the American version of the free enterprise system of organizing an economy or the belief that our own particular kind of democratic institutions are necessarily the only, or even the best, political arrangements human beings can produce. Seeing the world from the point of view of the other makes it much less likely that we can claim that ours is the "one best system." To place oneself in the shoes of the other, to try to assume others' perspectives on religion, culture, and politics, is surely part of the process through which we may lessen our sometimes arrogant stance on others' lives, commitments, beliefs, and values. To see the world through the lens of the other represents a transformation of consciousness in which a single truth that holds the key to all that is valid and worthwhile gives way to a recognition of the multiple perspectives through which human beings bring meaning, purpose, and order to their lives.

Floating in the Sea of Impermanence and Contingency

Although education is indispensable to this transformation of consciousness, I do not want to suggest that there is anything easy about the process. For one thing, we have to let go of our propensity to believe that our own "realist" version of truth constitutes the one and only accurate representation of what we call reality. In other words, we have to recognize that there is more than one truth "out there." This means accepting that there are multiple possible versions of reality, each of which is a construction of or interpretation of our minds. Daniel Gilbert[2] expresses this succinctly, if humorously. He writes that most of the time we do not realize that what we take to be the real world is actually constituted through a process of interpretation:

> Instead, we feel as though we are sitting comfortably inside our heads, looking out through the clear glass windshield of our eyes, watching the world as it truly is. We tend to forget that our brains are talented forgers, weaving a tapestry of memory and perception whose detail is so compelling that its inauthenticity is rarely detected.

However, the "tapestries" that constitute the world for each of us are not, at their root, our own individual creations. They are instead the stories or narratives that together constitute a *culture*. These narratives provide us with the *root metaphors* that give meaning and value to our world. To a large extent they are woven so tightly into the mental frame that gives our reality its coherence that we are frequently unaware of their existence as contingent, temporary, and often fragile phenomena. To recognize what we know and what we take to be the way things really are as only the chance product of history and culture is to be *critically aware* human beings. When we become critically aware, we begin to see that what we have taken to be reality is no more than one among a number of different possibilities for how we live together as human beings and how we define the purpose of human existence. Certainly, re-seeing our world in this much less sure and fixed way can be an anxiety-producing change. It means that truth and knowledge cannot be relied upon to give us any kind of permanent way of "mapping" our world. More than this, it suggests that there is no absolute veracity to the particular way that we, in our society and at this moment in time, give meaning or value to our lives. *It is surely a scary thing to let go of these kinds of mental anchors and feel ourselves floating in a sea of contingency and impermanence.* Indeed, it is perhaps a fundamental dimension of the human condition to seek the sense of security that comes from believing that our identity, our beliefs, and our values are not passing illusions or temporary phenomena, but instead represent a set of incontrovertible truths.

Schooling and the Culture of the One Right Answer

Whether or not this hankering after a secure and unchanging vision of what constitutes the world is programmed into human DNA, I have no doubt that it is one of the consequences of too much schooling. *The education that so many of us have received has been a long lesson in the idea that there is always one right answer to any question, puzzle, or problem.* The emphasis on standardized tests in our classrooms and homogenized textbooks had the effect of drumming into many of us the belief that there is one, and only one, correct answer to any question or problem. As a teacher, I am always saddened when confronted by students who are thoroughly socialized to believe that there is only one right response to my questions. And that their job is to ferret it out from all the other incorrect possibilities. Intellectual dullness is not the only result from this process of limited inquiry. Conformity of thinking and timidity of imagination are also consequences of striving to mimic someone else's idea of what is true or correct thinking. Education then becomes little more than an effort to memorize and regurgitate others' ideas or understanding. My own assertion in the classroom that all knowledge is a kind of "collective hunch" is sometimes met with stunned disbelief. My "story" about the nature of knowledge flies in the face of students' assumption that what is being communicated to them is an accurate or true account of reality. Whether the subject is history, math, social studies, or physics, students generally suppose that what they are hearing and reading is the way things *really* are, or were, out there in the natural or social world. I labor to explain to them that the only fact is that whatever they learn is someone's idea or interpretation of what is going on. What human beings know about reality is always filtered through the prisms of their linguistic, cultural, and ideological situation. There is no "history," only histories—a series of narratives that reflect the prejudices, concerns, and perspectives of those attempting to make sense of the past from the context of where the storyteller is situated. Literature is always a selection and interpretation from a whole range of possibilities of what is worthwhile reading made by a *particular* group of people at a *particular* time. Math is an imaginative and creative series of language games with specific sets of agreed upon rules about how valid mathematical knowledge can be generated. In each case assumptions must be made about reality even while it is understood that such rules are only heuristic devices. In other words, they are useful ways to solve problems that have only a limited relationship to things in the real world (there are different kinds of geometries and algebras depending on what rules we lay down as the starting point for problem solving). Even the sciences are shaped by cultural values in ways that reflect prevailing social metaphors. Think of how the brain is now popularly conceived of as an information processing machine akin to the computer; how those who study the fundamental nature of matter periodically adopt new and creative images for describing the building blocks of the physical world; or how ecological values that emphasize interconnection or holistic models now abound in physics and biology and replace the older jungle or Darwinian view of a predatory world.

What we know about anything should not be construed as an objective statement of fact so much as reflecting the extraordinary human capacity to give metaphorical expression to our experiences and interactions. And these expressions can never be fully separated from the time, place, and ingrained assumptions of those weaving the metaphors. As one wit expressed it, where we stand in terms of our views and beliefs depends on where we sit. In other words, our knowledge is always shaped and limited by the concepts made available through our particular language, or by the assumptions about human nature we may hold, or the religious, cosmological, political, or cultural images that shape our worldview. There is no God's-eye view through which to see and know our world. *Simply put, there is no place that human beings can find to observe the world so that they stand outside or apart from society's influence.* This is readily grasped by students when I remind them of how much our belief in legitimate knowledge in the modern world assumes that it must be measurable. It is the capacity to measure something that gives knowledge its supposed veracity. Yet this seems to exclude all those far more ephemeral but arguably equally important dimensions of the human experience that move, inspire, and shape our lives. This includes things like love, compassion, our spiritual lives, or the sense of oneness that connects all life on our planet. It also excludes self-knowledge—the exploration of our own interiority with all of its mysteries and uniqueness. It also explains schools' obsession with making every part of the curriculum testable, demonstrable, and measurable. In the immortal words of Einstein, "If we can't count it, then it doesn't count!" (He also went on to say that not everything that counts can be counted!) I don't have to elaborate on the damaging effect this kind of thinking has had on education. In short, it has compressed the curriculum to those areas that seem most amenable to standardization and measurement (not surprisingly, the arts have been at the short end of this emphasis, as well as children's play and other non-directive or less structured experiences). It has also made the classroom a place of increasing drudgery as instruction has become little more than an endless process of testing, and learning has become increasingly devoid of the opportunity for creativity, imagination, and the Socratic arts of dialogue and critical thought. Sadly, the current approach to education does great harm to those very qualities that are crucial to the kind of development that might encourage more empathy and understanding among human beings. Such development depends on those very qualities that current practices and policies squelch, such as the ability to listen and hear how others experience their lives. It offers little to the process of grasping how others who share our world might have very different ways of seeing and understanding things, or recognizing that far from there being a single true reality that we all agree on, human beings quite often arrive at very different takes on who we are, what our purpose in life is, the origins of existence, and so on. All of this requires that we teach in ways that dismantle, rather than reinforce, the idea that a single unalterable truth exists regarding just about anything we can point to in the living world. *Breathtaking multiplicity characterizes how human beings see, understand, and give meaning to reality.* We continually learn how much harm is done when we insist that it is *only we* who have the correct version of how things are (or ought to be). Or it is only we who have the facts or who really understand what or who is right as we look out at the world.

Power, Knowledge, and Compassionate Understanding

I do not want to suggest to my students that knowledge is just something arbitrarily thrown together. Indeed, I strongly disagree with statements that suggest that what we know is all "just a matter of opinion." Scientific knowledge, for example, is arrived at through extraordinarily exhaustive thought, experimentation, deliberation, and collective discourse. Clearly there are ways of understanding that seem to correspond more accurately with reality and are far more effective at controlling or predicting natural processes. To say that evolution is a theory in no ways detracts from its power to explain and provide a compelling framework for investigating nature. As one writer[3] notes:

> Without evolution biology is merely a collection of disconnected facts, a set of descriptions. The astonishing variety of nature...cannot be probed and understood. Add evolution—and it becomes possible to make inferences and predictions.... All of a sudden patterns emerge everywhere, and apparently trivial details become interesting.

Evolution may be an interpretation of events—a story, if you will—but it is an extraordinarily beautiful and compelling story that allows us to shape disparate phenomena into a meaningful whole. In this sense it is no different from other scientific theories that are powerfully illuminating but always tentative, provisional, and subject to revision. At the same time we need to recognize that the power of these ideas is undergirded by the validation they receive from a community of interested scholars. Indeed, without this validation, there can be no agreement on the truthfulness (albeit tentative, at least until it is proved otherwise) of the ideas. Scientific discourse is, in this respect, no different from other kinds of knowledge. We have increasingly come to see just how much what we call knowledge, in any area of human experience and endeavor, depends on a community of interested participants. Postmodern philosophers like Richard Rorty and Thomas Kuhn on this side of the Atlantic and Michel Foucault and Jean-Francois Lyotard in France[4] have made clear that what we think of as our knowledge of the world, both natural and social, is simply inseparable from a community that shares a common way of understanding reality. This community of understanding, they further suggest, is always a manifestation of where the dominant power is in the culture. Whether in the world of scientific inquiry or in our apparently common sense view of our day-to-day lives, what is taken to be true is always an expression of who controls the flow of ideas and who is able to shape our expectations and imagination of what seems plausible. This is a critical step in the process of sensitizing students to the relative or situational nature of our knowledge about the world. The golden rule here is not simply that those who have the gold rule, but that those who can define what gives gold its superior value hold the real power. They are able to control the ideas that tell us who we are, who belongs in our community, what our community values are, and where and how we may find the true meaning of our lives. Truth here is no longer the product of a disinterested process of rational inquiry that is enshrined in our enlightenment-bequeathed vision of objective knowing, unsullied by human emotions and prejudices. Instead, we see that knowing is always mixed up in the much messier business of human interests, passions, subjective beliefs, and values.

What this means for those of us who are interested in educating for peace is helping our students understand that conflicts invariably imply that human beings are making sense of the same situation, context, or issue in very different ways. And no simple appeal to the facts or evidence will produce agreement or common understanding. What we have come to see is that knowledge cannot easily be separated from the knower (or as the philosopher Friedrich Nietzsche put it, the dancer cannot be separated from the dance), whose view of the world is profoundly influenced by the history, social experience, and cultural assumptions that constrain and shape the way we understand things. Rational inquiry as to the true nature of a problem or conflict will rarely assuage protagonists of the other side's sense of injustice. Truth in the context of human conflict cannot be separated from the deep emotion that frames and distills the very meaning of truth itself. (The satirist Stephen Colbert has coined the wonderful term "truthiness" to refer to the inevitably emotion-laden nature of what we take to be true—things that appeal to our preferences and prejudices as much as to our rational intellect in deciding what are valid claims.) The question then is no longer who is right or who is wrong. Instead, we have to discover the "truth" of each side's suffering, fear, anguish, and sense of injustice. It is in this realm of multiple and colliding truths that the struggle for peace and reconciliation is found. To find the truth that is held so tightly by each side means that we must "excavate" each side's view of reality and truth. This is no easy thing to do. It is even more difficult when we, ourselves, identify with one side or another in a conflict or struggle. Understanding here means not a cool, detached, objective hearing, but an active listening that allows us to enter the emotional world of the other. I am speaking here of a *compassionate knowing* that seeks to grasp how it feels to live in the world of the other with all of its hurt, pain, humiliation, blame, and suffering. Compassionate knowing means that, as much as possible, we have to try to suspend what we assume about the other and instead attempt to share the other's worldview with all of its complex emotions. Such knowing brings closer the possibility of finding the middle path of compromise between two competing worldviews and overcoming the intransigence of mutually exclusive claims about truth and reality.

HEALING ISRAEL/PALESTINE: THE HERMENEUTICS OF PEACE

For many years I have been deeply connected to the struggle between Jews and Palestinians around the question of the Israeli state and Palestinian rights. As a Jew, I have had to constantly struggle with my own emotional and intellectual one-sidedness in this conflict and the difficult task of seeing the world from the perspective of Palestinians and Arabs. For most Jews, including myself, Israel represents a haven created to safeguard the remnant of a people brutalized by history—a land that offered those who survived the Nazi genocide and other anti-Semitism the promise of a normalized and secure existence in a country of their own. It was a place where the ancient and historic attachment to the land (of which Jews are constantly reminded in their prayers, recitations of the sacred books of the Torah, and in the celebration of their holidays and commemorations) promised to be renewed through the creation of a modern and flourishing oasis in the sand. For Palestinians in particular, and Arabs in general, the Zionist state (as Arabs commonly refer to it) was nothing less than another European settler state imposed by the very colonial powers that had exploited and oppressed the people of this region. In this narrative the Jews were not the victims of history, but one more incarnation of imperialist arrogance and disregard. I concluded long ago that peace in this seemingly endless conflict, which has taken the lives of thousands of men, women, and children, requires a recognition of the "hermeneutics" of conflict in which there is no final truth but only conflicting interpretations of experience and of history.[5] *After listening to the endless and conflicting arguments of Jews and Arabs over many years, I have come to believe that my enemy is someone whose story I have not yet heard.*

While the guns continue to fire and bombs continue to explode, and as bodies are broken and lives are destroyed, it is very difficult to achieve the attentive and empathetic listening that hermeneutical understanding requires. Although, it should be said, I know of many brave and extraordinary people who manage to do just that—listen with compassion and openness to the pain, as well as the anger, of the other side. These people are able to break out of the closed "bubble" of understanding and attitudes that seem to permanently leave each side in the grip of unrelenting suspicion and animosity. For most Jews, both inside Israel and outside, the experience of being under attack by Palestinians and other Arabs is difficult to distinguish, at least psychologically, from the history of brutal persecution at the hands of the *goyim* (literally, strangers, but the word refers to all those who are not Jewish). For them, this is but one more episode of attempted annihilation by those who hate Jews. But the strong hand of their own state will allow no passive acquiescence to the murder of the Jewish people. Every act of aggression will be met with force and returned violence. To the outsider, Israel appears secure and insurmountably strong, but to the Jew, the Nazi genocide is only a few years in the past. Fear and existential threat haunt the Jewish psyche. For the Palestinians, however, living under occupation, the sense of social and psychic destruction is much more than the feared return of history. It is nothing less than today's nightmare predicament in which they face the unending indignity of military control over their lives, checkpoints that makes mobility all but impossible, the misery of poverty and unemployment caused by years of occupation, the disproportionate firepower of a powerful army, and the continuing loss of land and homes to Israeli settlers. Amin Maalouf[6] expresses this anguish eloquently:

> At every turn they meet with disappointment, disillusion or humiliation. How can they not feel their identities are threatened? That they are living in a world which belongs to others and obeys rules made by others, a world where they are orphans, strangers, intruders or pariahs? What can be done to prevent some of them feeling they have been bereft of everything and have nothing more to lose so that they come, like Samson, to pray to God for the temple to collapse on top of them and their enemies alike?

The struggle of two groups of people for one small piece of territory can, finally, only be resolved through a compromise. Such a compromise will require each side in this bloody war to hear the story of the other and to recognize in it the human fear and loss that has led to endless violence and the deep historical and cultural claims that each side brings to the table. Of course, compromise requires the willingness to let go of deeply held convictions that only one side possesses right and justice. The ability to hear and let go is made much more difficult as pain and hardship continue to be inflicted. Such suffering hardens the heart. It does not soften it. Despite all of this, the middle path of compromise can be taken, and sometimes is. One can see this in Northern Ireland where after decades of bloody conflict, people exhausted by the bloodshed, although not entirely giving up their own historical narrative, agreed to share power and make political and social changes that mediated competing claims. The Catholic population accepts that, at least for now, Northern Ireland remains part of the United Kingdom. Protestants meanwhile agree to a sharing of political power and the beginning of economic and cultural cross-border links between the Irish Republic and the British enclave as an acknowledgment that Ireland is a single historic entity. One can see it too in the courageous willingness of the Dalai Lama to acknowledge Chinese hegemony over Tibetan territory while desiring in exchange only cultural autonomy and religious freedom for his people. And in 1994 the extraordinary moment of transformation in South Africa that converted the heinous apartheid state with all of the exploitation, oppression, and abuse of its African majority into the "rainbow nation" of the new democratic South Africa is also recalled. This transformation required the end of the narrative of the superior status of the white population and its replacement with a vision of equality and inclusion of all citizens of the country—a transformation that meant immense changes in terms of political power, economic life, culture, education, and general opportunity in that nation.

Neighbors Who Hate and the Possibilities for Peace

Yet the process by which we may come to hear one another and recognize the validity and authenticity of each other's concerns is no easy matter. Proximity or social contact between competing groups is no guarantee that there will be an openness of the heart or mind to others' experience and story. We often see how people who have lived closely with one another, frequently as neighbors, can remain or become violently hostile to each other. We have witnessed this in Northern Ireland among neighbors who are Catholic or Protestant; in what was Yugoslavia where differences in identity and religion led to a succession of wars and ethnic cleansing; in African countries such as Rwanda and Kenya where tribal differences have led to brutal wars and genocide; in India among Hindus and Muslims; among Sunni and Shia Muslims in Iraq; and in many other places throughout the world. Growing up, living, and working closely with others is no guarantee of the kind of human understanding and empathy that might forestall hatred and violence. Still, I must also point to the continued efforts of courageous and morally and spiritually inspired people to bring human beings together in communities and schools so that bridges of common understanding might be created and nurtured. There are many wonderful and moving examples of these kinds of efforts throughout the world. All of them attempt to go against the grain of deep prejudice and negative assumptions about the other, and instead try to build appreciation and positive recognition between different communities and encourage a sense of a shared humanity.

One moving example of this kind of brave commitment is found in the village of *Neve Shalom/Wahat Al-Salam* in Israel—a village that, intentionally, is known by its twin Hebrew and Arabic names. Neve Shalom/Wahat Al-Salam was the brainchild of a French Jew who was baptized into the Christian faith, Father Bruno Hussar, who arrived in Israel in 1953. Hussar was an extraordinary man of faith who devoted his life to peacemaking and mutual understanding. He was nominated for the Nobel Prize in 1988 and the Prix de l'Amitie Judeo-Chretienne in 1994. In an interview, Father Bruno explained that his vision of a community based on coexistence and mutual respect came from seeing that "both Jews and Palestinians are wanderers in the desert of war, but they have invented a place to 'be' here in this village—a shared enterprise of peacemaking through community and education." Father Bruno died at the age of 85 and was buried in the village's cemetery. What he advocated—a binational community of Israeli Jews and Palestinians and a school that taught and advocated peace and equality—has survived and even flourished, though not without struggle and difficulties. This community provides a powerful example of what it means for people divided by injustices, violence, and mistrust to come together and try to live with respect and in friendship. The school, which, uniquely in Israel, brings together children from these different communities, provides a metaphor for what is involved in trying to address the rights and needs of all the people who are citizens of this state in the spirit of social justice and democratic values.

In a wonderful book by Grace Feuerverger,[7] *Oasis of Dreams*, which describes the history and experience of life in this community, the author provides us with a moving and powerful account of what it means for a small group of people to come together and attempt to build an existence in which people confront and struggle with these issues. How can Jews and Palestinians live together in a spirit that recognizes the equal value and worth of all? This is a community that attempts to validate each group's national and religious traditions, history, and identity while building relationships of respect and even affection across the walls of misunderstanding and distrust erected through the years of conflict and war. Nothing describes the day-to-day struggle of mediating these differences better than Feuerverger's exploration of the elementary school in this community. She movingly describes how children share celebrations of each other's holidays, learn about the different ways they understand history, and come to play and build friendships with one another. None of this, she constantly reminds the reader, happens without addressing complex and often achingly painful tensions in relationships—among teachers, children, and families.

Yet in spite of the inspiring example of coexistence that the village of Neve Shalom/Wahat Al-Salam provides in this region of continuing mistrust, hatred, and war, the difficulties of achieving mutual recognition and understanding among human beings who are divided by distinct loyalties and beliefs are not easily eradicated. Shared human understanding and reciprocal communal affirmation are not easily won. I believe that the most powerful moment in this text exists in the interview that the author conducts with Rayek Rizek, a Palestinian resident of the village. The interview, in fact, is a painful and honest exchange between the Jewish author and her Arab interlocutor. In many ways this conversation sheds ample light on the fundamental tragedy of the Israel-Palestine struggle. Feuerverger conveys to Rizek the history of her own family's experience through the Holocaust with all of its loss and terror. She tells him of her parents' struggle to enter Canada as displaced refugees and her own subsequent sense of estrangement and alienation as the child of survivors. Israel, she explains, represents a coming home, a place to feel whole and connected and to be proud of one's Jewishness. In return, Rizek talks openly about the misery of Palestinian exile and the anger of Palestinians having to pay for what the Nazis did in Europe to the Jews.

For each of them their history is one of terrible suffering and victimhood and the tragic way their respective suffering has turned into an endless conflict and bloodletting. In reading Feuerverger's account I am reminded of Michael Lerner's comment in *Healing Israel/Palestine* about the way the tragic history of the Jews redounded into the oppression of the Palestinians. He suggests, metaphorically, that when the Jews jumped out of the burning house of Europe to escape persecution they landed on the backs of the Palestinians. The suffering of the Jews became the oppression of the Palestinians. And the desperation of the Jews in Palestine, and then Israel, left little room for compassion towards those who lost their land and homes and who now appeared to many Jews as one more incarnation of hatred towards the Jewish people.

Though he lives among Jews, Rizek acknowledges that never before had he heard a personal account of the emotional woundedness of the Holocaust from a child of survivors. In a revealing statement, the author declares,

> There is no justice in all this mess. I see it as a sick twist of fate that the Palestinians became the indirect victim of the Nazis too. We're both victims, but how do both Jews and Palestinians begin to discuss this in open dialogue...they can both acknowledge one another's pain and loss and fear. To me that's the real impasse. It takes compassion and real courage to do that. I don't know what else to say.[8]

In this light we may understand Rabbi Lerner's insistence that any resolution of this conflict requires not just a political settlement, but a process of reconciliation in which each side can learn and acknowledge the suffering caused to the other.

A Pedagogy of Engagement and Dialogue

Experiences like the one at this Israeli village clarify that the process of moving individuals towards greater understanding and empathy for the other is difficult and fraught with misunderstandings and frustrations. Yet the process of reducing hate, bigotry, and violence cannot happen without such efforts. And in spite of these difficulties educational programs that bring together young people across the boundaries of race, sexual identity, religion, ethnicity, and nationality to meet and explore their differences and recognize their similarities are of immense value and importance. Just ask participants (and teachers) at places like the Anytown program in North Carolina, or Seeds of Peace in Maine, or the Givat Haviva Institute in Hadera, Israel, to gain an appreciation of how profoundly they are affected in their attitudes and beliefs. These places can, and do, transform prejudice into sympathy and hostility into friendship. They indicate to us what can be achieved in educational settings when the goal is to promote peaceful relationships. School classrooms can join these efforts if that is what we as educators and citizens believe is an important enough goal of education in the twenty-first century. But the kind of engaged pedagogy that is too rarely found in our schools today will need to be practiced. In the first place, the classroom becomes a place in which learning comes not from the usual top down, "chalk and talk" kind of instruction, but from the process of dialogue among students. This is a classroom in which there is no single, right answer to any question. What is valued, instead, is the play of multiple and shared responses and views among all the participants. It is a process that facilitates and encourages the expression of diverse perspectives and vantage points. And in this setting no single voice can be allowed to dominate the conversation. This must be a place in which all voices, even the shyest and most withdrawn, are encouraged to join the flow of ideas, opinions, and shared experiences. The goal is always to promote the freest of expression and an uninhibited articulation regarding how one sees and experiences social reality. Truth-telling, or more precisely, the telling of one's own truth, must be encouraged and facilitated by both teachers and other students. What does it mean to be Black in America today? Or to be a young gay man or lesbian woman having to deal with daily harassment and insults? What does it feel like to be an observant Jew in a Christian world? How threatening is it to be a Muslim student in post-9-11 America? How is it to grow up as the child of illegal Mexican parents in today's climate of hostility and suspicion? How is one's commitment to evangelical Christianity treated by others in school? How do media messages shape or distort girls' sense of self, worth, and agency? Is disability a catalyst for mocking behavior? The list goes on. In each case the intent is to create a space in which one's story can be told. The classroom becomes a site for sharing one's struggles, shame, fear, humiliation, exclusion, and violent abuse. It is also a place in which there is a sharing of those things that give individuals the strength to resist and survive in tough circumstances—communal solidarities, friendships, spiritual and emotional resources—which allow them, as the singer Michael Franti says, to stay human.

All of this requires that others in the same room not merely hear what is said, but try to actively listen. They must enter, as much as possible, into the context and lives of the teller. They must move beyond their own zone of comfortable understanding and cross the border into the other's world of meaning and experience. As I have already noted, this is no easy task. Certainly we cannot ever fully know the life of another person; we cannot look out at the world through their eyes or hear the world through their ears. Yet the effort to gain even some partial sense of the other's viewpoint, to walk in another's moccasins, is enormously worthwhile, for this is how our empathy and compassion for others grow. We must, of course, deal with our own resistances to what we hear. In other words, students have to recognize their own prejudices, attitudes, and negative assumptions towards others. In our schools this means being able to see how such things as racism, sexism, homophobia, views about immigrants, views about other religions, and so on, color attitudes and make it difficult to really hear what others may be saying about their lives. Meaningful dialogue among individuals cannot be separated from the effort to suspend their beliefs and assumptions about others. Obviously this puts great responsibility on the shoulders of the teacher, who must coax students—sometimes gently and sometimes with greater directness—to acknowledge and own up to those things that get in the way of honest communication. For good reason this can be difficult territory for teachers. Such a process is fraught with emotion, including fear, anger, and frustration. As a culture we are not at our best dealing publically with such feelings. There is the sense that things can get "out of control" quickly, and the classroom can turn into a space for expressing rage and hostility. Here, laying down the ground rules for dialogue are critical. These must include the following:

- Students must maintain respect for each other's humanity even while serious differences of views emerge.
- There must be a refusal to allow any kind of personal attacks.
- There must be opportunity and encouragement for all students to voice their opinion.
- There can be absolutely no threats of physical violence.
- There must be a commitment on the part of students to listen attentively and with openness to what others say.
- There must be recognition of the way we approach social reality from multiple standpoints and perspectives, with humility towards the certainty of our own particular truth.

Change in how we see the world and how we relate to others comes at a cost. We must give up the comfortable and familiar ideological assumptions that shape our worldview with what may be negative and derogatory beliefs about others that structure the categories that shape our construction of reality. This process of change means letting go of the reassuringly familiar and entering a world of new uncertainties. This process may lead to some confusion and anxiety as we feel the need to jettison things that perhaps were part of family lore or our community's folk wisdom. This means students will have to confront the dilemma of letting go of family or social values, albeit ones that were demeaning of, or negative towards, others. In some cases it means confronting contradictory religious values that are incompatible with new forms of social acceptance and solidarity. My own experience, as a teacher, has been to try to ensure that students are neither blamed nor made to feel a sense of guilt. Such feelings more often close off the kind of honest and open dialogue I seek. I often open discussions about prejudice with the acknowledgment that it is difficult to grow up in this country (or in the United Kingdom, where I spent my childhood and youth) without absorbing the deep assumptions of a racist, Eurocentric, Christian-dominated, patriarchal, and homophobic worldview. So any discussion must reveal how we have all learned values and attitudes that demean, hurt, and exclude others. I emphasize that no-one, including myself as a teacher, is a saint regarding these things. Instead, I suggest, we are all travelers on the same road trying to undo the deep distortions in how we have learned to view others who are different from us in some way. I continue by saying that this is a journey we never fully complete. We are always in the midst of trying to uncover and disentangle ourselves from the deeply harmful and disfiguring way we have learned to view other human beings. So, to whatever extent we are able to free ourselves from these negative forms of consciousness and however much we can open ourselves to others' lives, it should be welcomed and affirmed. I have found that in acknowledging that making such changes can be a difficult, painful, even dangerous struggle, space is opened for individuals to speak honestly about what they believe, or were taught to believe, and their efforts to move beyond these harmful beliefs.

I must emphasize again here that all of this assumes a major change in our vision and practice of education. First, the classroom as a place where individuals can gain understanding of others' lives, as well as insight into their own identity, becomes paramount. Success in education is no longer understood as simply the vehicle for individual achievement and success. The moral purpose of education as a means to develop social relationships that are respectful, empathic, and compassionate becomes understood as a central purpose of schooling in the twenty-first century. Second, this means we must profoundly reorient our approach to pedagogy. Classrooms become places where dialogue and exploration into what shapes, or disfigures, our humanity assume far more importance. Students are encouraged to articulate their own experience in coping with the world, as well as that of their families and communities. Honest expression is valued and deep reflection is encouraged. And a critical problematizing of the assumptions and prejudices that individuals bring with them into school is demanded. And throughout the curriculum the uncertain, provisional, and interpretive nature of all knowledge is emphasized. And with this is the continuing attention to how knowledge about reality is always influenced and shaped by social interests, taken-for-granted assumptions, communal preferences, and ideologies. As never before, the twenty-first century will be a time in which human beings and diverse worldviews will meet, interact, and sometimes collide. To prepare young people for this kind of world will demand an education in which the hermeneutic process of hearing and attempting to truly understand the words and lives of others assumes unparalleled importance. The challenge of human survival in this new century is great, and education will need to take on a radically different shape if it is to contribute in a significant way to this challenge.

Voices of Anger: Hearts of Compassion

The challenge of listening more openly and empathically to the voices of others is, as I have indicated, enormously difficult. Yet our vision in education must constitute a horizon of possibility that offers us a direction and a goal, even if we are destined to always fall short of fully achieving it. We may set our compass in the direction of greater understanding across the borders of our lives, situations, and experiences, yet recognize that the barriers we set up to resist such understanding are very great. Our efforts are to be measured, not in terms of some absolute success, but by whether we can bring our students to at least a place of greater sympathy and understanding towards those whose lives are different in some important way.

I am writing this having just returned from a contentious town meeting on health reform in the United States. As I argued with people whose worldview and political sympathies were so different from mine, I could feel my blood pressure rising and the level of my frustration increasing. What is wrong with these people? Why can't they see things the way I do? If I shout a little louder or provide another set of facts, surely they will come around to my way of thinking! Of course, it works that way only in my dreams when the forcefulness and cogency of my argument makes immediate converts to my truth! Anyone who has ever been married knows the exasperating futility of arguments that seem to go in circles—each partner talks at, and past, the other, desperately seeking to bring the other to their point of view. The problem is that the particular issue that we are arguing over may represent just a sliver of a much larger viewpoint. Like an iceberg in which only ten percent is visible above the surface, so it is with our arguments, which often occlude the much deeper differences in how we make sense of our experience and world. The differences may appear to be matters of intellect and knowledge, but the glue that gives them their resilience is emotional and psychological. As a result, any serious challenges we may make to another's understanding of the world may be a challenge to some deeper aspects of their identity and the structure of their loyalties and emotional ties.

In the classroom, questioning students' prejudices around homosexuality often challenges something fundamental in their religious or moral worldview. More than this, it may well be experienced as a threat to the bonds that connect them to parents and other family members. Diggging into the roots of racism in our classrooms, as I have seen on many occasions, may well force students to confront painful and disturbing prejudices that run among their family members. Questioning the justification for American military interventions may rouse angry resistance in students whose siblings or parents have been, or are presently, risking their lives in a foreign war. Teaching in a state with a high number of military bases, I have more than once encountered the fury of students angered by my skeptical views of our reasons for going to war in Iraq. In a broader sense, my advocacy of greater social justice and preference for policies of greater economic democracy and social equality encounter angry responses because they appear to violate some students' deeply held beliefs about liberty and personal responsibility. The latter touch on some basic ideological differences in American culture about the nature of capitalism or the free-enterprise system and the proper role of government. In all these cases, what may begin as a relatively amicable disagreement about ideas or viewpoints is liable to quickly spill over into something far more hostile and contentious, and what comes to be at stake is something far more primal and visceral.

Developing empathy for the other's worldview is crucial to the possibility of overcoming irreconcilable conflicts. Yet empathy requires understanding of just how tightly the views, knowledge, and understanding of the other are woven into the emotional tapestry that forms one's identity. This identity binds together those primal allegiances of family and community. It is not difficult, given this, to see how much we strive to defend our beliefs and resist those who want to show us we may be wrong. It is not too much of an exaggeration to say that our lives depend on it. Who we are, who we care about, what it is that provides us with meaning—all are at stake here. And we will defend, sometimes to the death, those articles of belief. We will deny those things that might show flaws in our logic. We will deflect the idea that our beliefs or understanding about the world might be the cause of someone else's pain or oppression. We will find ways to blame or project onto others faults for which we may be culpable. We will rationalize and legitimize even the most flagrant acts of persecution or indifference perpetrated upon those outside of our community. All of this means that cultivating empathy often requires asking people to get "outside of their own skins"—to risk their own deeply held beliefs—in order to hear and understand someone else's experience, which may conflict or call into question things that seem to provide the existential ground upon which they stand. It is no wonder that the classroom work we undertake to encourage empathy for the other is such a difficult process. Teachers who do this day in and day out know how much patience it takes. How quickly the emotional pot can boil over. They know that humor is often needed to cut through the moments of sullen anger. That sometimes students who are the most unmovable in their convictions may turn around weeks, months, or even years later as they discover a different set of truths. Or that students who are the loudest and most belligerent in their resistance to another way of knowing are sometimes the ones who are struggling the hardest with the dissonance between what they have been taught and what they now hear. But, of course, there are no guarantees to this process. Indeed, sometimes what we do may harden convictions and freeze differences.

In the end the struggle to create greater empathy may lead us to some even deeper insights—ones that demand more from us than even this capacity to know or see the world from the perspective of the other and the recognition that ours is not the only truth. It demands from us compassion and forgiveness. As the song goes, "There but for fortune goes you or I." The message is a simple one though immensely demanding. It is to see human actions not as the result of evil inclination or the desire to hurt others, but as the consequence of the situations into which we are born or in which we find ourselves. It is what any of us could or would do, and believe, if this was *our* situation and *our* experience, and if we understood it as what was expected of us. It is what we would likely believe if we had been led to understand that this is the nature of the world. It is what we would embrace if the elemental ties of family and community were bound up in this particular set of beliefs. Once this is understood, our anger at others for the stupidity, callousness, and oppressiveness of their beliefs can give way to compassion for others' lives and the beliefs they have produced, and forgiveness for the hurt that their beliefs have caused. This is the extraordinary message of groups like the Truth and Reconciliation Commission, which attempted to produce reconciliation and healing at the end of South Africa's apartheid regime. Forgiveness for human acts of brutality is possible if the perpetrators can hear the pain of those who were hurt by their actions and acknowledge with contrition their participation in these acts. By their nature these individuals are not irreconcilably bad. They, too, were the "victims" of an evil system in which brutal behavior was normalized and expected. This is what former President Jimmy Carter meant when he said that the end of segregation and Jim Crow in the southern United States liberated not just Blacks—it also liberated whites from their roles in a vicious social system. As a result, both Black and white citizens of the south would be able to regain their humanity. Perhaps it is the Vietnamese monk, Thich Nhat Hanh, who said it best:

> ...everyone is a victim. If you are not a victim of this, you are a victim of that...when you have anger and despair in you, you are a victim of your anger and despair, and you suffer very deeply....We may be the victim of others, and we may be the victim of ourselves. We tend to

believe the enemy is outside of us, but very often we are our own worst enemy because of what we have done to our body and mind.... The practice recommended (in Plum Village) is not to destroy the human being, but to destroy the real enemy that is inside the human being.[9]

For Thich Nhat Hanh, the real enemy inside us is fear, anger, and despair. It is these that have to be faced and removed:

When we cultivate the energy of mindfulness, the first insight we have is that the main cause of our suffering, of our misery, is not the other person—it is the seed of anger in us. Then we will stop blaming the other person for causing all our suffering.[10]

Our compassion for the other comes from recognizing the fear and anger that we have inherited and has been inscribed in us, the fear and anger that have become written into the DNA of our belief systems—religious, cultural, and political. And these cause suffering, not just to those who find themselves castigated as the objects of these beliefs, but to the perpetrators themselves who live under the constant danger of a world that must seem so perilous or threatening. Empathy in a world so filled with conflict, anger, and violence means allowing ourselves to enter into the lives of others with all of its terrors, insecurities, and perceived dangers. It means allowing the stories of rage, resentment, and hostility to be told and to hear them with compassion and even forgiveness.

Educating the Ear (Not Just the Eye!)

When I was in Cape Town, South Africa, I was fortunate to have a chance to talk with Archbishop Desmond Tutu, a Nobel Peace Prize recipient and leading anti-apartheid activist, about the meaning of peace education. In his reply to my first question about the nature of peace education, he suggested that peace education meant simply allowing the stories of those who have been scarred by violence and oppression to be heard. "Make it possible," he said, "for those who suffer, to speak." His simple suggestion made me realize to what degree school emphasizes the capacity and disposition of the *eye* over the *ear*. While the ear remains open to whatever stimulation is in its range, the eye can close and shut itself off from the world. Through dialogue the ear brings us closer to others, while the eye is trained to permit the individual to unemotionally distance the self from what is seen. The ear is about the messy and visceral nature of relationships, while the eye is about the precise measurement and dispassionate analysis of an object. The emphasis on the education of the eye represents the legacy and continuing dominance of our enlightenment tradition (even the term enlightenment relates to what is seen or illuminated). It has quite obviously brought to our lives the immense benefits of science and technology. Yet Archbishop Tutu's suggestion speaks to our civilization's need to allow more people to speak and share their stories and for more voices to be heard. We need, simply, for there to be more *ear* in our education (and perhaps less *eye*). In the classroom its meaning is clear. We need to recognize the importance of the classroom as a place where stories can be told, lives can be shared, and the experience of others can be communicated. This would, of course, make the classroom a far richer, more stimulating and relevant place for our students. But beyond this it would mark an important shift towards the making of a culture of peace—one in which we release and nurture the voices of all those who share their lives with us in our communities, nation, and across the planet so that we may hear their pain, struggles, and hopes. In the end, a culture of peace will rest on the degree to which our children are brought up to know, and to communicate, the values of mutual understanding, empathy, compassion, and, yes, forgiveness. Quite clearly our educational focus today is very far from this, yet a culture of peace should be the horizon of possibility for our work tomorrow.

Chapter Three

Undoing the Narrative of Competition

You want peace. There is no one who does not want peace. Yet there is something else in you that wants the conflict. You may not be able to feel it at this moment. You may have to wait for a situation or even just a thought that triggers a reaction in you; someone accusing you of this or that, not acknowledging you, encroaching on your territory, questioning the way you do things, an argument about money... Can you feel the enormous surge of force moving through you, the fear, perhaps being masked by anger or hostility? Can you hear your own voice becoming harsh or shrill, or louder and a few octaves lower? Can you be aware of your mind racing to defend its position, justify, attack, blame? In other words, can you awaken at that moment of unconsciousness? Can you feel that there is something in you that is at war, something that feels threatened and wants to survive at all costs, that needs the drama in order to assert its identity as the victorious character within that theatrical production? Can you feel there is something in you that would rather be right than at peace?

—Eckhart Tolle, *A New Earth*

War is the calculated and condoned slaughter of human beings too often sent into combat as "cannon fodder" by politicians who should have settled their conflicts by dueling among themselves. War isn't worth one life. Too many have died. Irrespective of the uniforms we wore, we were all victims.

—From a BBC interview with Harry Patch, the last remaining British soldier of World War I who died in 2009

The Olympic Games: A Manichean Tale

I began writing this chapter shortly after the end of the Beijing Olympics. These games provided a riveting spectacle of extraordinary

Chinese pageantry and organization, for me and for many people around the world. But they especially offered to literally billions of people an enthralling show of incredible athletic skill and competitive spirit.

Even now, it is difficult to forget Michael Phelps' fantastic swimming success or the unbelievable speed of the Jamaican runner Usain Bolt. The Olympic Games, as we are often reminded by media commentators and the official organizers, offer us a picture of a world come together in peaceful harmony to celebrate the shared human drama of amazing sporting ability and extraordinary dedication. One of NBC's commentators described it as a two-week holiday from the world's divisions and troubles. There is much to be believed in this statement. After two weeks of intense competition between individuals and the nations they represent, the finale of the games has, since the 1956 games in Melbourne, Australia, featured all competitors entering the stadium as a single mass, not separated into national squads as they are in the opening ceremony. The message is that the whole world's youth has come together in celebration undivided by national flags and identities. (Dara Torres, the Olympic swimmer, noted that the games are both metaphorically and literally a *love fest* for the participants!) It is, in my belief, a lovely image and one I find moving in its vision. There they are, thousands of attractive and ecstatic young people ambling around the stadium conveying an unalloyed joyfulness and energy—an image so at odds with the everyday pictures of division, hostility, and violence that seem to pervade our world.

It is easy to forget, in this moment of happy unity among people from every corner of our planet, that the most compelling dynamic of the games is *not* the oneness of humanity, but national identification and separation and the competition for national glory. I confess that I found myself taking sneak peaks at the so-called "medal table" in my morning newspaper, which provided a ranking of nations according to each one's success at attaining gold, silver, or bronze in the events (a habit, my wife assures me, that is much more common among men than women). It was no accident that China this time was at the top of the table in terms of the number of gold medals won by its athletes. This was a clear result of the "athletics machine" that had been set up to ensure a large number of victories. The "machine" was established to identify potential outstanding athletes at a young age and then subject them to almost military discipline and training to ensure their success. To be fair about this, China is not alone in this ferocious effort to find winners. For countries such as the United States,

Russia (and its forerunner, the Soviet Union), Germany, Australia, Britain, and even smaller countries such as Cuba and Korea, showing the world their superior athletic prowess is no game. It might be said that Olympic competitiveness is war by other means. National status and glory rest on how many medals a country can claim. Victory in the sports arena is a deadly serious business. Somehow the ability of a country's citizens to run or swim faster than others, to outscore others on the soccer field or basketball court, or to show greater skill with a sword, on a horse, or in a boat allows a nation to bask in the reflected glow of success and superiority. Not just the athletes, but all of their compatriots as well can feel better about who they are. For countries that do well there is exaltation; for those that have meager successes there is an agonizing contemplation of national humiliation. And for the athletes who bring home the gold medals there is the adulation of a grateful nation (and frequently the opportunity for very lucrative gain).

As everyone knows, the Olympics, like other professional sports, have become a vehicle of huge proportions in terms of their commercial value, involving enormous corporate investments in facilities, athletic materials, and sponsorships. Such support in turn produces tremendous returns in corporate profits and visibility. Clearly it is in the interest of such corporate interests to grease the wheels of competition between nations. The more that is at stake in such games the greater the public's interest, and the more exposure there is for the commercial products that support the athletes' quest for success. Yet beyond this, events like the Olympic Games take on a quasi-religious aura in the way sport becomes linked to some transcendent purpose. Look at the rituals of flag raising, hymn singing, and pious speech making that accompany the events themselves. The U.S. basketball team's unofficial designation in Beijing as the "redeem team" spoke in an immediate way to the sense that earlier losses can be overcome; humiliation and shame can, through victory on the court, be redeemed and made good. One may remember how the famous ice hockey game between the Soviet Union and the United States at the 1980 Olympic Games became something much more: a playing out of the struggle between the supposed forces of light and evil in the world. Or at least that was the way it was portrayed in the American media. Other examples abound of the way a simple game becomes a moral tale of good versus bad, of the virtuous against the duplicitous. Sporting victory becomes a morally ennobling and humanly elevating pursuit, not just a game played with a ball, between tracks or a net, or with a stick, bike, or bat.

If the official rubric of international sporting competition is unity among people and nations, its real purpose is probably to indulge in that most pervasive and popular pursuit of sorting out winners from losers, the outstanding from the merely mediocre. Even the extraordinary athletes who end up on the podium as second or third best in the world are rarely remembered or lauded. Yet at the same time, perhaps the global dimensions of events like the Olympic Games should not be dismissed out of hand. Perhaps the global event has an appeal that really is more than TV network hype. Maybe there is a genuine and widely shared feeling of celebration and delight at the idea of a world coming together to appreciate extraordinary human abilities and skills that does, at moments, transcend borders. Perhaps there is a taste here of a global community brought together to celebrate human accomplishments across and beyond all of our differences. And through the wonders of technology, the virtual community can now embrace billions of its fellow beings simultaneously as these moments intimate to us the oneness of the human race and our closeness and connection as inhabitants of the same planet. Perhaps these moments offer us just a glimpse of a world made whole, in which fractiousness and destruction give way to the shared pleasure of viewing the amazing capabilities and feats of human beings regardless of their home country.

COMPETITION: THE ONE AND ONLY SYSTEM

The overwhelming power of competition to compel our attention and to stimulate our passions in the modern world is undeniable. International sporting competition is but one, though enormously visible, example of competition's grip on human emotions and imagination. This is powerfully reinforced and daily legitimized by our experience of life in a capitalist or market-dominated society. Throughout our world the market is increasingly seen as the single best way to organize the production and distribution of those goods and services upon which human life depends. The market has increasingly come to be seen as the most efficient, innovative, and productive means through which societies can meet the expectations of a good life for their citizens. Certainly there can be little doubt of the extraordinarily innovative power of capitalism and its historically unparalleled capacity to develop new technologies and products and make these available to millions, or indeed billions, of consumers throughout the world. Capitalist markets have transformed every aspect of human life, from the production of food to our means of transportation, and from the media of communication to the extraordinary development of medical technology. They have supplied us with fantastic new forms of electronic gadgetry, energy sources, and popular entertainments. And capitalist markets have raised the living standards of millions of people across the globe. There can be little doubt that millions of human beings today live material lives that could hardly be dreamt of just decades ago.

Yet despite its amazing power to materially transform lives and improve living conditions for so many, there is also a much darker side to the marketplace and its dominance as the engine that shapes our world. At its heart is the view that what sustains human activity and productivity is the will to compete—for more profit, more status, more influence, and more control. What drives capitalism is surely a dismal view of human motivation: the desire to beat out one's competition in order to have more, appear superior, own more, and have more power. Capitalism, for all its extraordinary productivity, offers us a vision of human life that is endlessly driven by egotistical desire: the drive to fulfill one's self-interest without concern for the wider social or communal consequences of what one does. The accumulation of profit, not human welfare, guides the markets' calculus of decision making. Selfish aggrandizement of the few, not broadly distributed improvement of the lives of the many, has always been at the cold heart of capitalism's system of organizing society. Certainly, as we see more clearly every day, concern for the well-being and long-term preservation of nature and our planetary environment has never been capitalism's concern. It is not for nothing that some who study the concentration of the world's economic resources in the hands of a few giant corporations refer to these corporations as pathological institutions.[1] Corporations, they argue, are institutions dedicated to maximizing their own wealth and influence regardless of the dehumanizing effect on the lives of workers and the corporation's lack of responsibility towards the well-being of communities. Only under intense political pressure do corporations respond to consumer safety issues, the destructive effects of their activities on the environment, and their obligation to provide safe working environments. They will ally themselves with even the most militaristic and repressive regimes in order to ensure their ability to maximize profits, and they are ready and willing to supply the most deadly of products to anyone who wants them if it ensures a healthy monetary return.[2] (It's certainly paradoxical, if not revealing, that the advertising jingle for a company that is one of the world's largest arms manufacturers, GE [General Electric], is "We Bring Good Things to Life"). Corporations spend literally billions of dollars each year to shape the values and human desires of the culture. The "educational" goal of this advertising is always to convince us that more is better, that happiness comes from material things, and that we can be smarter, more attractive, and more secure if only we buy the right products. The focus of this improvement is always the individual, or the individual's family. Rarely is it the community as a whole.

Although the market promises to lift all boats, in fact it doesn't. It produces a world of winners and losers. In the United States, the separation between the richest and the poorest is the greatest it's been since the 1920s. The top 1 percent of households owned 47 percent of all financial assets, which is more than the entire bottom 95 percent. David Korten,[3] one of the most insightful observers of business and the economic world, notes that

> ...in the decade between 1989 and 1999 the number of U.S. billionaires increased from 66 to 268. The number of people below the pitifully inadequate official poverty line (about $13,000 for a family of three in 1999) increased from 31.5 to 34.5 million. The ratio of CEO pay to the pay of an average worker rose from 141 to 1 in 1995 to 301 to 1 in 2003.

Another observer, Riane Eisler,[4] notes that by 2004 the salaries of CEOs had jumped to unheard of levels. Their pay, she says, in salary, bonus, and other compensation averaged $10.2 million in 2004. That same year, full-time worker pay averaged around $32,000. She continues:

> This widening of the economic gap between those on top and those on bottom both in the United States and other nations is not an isolated phenomenon. It is part of a larger regression towards more rigid top-down rankings in all spheres of life.

We have all seen, even in the midst of the worst economic downturn since the 1930s, the way that bankers have continued to pay themselves bonuses in the millions of dollars during a time when so many of their fellow citizens are losing their jobs and homes. David Korten notes that in the United States there are now (2008–2009) 12 million children (nearly 17 percent of the total) who live in families that fall below the official poverty line, which means families that cannot supply even the most basic needs to their children. An estimated

4 million children in this country experience prolonged periodic food insufficiency and hunger each year. By now the catastrophic situation with health care is widely known. At any one time somewhere around 50 million Americans have no health insurance. Anyone who has seen Michael Moore's brilliant exposé of the health insurance industry, *Sicko*, can have no doubt of the industry's inhumanity and inequity. Beyond the United States things are much, much worse. As Korten notes,[5]

> Globally, UNICEF reports that of the world's 2.2 billion children, 1 billion, nearly every second child, are living in poverty. Six hundred forty million children live without adequate shelter. Four hundred million have no access to health services. More than thirty thousand die each day, eleven million a year before the age of five, mostly from preventable causes.

There is no doubt that the ethic of competition has left a grotesque and ethically insupportable world of huge disparities in the lives of human beings. Whatever the praises sung by supporters of the free or unregulated market, the evidence of human misery and deprivation confronts us on every side. The quiet violence of lives destroyed and blighted by the ethic of competition and the moral economy of greedy self-interest are there for all who care to look.

Educating the Self for Competition

The market economy produces a market society—a society in which our lives are increasingly shaped by the uncertainty and insecurity of harsh competition. It is not just access to medical care, mortgages, jobs, and education that is the result of our capacity to be winners in the race for a decent and secure life. It is our very *being* that is shaped by our capacity to compete and succeed in the frighteningly precarious world in which we now live. We have, ourselves, become salable commodities that must compete with other commodified selves in order to prove our worth and value in the world. So-called reality TV (on both sides of the Atlantic) provides us with a mirror to see the kind of competitive world that we have created. In these shows individuals fight to survive and win—to be hired for a job, to find the perfect mate, to become rich, and so on. Entertainment comes from watching the manipulative, scheming, and frequently dishonest manner in which individuals attempt to remain in the hunt. It seems that there is no behavior too degrading or corrupt that competitors will employ in order to beat out their rivals; there is no behavior too venal for individuals in these shows in their efforts to become winners. Of course, the popularity of reality TV is no accident. It is only a small step removed from what most people face in the real world. In the increasingly insecure and uncertain world of global capitalism we feel more and more pressured to sell ourselves in order to survive. We are continually urged to make ourselves "marketable," to become masters of the game of what Erving Goffman[6] years ago called "impression management." We must become adept at the art of *appearing* to be smart enough, attractive enough, inventive enough, hardworking enough. Whole industries now exist that offer to teach us how we might learn to manage the impression we make on others: how to write a resume, how to perform at an interview, how to sell ourselves. Even in our most intimate relationships we are taught to act strategically and to treat others in instrumental ways so we can get them to give us what we want. And our political culture is almost indistinguishable from the exaggerated and over-hyped language of advertising as winning public office has become all about the capacity of one candidate to outhustle another through empty slogans, sleazy personal attacks, and the use of buzz words and expressions.

The famous French social critic Jean Baudrillard once described our culture as entirely taken over by public relations (PR). It is not difficult to understand what he means. Acute observers of our culture like Peter Gabel[7] have described the terrible damage that is done to the human psyche as we come to view our fellow human beings as competitors who must be beaten and outhustled to achieve what we need. This is a world in which we have become strangers to one another. The other is no longer a fellow human being possessed of infinite beauty and value, but an adversary to be outmaneuvered, outperformed, and outshone. And it is not just others who have become strangers to us, unknown beings who appear as a threat to our own well-being. We have become, says Gabel, strangers to ourselves. Filled with the dread and anxiety of a world in which we hardly know ourselves, we constantly attempt to impress strangers with how we speak, act, look, or perform. This is a double form of alienation, says Gabel. We are estranged from others as we become estranged from our authentic selves. It is no wonder that so many individuals enter the therapist's office complaining that they have become numb to themselves. They feel de-centered and emptied of emotion or passion. (It is interesting how some of the most influential spiritual teachers of our time speak of the need to come back to ourselves in the sense of being present in the "now" rather than always living for some future result or achievement—a process that seems increasingly challenging for most of us.) Paying too much attention to how we appear on the outside turns us into shells of people. It also reinforces our inability to come together with others in the fullness of our humanity. Our interactions are stunted by the nagging sense of distrust and vulnerability that characterizes social life. We approach others with wariness and suspicion as to their motives and interests, which mirror what we ourselves have become in a predatory and hyper-competitive world. In the end we seek the destruction of others just as they seek our destruction.

Schooling for Life as a Race

No institution teaches us to see the world through the lens of relentless competition more than school. It certainly can be argued that the most significant ideological purpose of schooling is to shape us as beings who take as a given that life is an endless race—for success, achievement, and self-worth. From the moment students step into the classroom the central message is that they are in an arena that will sort and select them, measure them, and ultimately allocate to them a "badge" of social value. Although we try to assure students, especially the very young, that everyone is loved and cherished, the truth emerges very quickly. Whether they like it or not, they are now participants in the deadly serious game of being assessed as to their worth: Who deserves to be praised, receive accolades, and be provided with special attention and who does not? In the world of small people the rewards are small—gold stars, permission to go play, or permission choose an activity for themselves. But the message could not be more profound. The apparent focus of attention is the student's academic skill, knowledge to solve a problem, or capacity to memorize some information. Yet the deeper consequence of the competitive classroom, which starts in such apparently innocent ways, is the making of our sense of worth and value. As we progress through school the markers of this worth become ever more indelibly attached to the very nature of who we are.

Beyond the ostensible academic concern of education is something far more consequential for young people: the formation of identity. It is an identity that is shaped through the endless process of invidious comparison in which children, and later adolescents, are taught to see themselves through the lens of a process that compares, evaluates, ranks, and orders the worth of a person. I have remarked elsewhere that the concept of No Child Left Behind, the educational legislation enacted by the Bush administration in 2001, contains an extraordinary paradox.[8] One is left to wonder how it is that no child can be left behind in a system that relies so heavily on a testing process that endlessly sorts and ranks students and schools. Given that all this testing is done against a standardized norm of what constitutes a correct response, we are left to wonder how this cannot produce winners and losers. Indeed, in my own state of North Carolina, too many students doing well on the standardized tests has created a bizarre problem—how to reduce the scale of success in order to maintain the competitive and selective results that the tests were designed to produce. One is reminded of Garrison Keillor's ironic description of Lake Wobegon in which it is asserted, "all the children are above average!"

School is that place where we learn that there must indeed be winners and losers. Whether we take a course in statistics or not, we learn pretty quickly, and at a young age, that in school its all about the normal curve of distribution, or more commonly, what we call the bell curve. Only some can be winners, and the remainder must fall somewhere between mediocre and failure. That's how the bell curve works. It's about sorting people out and ranking them on a continuum of success or failure. That's the "hidden curriculum" (and nowadays, not so hidden curriculum) of grading and testing. School promises *everyone* the chance of success, but at the same time reminds us that success is a scarce commodity that *cannot* be available to everyone. If it were, it would devalue the meaning of success. *So whatever else we may learn in school, the most powerful message is that education is a race in which only some may win.* Who wins is another story. We know very well that in this game the dice are heavily loaded in favor of those with greater resources and the "right" appearance, dialect, and background. School most often reinforces the inequities of social class and ethnicity in our society rather than disrupting them. Elizabeth Dodson Grey[9] perceptively describes the competitive classroom as a "culture of separated desks." She continues:

> Each child at each desk is running a lonely race from an early age, straining towards a future prize, gobbling up facts and figures and proficiencies so he (or she) can out-perform all the other desk-runners. No communication from desk to desk ("talking") is allowed. The ethos is serious, the competition is assumed, the "play" of early childhood is obliterated, the wonderful diversity of human curiosity and talent and interest and personhood is trampled beneath the constant

naming of the right answer or the correct way to do this or that, and all this is sealed as excellence, complete with grades, graduations and approval.

The Road Runner reigns supreme. The dutiful take up the imperative to race and start out upon an endless obstacle course that becomes a life of achievement, first in school, then college/professional school, and then career. The rebellious are labeled as dyslexic, disruptive, hyperactive, hard to teach or simply dumb.

Thoughtful observers of our schools such as Alfie Kohn, Henry Giroux, David Purpel, Jean Anyon, and others have given us a vivid account of to what degree education is about the ideology of winning and losing. It is quite simply the place we send our children to be inducted into a world in which they learn to see their neighbor as a competitor or adversary for success, recognition, and status. Almost everything in school reinforces this particular view of the world. It is a world in which sharing one's knowledge with others is considered a violation of the rules; in which there is only a limited availability of positive recognition; and in which there is a never-ending process of evaluating one's place in the hierarchy of rewards. It should go without saying that in this setting the concern with "what d'ya get?" preempts any real concern with learning. Grades, test scores, GPAs SATs, EOGs, etc., become the main concern of students' academic lives, but usually have little to do with thinking critically about the world we live in, finding meaning in our lives, becoming more socially responsible human beings, or awakening our imagination or capacity for creative activity. The educational philosopher Maxine Greene talks about the way school inculcates in us a set of assumptions about the world that become the taken-for-granted beliefs about what it means to be human and how we should relate to those who share our world. The pervasive presence of competition in school persuades us that to be human is to be in a perpetual state of rivalry with others. Sorting, selecting, and ranking are, we learn, the *inevitable* nature of the social world. And, we are told, the "sorting machine" that is school can be operated in a way that fairly divides up and allocates success and opportunity.

COMPETITION: THE UNALTERABLE REALITY

We need to ask what this hyper-competitive experience does to the emotional formation of young people. How does it shape their affective identity and the way they see themselves and others? In the first place it instills in them the belief that competing with others is simply the natural and expected way in which individuals relate to one another. Competing with others for recognition, achievement, affirmation, and even love come to be seen as the fundamental, unalterable nature of human reality. The sooner one comes to term with that and learns the rules of the game, the more successful one can expect to be both in school and in the world. What goes along with this is a cynicism about any idea that the world can be radically different. Notions that the world could operate on the basis of care and compassion for others becomes an entirely unrealistic idea that only out-of-touch dreamers would entertain. Being practical and hardheaded means embracing the apparent fact that self-interest and aggressively striving for one's own individual success are what maturity demands.

The ethos of competition, which is the powerful if unspoken curriculum of schooling, is the recipe for an enormous amount of personal stress. We are increasingly aware of just how much anxiety is stirred up in schools today as they become ever more deeply enmeshed in the culture of endless testing. Interestingly, in the United Kingdom, which has undergone a parallel process to our own of believing that more and more standardized testing would produce a better educated populace, there has been a widespread revolt against this trend because of the enormous increase in stress it has inflicted upon young people. Anxiety is a dreadful condition that produces a myriad of physical ailments and emotional suffering, including violent behavior both towards oneself as well as others. There is certainly a connection between this heightened anxiety and increasing levels of depression and suicide among young people. Recent reports from China show that the increasing competitive pressures in the economy and in schools are resulting in a surge of suicides and depression among young people. Japan has a long history of suicidal behavior stemming from the extreme competitiveness of the educational system.

At its root, this anxiety cannot be separated from heightened levels of fear—of appearing inadequate, incompetent, or stupid in the eyes of others. The culture of school with its relentless emphasis on invidiously comparing self with others turns one's neighbor into a threatening presence—someone who shines more brightly when your star dims. Much of the time the emotional consequences of all this exist below the surface of our daily interactions. Yet when reminded, it is not difficult (as my students often tell me) to remember the way that they, as young children, put their hands over the pages of their notebooks to avoid the embarrassment of a wrong or inappropriate answer and subsequent subjection to the giggles and ridicule of their peers. This psychological violence left its enduring scars of shame and hyper-vigilance that are awakened again and again in the competitive environment of school, and often later in other situations in our lives. This kind of experience is not the only one in our young lives. There are the warmer experiences of friendship and the joys of romantic intimacy, shared loyalties, and support of one's peers, including the solidarity of the young in the face of adult authority. At the very least such things make young life bearable. They also provide the joys and thrills of youthful experience. But the heavy emotional effects of learning to see the other as an actual or potential rival cannot be underestimated in the way it drills into us a sense of the adversarial and damaging nature of human relationships. We must always be on guard because we live in a world in which we are taught, whenever necessary, to maximize our advantage at the expense of the other.

In the graduate program in which I teach, students give a great deal of attention to the negative consequences of our hyper-competitive culture, and students are encouraged to examine the effects of this culture on their own lives and relationships. Yet I am always amazed at the distrust and hostility, and sometimes anger, towards fellow students that continues to lurk beneath the surface of the student culture. "Is someone getting more attention from a teacher than I am?" "Why are my grades lower than hers?" "Isn't that student deliberately flaunting the knowledge or books he has encountered?" Sometimes the level of suspicion and paranoia becomes so unpleasant I feel the need to escape from it. As the great cultural critic Raymond Williams once noted, if the dominant ideology could be peeled off like the skin of an onion, personal and social change would be relatively simple. In reality ideology "interpellates" us emotionally and cognitively so that even after we see its damaging effects, shedding it from our thinking or behaving is no easy matter. We continue to act and feel in ways that we may well recognize as destructive to ourselves and others.

Killing Bodies and Souls

How students behave towards one another in a graduate program may seem fairly unimportant in the bigger scheme of things. Nonetheless, it points to a culture that is pervaded by suspicion, distrust, and resentment. There is the always-present feeling that someone is getting something (rewards, recognition, approval) that you are not receiving. And it is not difficult to grasp how, in certain circumstances, such feelings can shift from words and attitudes towards more lethal forms of expression. The horror of gun violence on school and college campuses remains vivid in our minds. When I wrote about the tragedy at Columbine High School nine years ago, my concern was to try to get beyond the way the media was representing the awful events as something that could only be understood in psychological terms—the mad rampage of sociopaths. Such an approach led to legions of experts who spoke to how we must be on the alert for individuals showing signs of antisocial behavior, dissociative affect, depressed or suicidal tendencies, and so on. We witnessed again, after the killing spree at Virginia Tech, the same tendency to bring on the psychological experts who can alert us to the "warning signs" of dangerous behavior. And, as with Columbine, there is a similar discussion about whether we have the right systems in place to identify and counsel psychologically troubled individuals, as well as the most effective means of policing and responding to sociopathic behavior. Yet all of this discussion enables us to avoid what these murderous rampages might tell us about our culture. We should not forget that Virginia Tech and Columbine are part of a harrowing line of massacres at schools in Colorado, Arkansas, Oregon, Florida, Minnesota, Wisconsin, and Pennsylvania. Sadly, we can expect more.

These terrible events cannot be separated from things like the easy availability of guns in our society or our toxic notions of masculinity and our violence-obsessed media culture. Here I want to emphasize the way that school violence is linked to a competitive culture and the deep sense of invalidation felt by so many. Years ago when I wrote about Columbine, I talked about the way schools in our society represent an arena in which there is constant struggle for recognition and validation of students' worth. So many times violent outbursts come after a history of belittlement and marginalization. High schools in particular can be brutal experiences for students who are marked as misfits or failures in the culture of the school. The exclusion, ostracism, or shaming takes a serious toll on the emotional life of young people at this extraordinarily vulnerable developmental stage. And it is no surprise that such treatment is the catalyst for an angry and sometimes rage-filled response. The "Trench Coat Mafia" at Columbine represented one such way to construct a "counter life" that validated and affirmed students who felt themselves belittled by the school culture. We learn from our first days in school that some will be rewarded, recognized, and lauded for who they are, and others will feel the sting of low standing and, in some cases, their sheer invisibility as persons. Since school is ostensibly about academic learning and the mastery of skills, it is easy to miss the much more profound and lasting consequences of schools on our psyches and identity. While the former is often quickly forgotten by the end of the course or semester, the latter influence can stay with us for much of our lives.

In a commentary on the Virginia Tech killings, James Alan Fox, a professor of criminal justice, notes that the United States has become an increasingly competitive, dog-eat-dog society. Our society has become a place, he says, that admires those who achieve at any cost and has less compassion for those who fail. The popularity of reality shows like *The Apprentice* or *Survivor* seem to reflect this increasingly shark-like national ambience. The increasing emphasis on testing in our schools both reflects and contributes to this phenomenon. None of this is meant to excuse the horrifying violence in our schools. Nothing can begin to justify such things. But we must allow ourselves to recognize that these incidents do have some connection to the larger culture in which we live our lives. They are not just the manifestation of crazy and violent loners. They tell us something, not just about who these individuals are, but about *who we are* as a society. For so many of us, the "religion" of a heartless and morally unrestrained capitalism shapes our lives. It is not difficult to see how much this has coarsened and hardened the way we deal with one another. The resulting brutality takes many forms. Sometimes, as we have seen recently, it is horrifyingly and vividly lethal, and sometimes the brutality is a slower and less visible erosion of the bonds of human care and responsibility that affect untold numbers of citizens.

THE DESTRUCTION WITHIN AND WITHOUT

A hyper-competitive culture dehumanizes the lives of others. Other people become objects to be overcome and bested within, or eradicated from, the competition. They become obstacles in the way of our achieving what it is we want. This culture encourages us to be hardened in our resolve to not let others stand in our way. We may consider how cheating becomes increasingly endemic in school and business as individuals feel encouraged to do "whatever it takes" to maximize their advantage over others (a recent survey by the Josephson Institute of Ethics found that 45 percent of students agreed with the statement that "a person has to lie or cheat in order to succeed"). In professional sports the abuse of performance-enhancing drugs is endemic. A culture of spite pervades female relationships as girls compete for popularity and sexual attractiveness. We may consider how workers who have given their best energies to a company are so easily shunted aside for cheaper employees elsewhere in the country or in the world; how workers are cheated of their retirement savings as corporations declare bankruptcy and "restructure" their financial obligations; or how health insurance companies dump those who get sick or have pre-existing medical conditions. We may look at the continuing and pervasive degradation and objectification of women who are reduced to demeaning images that are used to sell just about everything (pornographic sex often involving girls or women who are victims of the global sex trade is the most lucrative aspect of the Internet). We may recognize how we so readily employ migrant workers to take care of those things that are too onerous or too poorly paid for domestic workers, and then callously demonize them and their children for "invading" this country. The ideology that turns every relationship into one of competition primes us to see everyone as a threat, or potential threat, to our well-being or our success. In such a world, other countries, religions, and ethnic groups are easily transformed in our imagination into forces that threaten us. The relentless propaganda of competition is easily mobilized by politics that turn others into groups that want to harm us, deprive us of what is ours, or undermine our economic well-being. In such a world, all relationships become a zero-sum competition for power, resources, and control. When our imaginations are ruled by this kind of worldview it becomes very difficult to envisage a planet in which compassion and not fear shapes our politics, and in which we see ourselves as part of a global community in which resources and power are shared justly.

The culture of competition also produces lives of gnawing dissatisfaction with who we are. Invidious comparison rules our lives. We are urged to constantly see ourselves in relationship to the success and achievement of others. School, advertising, and popular culture are never-ending lessons for how we lack something that others have: desirable possessions, attractive looks, perfect health, the opportunity to attend the best college, exciting travel experiences, and so on. Our lives are ruled by envy for what others have, or what they appear to have. We feel ourselves to be in a state of permanent lack or inadequacy. We view our own lives as being full of missed opportunities and failed efforts. Self-blaming for our failures and inadequacies leave us at war with ourselves and dissatisfied and angry with our lives. "If only I had worked harder, tried harder, made more effort, taken better care of myself, I would not be where I am now." It is not surprising that therapies, both psychological and spiritual, that promise release from oppressive egos that relentlessly remind us about our own inadequacies and the need to work harder in order to satisfy them have become increasingly popular. "How can I feel at one with myself and in harmony with those around me?" is the pressing concern of so many of us. "How do I live fully in the present moment without spending all my time anxiously wondering about, or planning for,[10] my future?" "How do I not become addicted to those things that allow me to escape from the awful feelings of pressure, anxiety, and dissatisfaction that are the consequence of our driven culture?" A culture that breeds such negative emotion and conflicted self-regard must inevitably produce a great deal of rage. Such rage can be turned inward in the form of depression, as well directed at those outside of ourselves, whether intimates or strangers. In each case, anger and violence are not far away. For some the violence is turned against the self who, it seems, they can no longer live with. For others anger at the self is vented through abuse of one's family members. Such violence against spouses and children is of epidemic proportions in the United States. Or the anger is externalized on others who provide scapegoats for one's fury, whether these are gays and lesbians, Jews, immigrants, Muslims, women, or ethnic or racial minorities. Whatever the direction and form in which anger is expressed, we must assume that a culture that systematically encourages and breeds so much dissatisfaction with who we are must inevitably produce large numbers of individuals who view the world with hostility and negativity.

Undoing the Culture of Competition

I should say at the outset that I do not propose, or even envisage, a world without competition. I myself am a lover of soccer and an ardent fan of a team in the English Premier league. Enjoyment of, and desire for, competition is a powerful component of the human psyche. Certainly there is nothing I can say or do that will somehow erase this from the human experience or weaken its draw. It undoubtedly provides, for millions of people, a hugely compelling, exciting, and joyful dimension of their lives. I am not advocating the end of sport or those other diversions that rest on pitting human beings against one another in a test of skill, athletic prowess, courage, or chance. *My concern is not whether we have a culture in which competition plays a role, but whether we have a society, and a world, that is defined, organized, and shaped by the play of competitive relationships.* In a parallel sense, the issue is not whether we will have a market-based *economy*, but whether we will have a market-based *society*. Our challenge, I believe, is whether we can imagine a world that is not based on competitive relationships between human beings, but instead is organized around the principles of a loving and caring community. Can we have a society in which there is much less focus on winners and losers and much more emphasis on the ways we can cooperate with one another and act in a spirit of solidarity and partnership? Can we imagine a world that is not ordered in the manner of cutthroat national or ethnic self-interest and instead around a shared sense of responsibility?

Such thinking might seem utopian and entirely detached from reality. Yet human behavior and motivation is not one-sided. Whatever the other motivations, human beings know and experience the importance of loving and caring relationships. Indeed, without such relationships the world would be an unbearably brutal place. For many of us family life can be what Christopher Lasch[11] once called *a haven in a heartless world*—a place where the love of a partner or children can restore and heal our buffeted lives. Nor do people only act from selfish intent. We see our fellow citizens frequently giving generously to help those in need—both at home and abroad. Millions of our neighbors devote long hours in volunteer capacities to build homes for others, serve meals to the aged, work in shelters and hospitals, raise funds for disaster relief, and other kinds of human deprivation and give of themselves selflessly for the benefit of others. And one continuously hears how this kind of generosity brings deep fulfillment and joy to those who engage in it. In many ways we are divided creatures driven by the market values of selfish interest and competition with others, while at the same time finding meaning and purpose through how we unstintingly help others. Millions of us hear the religious or spiritual call for lives of service and compassion towards others while at the same time embracing and participating in a world of ruthless competition.

If we are to more fully embrace the concept of a world that is less about winning and more about caring, we will need to problematize the idea that competition is in the basic and unalterable nature of being human. And we will need to deconstruct the belief that *only* competition provides the motivating force to energize us as creative and agentic beings. We will need to challenge the belief that without the motivation of winning (and the fear of losing) we would all quickly become lazy and passive. The goal is not just to question the widespread assumptions about competition, but also to help students *re-imagine* the alternative possibilities for human relationships and behaviors.

Teaching Peace: Challenging the Assumptions

It might be useful to enumerate some of the challenges that face teachers of peace within this culture in which competition has such a penetrating and overwhelming presence:

1. Students, like most of us, have come to believe the ideology whose fundamental assumption is that competition is the only, or most important, means to motivate human efforts and energies. I am always surprised, and somewhat amused, when I ask students what would be the effect of removing grades from their education. Their first response is delight at the prospect. But then they argue that no one would bother to do anything. People would not study or learn anything. I suggest to them that this may have more to do with their disinterest in what they are studying rather than the need to compete for grades or approval from the teacher. I follow up by asking them to think of things they do out of pure interest that have nothing to do with being graded for their accomplishments. Their answers quickly become a flood of suggestions—books they like to read, things they like to make, poetry or stories they write, computer-related problem-solving and creativity, travel plans, community service work, artistic activity. In fact, the list of things that they do without the motivation of grades and tests are nearly endless. We then discuss the things that people in society actually do that have nothing to do with competing. Again, there is no problem in coming up with a long list of items, including volunteer work, creative activity, spending time with family and friends, and sport that is not so much about winning or losing but the sheer joy of participating. Through these kinds of questions it does not take very long for them to break through the ideological conditioning and begin to question the idea that without competition people would become lazy or inactive. In fact, they frequently come to an opposite conclusion, that it is precisely when they are not forced to compete that they find the most joy in what they do and exercise the most active and creative parts of themselves.
2. They also discover in this process the part that fear of failure has played in their lives. We begin to talk about how competition promotes an ethos of suspicion and distrust towards others—how they come to suspect others around them of seeking to gain some advantage over them. I ask them to imagine classrooms in which there is no need to worry about others getting ahead of

them in some way. There is an audible sigh of relief. The stories of how oppressive to them this endless process of invidious comparison has been tumble out—the ulcers, headaches, back aches, and anxiety that have blighted their lives. What they become much more aware of is how much the fear of failure and the shame of "looking bad" affect their lives. I ask them how much their parents' psyches are shaped by a fear of losing, and how this has been passed on to them? Considerable, they typically respond. I ask them to look more broadly at the way these emotions shape how Americans see the world. It does not take long for them to recognize how much the fear that others want to take away what we have as a nation produces aggressive and distrusting political attitudes. Ours, they have learned, is a predatory world in which others who are waiting to take advantage of us, both individually and collectively, surround us. We often end up talking about the war in Iraq and how much our country's motivation to become involved there was connected to the fear that we won't have enough cheap oil to allow us to continue with our current way of life. In both our individual and collective lives it becomes clearer to them how much our thoughts and actions stem from the belief that we need to defend ourselves against others who, we fear, want to deprive us of what we have. As a result of this discussion students begin to question this "zero-sum" way of thinking in which "my" gain depends on "your" loss. I ask them if it is possible to imagine a world in which we are not motivated by fear of the other. Could fear of the other be replaced by an attitude of trust and caring? And, teaching in the Bible belt, I ask them how they reconcile Jesus' teaching about loving one's neighbor in a world in which we are constantly taught to see others as a threat to our well-being. These are tough and disturbing questions for students who have never been asked to look deeply at the ideological values that shape who they are and how they think.

3. At some point it becomes necessary to explore the ideology of scarcity and the way this deeply shapes our assumptions about the unequal distribution of rewards and success. This inevitably brings us to the question of what is human nature. To my initial question to them about human nature they typically respond with a negative and dispiriting list of what they believe are the unalterable aspects of being human. Usually they include things like selfishness, greed, competitiveness, and aggression. Its interesting, I respond, that such negative qualities, rather than

generosity, love, compassion, and a desire for peace, are mentioned, even though the latter qualities are certainly not uncommon among human beings. Although we are quick to describe the most antisocial behaviors as the inevitable consequence of human nature ("What can you expect, people are just out for themselves?"), we rarely attribute selfless, generous, or compassionate behavior to the same human source. I suggest to my students that this negative view of what it means to be human is more than simply common sense. It is a deeply encoded ideology that tries to convince us that any attempt to imagine a world in which love and generosity shape the culture simply flies in the face of what is possible. It is a pie-in-the sky utopianism—a hopeless and impossible dream. So-called realism demands that they accept that greed, self-interest, and aggressive defense of what they have is the only possible kind of world that is possible. Anything else is pointless dreaming! Don't even try to imagine, let alone create, a different kind of world.

While I suggest that all of these qualities, both negative and positive, are found in human beings and in just about all cultures, the emphasis on the negative view of what it is to be human is no accident. It is maintained and reinforced by our belief in a particular and pernicious story that is transmitted through our culture from the moment a child enters the school classroom. This narrative of scarcity tells us that there is simply not enough of what human beings need to be happy and satisfied to go around. Whether it is about the recognition of our worth or access to those things that ensure a good and comfortable life, we will need to compete for the limited supply of what is available. This narrative tells us that life is a race, and in order to get what we need (or think we need) we will have to compete aggressively against others who want the same thing. It sometimes surprises students when I point out that from the time they step into the classroom as young children they begin learning that success is a scarce commodity; only *some* of them can receive a gold star or smiley face. In fact, school becomes a continuous lesson in the mentality and consciousness of scarcity. We learn that only some of us can be successful; some of us must end up on the negative side of the account sheet. The fact that rewards are handed out to a relative few keeps their value at a high level. In the same way that gold or diamonds maintain their preciousness because only a very limited quantity is available, it is the scarcity of the rewards that maintains the value of their currency. This is the real power of the bell curve—the idea that no matter how hard you work only some individuals can be successful. The rest must fall somewhere between average and poor. And, as I have already pointed out, this makes a mockery of the idea that schools can be places where "no child is left behind!" Although we emphasize the idea that *anyone can be successful, it is also understood that not everyone can be.* This is built into our basic way of thinking about the world: there is only so much success, opportunity, or recognition available. You will need to fight, battle, claw, or in some cases cheat your way to success. At the end of the day, we are led to believe, there must and will be winners and losers, somebodies and nobodies, those who make it and those who don't. And just because you end up on the upper rungs of the ladder, don't become complacent! There are always people just behind you ready to knock you off your perch!

Imagining a Partnership World

A pedagogy of peace must help students understand and challenge the pernicious story our culture tells about how competition is the single best way to motivate human effort. It must encourage students to question the way the culture inculcates a distrust and suspicion of others and the ever-present anxiety that comes from the endless process of invidious comparison. And it must develop in them the capacity to question the stories that shape our lives— stories that tell us that the supply of those things that signify our worth and value in the world are limited, and that we have no choice but to battle our neighbors to get a share of recognition and well-being. In her wonderful book, *The Real Wealth of Nations*,[12] Riane Eisler notes Gandhi's assertion that we shouldn't mistake what is habitual for what is normal. We were not born with unhealthy habits, Eisler says. We had to learn them and we can unlearn them. She continues[13]:

> ...unselfish acts of kindness counter the conventional belief that a more caring world goes against our inherently selfish, evil nature. Yet this belief is deeply entrenched in popular stories about human nature: from the religious myth about a fatally flawed humanity guilty of "original sin" to sociobiological theories that human evolution was driven by "selfish genes" that program us to only help others when it directly or indirectly benefits us.
>
> But there's much more to human behaviors and human nature than pure selfishness. We're certainly capable of insensitivity, cruelty, greed

and violence. But we're also capable of sensitivity, caring, generosity and empathy.

Our capacity for caring is just as wired into us by evolution as our capacity for cruelty—perhaps even more so. Caring is required for the perpetuation of our species.... By the grace of evolution, we humans are equipped with a neuro-chemistry that gives us pleasure when we care for others. We've all experienced this pleasure. We feel good when we care for a child, a lover, a friend, even a pet. We feel good when we're helpful, even to strangers.

Eisler argues that although humans are strongly programmed by their biology to act in caring and helpful ways, we have to look to culture to understand why there is such a lack of helpfulness and caring in the world. When people grow up in cultures that do not model partnership or cooperative relations between people, they will believe that human nature is uncaring and violent. They will believe that the world is a predatory one in which the rule is either to dominate others or be dominated by them. In such a world, others are seen as adversaries out to control or assert their superiority over us. The world is a dangerous and hostile place.

Yet as Gandhi reminds us, what is habitual can be unlearned. We can educate to challenge the myths of an unalterably hostile or adversarial world. We can undo the taken-for-granted assumptions about human nature. We can point to the complexity of human intentions and the way that human beings are not impelled by any one single motivation. We do exhibit loving, caring, and generous behaviors towards others, and even strangers. We can contemplate how unbearable life would be without the loving care of others. We can look at societies such as those in the Scandinavian countries in which competition and the ethic of the marketplace do not determine social policies and in which, as a result, there is relatively little poverty, few people go homeless, there are strong supports for the unemployed or those unable to work, and there is universal access to health care. We can point to societies and cultures that do not make competition the lynchpin of their social and economic policies and instead prefer the values of social justice, compassion, and solidarity among citizens. We can also explore those traditional and native cultures in which the organizing moral principles were cooperation, mutual support, and the sharing of material resources. Anthropology also provides us with examples of matriarchal societies in which cooperation, not competition, was the dominant value.[14] Both the questions teachers pose and the examples we provide can challenge the assumptions about the inevitability and unalterable nature of competitive societies. Human beings are reflective and malleable beings who can *choose* their way of life. We are not fated to always live as competitors and adversaries in a world in which self-interest must come first. The difficulty in moving away from a competition-driven culture is that it is a challenge to masculine values that uphold the importance of independent and self-sufficient individuals who can survive and win in a world of endless conflicts and contests. "Real men," as the saying goes, are those who are battle-hardened and emotionally invulnerable to the consequences of this endless struggle and have little need for the support and care of others (indeed, needing such care is indicative of a man's weakness and inadequacy). The notion of a society that emphasizes mutual responsibility for one another and compassion and support for all, especially the most vulnerable, from this point of view appears to represent a rejection of masculinity and its replacement with values long associated with femininity. It is surely no surprise that jobs most clearly identified as "women's work," such as caring for the very young or the old, are typically poorly paid and have low prestige. It is indicative of society's low regard for the act of caring and attending to the emotional and physical needs of others. Transformation of our culture from its emphasis on competition and winning would indeed mean greater concern for nurturing emotionally sensitive, cooperative, compassionate, and socially responsive behavior among all human beings. Such an emphasis would, I believe, enhance the quality of lives of us all, regardless of gender.

In school and in the classroom we can go further than merely considering these issues theoretically. There are still schools that prefer cooperation to competition. Although such schools do not eliminate all forms of competition and recognize the enjoyment of competitive sports, for example, they place far more emphasis on students working together in helping ways, in group projects, in peer tutoring, and in community service in which the goals are sharing and giving rather hoarding and winning. There is no doubt that we learn most profoundly when we actually live something practically rather than merely hear about something. For that reason it is important that young people experience learning in situations that are free of grades and the pressure to be better than someone else (or the fear of being worse). When students come together without the sense that they are being compared, judged, and ranked there is a real possibility that they can understand more fully and deeply the beauty and power of human beings who share their insights, creativity, and imagination. In these situations young people can truly glimpse the possibility of a world in which the human ascent occurs as a result of our common efforts and mutual responsibility rather than the aggressive and self-interested acts of egoistic beings. And in actually living as a community of caring and compassionate individuals, students come much closer to seeing the ethical, social, and spiritual choice that confronts all of us in our divided and violence-torn world.

Chapter Four

Justice Then Peace

I would further advise you not to take on other people's enemies. Most damage that others do to us is out of fear, humiliation and pain. Those feelings occur in all of us, not just in those of us who profess a certain religious or racial devotion. We must learn actually not to have enemies, but only confused adversaries who are ourselves in disguise. It is understood by all that you are commander in chief of the United States and are sworn to protect our beloved country; this we understand, completely. However, as my mother used to say, quoting a Bible with which I often fought, "hate the sin, but love the sinner." There must be no more crushing of whole communities, no more torture, no more dehumanizing as a means of ruling a people's spirit. This has already happened to people of color, poor people, women, children. We see where this leads, where it has led.
—From an open letter to President-elect Barack Obama by Alice Walker

World peace will not be built on empty stomachs or human misery.
—Dr. Borlaug, leader of the Green Revolution in wheat production and Nobel Prize laureate

Poverty is the worst form of violence.
—Mahatma Gandhi

The Long Struggle for Equality

The election of Barack Obama as 44th president of the United States in November 2008 was nothing short of a breathtaking moment in the history of this country, whose very creation is inseparable from the brutal horrors of slavery and generations of oppression, violence, and discrimination. It is a saga that reveals and illustrates much about how violence and injustice are inextricably connected in our culture as well as in human cultures throughout the world. Hopes for a more peaceful world depend on our capacity to transform and end the terrible inequities that continue to scar our social landscape. The United States has been a country with "two souls", speaking to the ideals of freedom, constitutional rights, and the basic equality of all citizens while simultaneously being a nation in which all of these had long been denied to those of African descent. When Michelle Obama commented in an interview that for the first time in her life she was proud to be an American, it pointed to the fundamental divide in the consciousness of Americans. For many white citizens this country's mythology, plausibly, spoke to the opportunity and relative affluence that the United States provided. For African-Americans the truth was very different. It was of a history in which opportunity was systematically denied and the ideals of freedom and equality were constantly betrayed. It was understandably impossible for her to join in the flag-waving patriotism of a country in which, to this day, Black Americans are so enormously disadvantaged on every index of human welfare from family income and economic opportunity to health and longevity; from educational opportunity to the fairness of the justice system; and in the way in which African-Americans are represented in our media and public culture. Even though most of the obstacles to full political inclusion have been removed, and there have been important gains among this group in income and education, the relative position of African-Americans remains significantly worse than that of their white counterparts. The median income, for example, of the Black middle class is only 62 percent that of the white median. The Black poverty rate rose from 21.2 percent in 2000 to 24.5 percent in 2007. In 2002 the median net worth of white Americans ($88,000) was 14.5 times that of Blacks whose net worth was just $6000. More than half of all Blacks born to middle class parents are downwardly mobile.[1] Although the effects of the 2008–2010 recession have been terrible for all working people, they have been catastrophic for the Black community.

Yet the truth about the African-American experience is not just the horrifying brutality and inhumanity of slavery and "Jim Crow" and the generations who, even with the removal of legal forms of discrimination, have had to struggle to survive in a harshly prejudiced and discriminatory world. It is also the extraordinary human resilience and the indomitable will to assert a humanity equal in worth to that of all others. The story of Blacks in America is not only the saga of unimaginable suffering and oppression. It is also the narrative of courage, spiritual fortitude, and communal organization in the quest for equality of treatment and regard in the United States. It is a story that speaks of the persistent struggle against unimaginably brutal forces to maintain human dignity and to expand the possibilities of a decent and secure existence. It is unlikely that the election of a Black president, as surprising and magnificent an achievement as this is, means the end of a society in which there are profound racial inequities. Yet we would be wrong to pass over the powerful tides that have brought us to this moment in history and miss the persistent and determined struggle for social justice that provides inspiration to so many, both in this country and globally. The Black experience in America is one of those extraordinary stories of survival in the face of terrible oppression and denial of human equality. It is a story of the power of an idea that asserts quite simply that human beings, in a fundamental sense, deserve dignity, respect, and opportunity that is the equal of that accorded to their fellow beings.

Thinking about the African-American experience in America, with all of its pain and also its fortitude, provides us with a powerful example not just of the human proclivity to create and sustain societies marked by terrible inequalities, but also the tendency for human beings to resist social injustice. Karl Marx noted in one of the most influential passages ever written that[2]

> The history of all hitherto existing societies is the history of class struggles. Freeman and slave, patrician and plebian, lord and serf, guild-master and journeyman, in a word, oppressor and oppressed, stood in constant opposition to one another, carried on an uninterrupted, now hidden, now open fight, a fight that each time ended, either in a revolutionary reconstitution of society at large, or in the common ruin of the contending classes.

Yet the awareness of how social injustice offends our moral and spiritual sensibilities extends much further. The Hebrew prophet Amos angrily denounced those who exploited the poor and the vulnerable:[3]

> *Hear this, you who trample upon the needy,*
> *And bring the poor of the land to an end,*
> *Saying: When will the new moon be over*
> *That we may sell grain?*
> *And the Sabbath,*
> *That we may offer wheat for sale,*
> *That we may make the ephah small and the shekel great,*
> *And deal deceitfully with false balances,*
> *That we may by the poor for silver,*

*And the needy for a pair of sandals
And sell the refuse of the wheat?*

It seems that the passion for a socially just world emerged at an early moment in the evolution of human civilization. We know that the prophetic voices in the ancient Israelite society raged against those who did not live ethically, meaning that no one was excluded, taken unfair advantage of, or treated without compassion. Indeed, among the radical demands placed upon the ancient Hebrew society was the notion of the Jubilee year in which, in every fiftieth year, land would be redistributed so that there would be no permanent concentration of property wealth, and all debts would be cancelled. Still, it was not until the emergence of modernity in the form of the American and French Revolutions, and the transformation of English society from a feudal to a bourgeois society,[4] that there arose an insistent and mass demand for equality. From that time forward, there has been no moment without broad-based social movements challenging the inequitable distribution of political and economic power and questioning the way this power is concentrated in too few hands. Such movements have continuously demanded a wider allocation of the franchise and that decision-making authority be put into the hands of those who are more adequately reflective of society's composition. Challenges to political power have quickly spilled over into questions about economic power. From the American Revolution on it was understood that there could not be equitable distribution of political power if control of economic resources remained in the hands of the same classes or elites. Socialist and working-class movements have, historically, continued to assert that political democracy also requires a more democratic sharing of wealth within a society. Democracy would mean little if the "commanding heights" of the economy were not made accountable to the needs and concerns of the majority. Democracy, in other words, has little meaning if it does not infer a more socially just distribution of wealth and income. Without this the "golden rule" (as one wit defined it) would apply; he who had the gold would indeed rule. This posed a fundamental and enduring question as to the extent that a capitalist society with all of its inequalities of wealth could be truly compatible with a democracy in which power would be widely distributed among the citizenry.

With the emergence of anti-colonial movements came the recognition that equality meant not just the end of the political and social power of the imperial elites, but also the end of the cultural dominance of these groups. The problem of inequality was not just a matter of who owned the land and resources and maintained control over the indigenous people of these territories. It was not just the terrible physical brutality that usually marked colonial control. It was also the linguistic and cultural hegemony that denigrated or suppressed native religions, art forms, education, and other forms of expression. Local people, to one degree or another, internalized the message that the manner in which they thought, spoke, and believed were aspects of their social inferiority. This "internalization of oppression"[5] represented a self marked by shame and the subjugation of one's own identity. Inequality was to be found not just on the outside in the form of our social and economic relationships, but also on the inside in the very way people viewed and felt about themselves.

Feminism, too, understood the complex and multi-dimensional way that inequality functioned. It subordinated women in terms of their public role; fostered inequities in income, opportunities in jobs, and professional advancement; limited their access to political power; and so on. But it also debilitated them in terms of their personal roles, leaving them to carry the overwhelming burden of child-rearing and responsibility for family life. Most insidiously it inculcated in women a distorted view of their own capacities and abilities, emphasizing their inferiority in terms of intellectuality and rationality and focusing instead on how they were judged for their sexual allure and physical attractiveness. Generations of women have continued to suffer from the consequences of a culture that encouraged girls and women to internalize the message that their value was preponderantly dependent on the gaze of men. The long struggle against "essentialist" views of gender, which asserted that men and women had fixed and unalterable kinds of emotional and cognitive dispositions (and which advantaged so-called male capabilities of men over women), has more recently been joined by those struggling against the subordination of gays and lesbians in our society. The struggle against homophobia is, at one level, a struggle for equality and human rights in every realm of our social lives. It is also a struggle against the internalization of oppression through the attempt to find pride, not shame, in one's sexual orientation. Like feminism, it is a cultural struggle against deeply insinuated notions of what constitutes normal or natural ways of being and acting. It is a struggle against the assumptions of "heteronormativity" that defines only one kind of sexual behavior as natural. But beyond this, "queer" politics represents a calling into question society's "binary" classification, which defines a clear and unambiguous dividing line between those who are sexually "straight" and the rest who represent some kind of abnormality. Contrary to the neat dividing line that seems to separate homo- from heterosexuality is the assertion that sexual identity is a far more fluid and complex phenomenon. This changing and multidimensional view of human identity offers some very important lessons for those who want to think beyond the simplistic ways in which we categorize and distinguish human beings.

What is clear from all of this is that the domination of human beings by those with more power is always, in some form, a violent process. It limits and restricts people's capacity to shape and direct their public lives. At the same time it disfigures the sense of worth, precious value, and inner beauty that belongs to each human life. Whether in the form of overt physical violence or in the more insidious forms of economic deprivation or the exclusion or denigration of one's culture, social inequality drives our world of anger, rage, and conflict. In a recent study across several nations as well as states within the United States, two British epidemiologists, Richard Wilkinson and Kate Pickett, demonstrated quite clearly that the level of violent behavior in a society (as well as other problems such as drug use, teenage pregnancy, illiteracy, illness, etc.) are directly correlated with the degree of social and economic inequality in that society.[6]

THWARTING EQUALITY: QUIET VIOLENCE

Whatever the origins of the drive to ensure equality in our human relationships, there can be no doubt of its enormous power. As we look back on the tumultuous events of the twentieth century we must see how the quest for greater social justice in the way societies are constituted has repeatedly challenged, disrupted, and overturned existing political, economic, and social relationships. And although this process has been roiling society for hundreds of years, we cannot in any way view it as being finished. The struggles against imperialism, neo-colonialism, racism, ethnic subordination, capitalism, patriarchy, and sexual oppression continue, in one form or another, unabated into current times. Although the hopeful and uplifting face of this drive for equality is the unfolding saga of a world in which human beings can be seen and treated in the fullness of their worth and ability, there is also a much darker side to this process. The struggle for social justice is almost always accompanied by a violence that seeks to suppress the human will for respect and dignity. Time and again we see this violence in the repression of those whose voices are raised to demand recognition of their rights and a fairer distribution of wealth and opportunity, or in the demand for an end to the environmental destruction of people's homes and communities. We see it in the refusal to permit full inclusion of an ethnic or religious community into the culture and polity of a nation. And we see it in the desire to maintain the subordination, vilification, and exploitation of a group considered as "outsiders." The violence is sometimes overt and seeks to maintain a group's dominance through assassinations, torture, rape, jailings, or military force. Or in forcing people from their homes when their land is appropriated by governments or corporations in order to concentrate agricultural holdings. We see it when businesses act with little thought of responsibility to their workers when shutting down a plant in order to move to a location with less expensive "overheads." Such brutality continues to blight human existence in many places around our world. The complicity of the United States' government in processes of violence is often kept hidden from the spotlight of public scrutiny, as in the guarded secret of "extraordinary renditions," in which American-held captives are sent to prisons in foreign countries where they can be tortured to give confessions or information away from the spotlight of judicial process. Or in the role of the "School of the Americas," which trains police forces from Latin American countries in methods of surveillance and interrogation of those deemed as threats to ruling elites.[7] And there is this country's periodic military intervention into, or occupation of, other countries in order to maintain the dominance of political and economic elites who are friendly to the United States, or to depose the emergence of regimes with their own national interests in places such as Nicaragua, Panama, Iran, Lebanon, Chile, Indonesia, or Iraq.

More often, however, the violence is ideologically and culturally insinuated into the way society functions so that the inequality seems to be justified by how institutions work and distribute rewards. When this happens there is usually a quiet, symbolic violence at work that makes it much harder to question, contest, or even identify how the process works to maintain some people's privilege over others. This is what we refer to as maintaining domination through "cultural hegemony"—the moral consent of those who are governed.

In a well-known piece by Peggy McIntosh, *White Privilege: Unpacking the Invisible Knapsack*,[8] the author notes the following:

> Whites are carefully taught not to recognize white privilege, as males are taught not to recognize male privilege.... I have come to see white privilege as an invisible package of unearned assets which I can count on cashing in each day, but about which I was "meant" to remain oblivious.... It seems to me that obliviousness about white advantage,

like obliviousness about male advantage, is kept strongly acculturated in the United States so as to maintain the myth of meritocracy, the myth that democratic choice is equally available to all. *Keeping most people unaware that freedom of confident action is there for just a small number of people props up those in power, and serves to keep power in the hands of the same groups that have most of it already.*

Although the society we live in is deeply marked by the unequal way in which we live, are treated, or are regarded, there should be no doubting the fierce and powerful drive that exists for greater fairness in the society and equal recognition. We live with a deeply schizophrenic worldview in which we are reminded of our inherent equality as citizens, while being constantly aware of the way society functions to privilege a few over the many. In this sense our democratic values are contradicted by the realities of capitalism, racism, ethnic prejudice, patriarchy, and homophobia, each of which undermines and thwarts our desire to live and be recognized in the fullness of our being and potential. *This conflict in our status means that there is a permanent tension between the reality of our lives and our hopes and expectations as citizens.* It is a tension that is managed through institutions that seem to embody our hopes for fairness and opportunity, while paradoxically also justifying and legitimating hierarchy and inequality. In a sense these institutions paper over the cracks in society, making socially acceptable that which seems to violate our moral norms about the deeply inequitable differences in the way we relate to one another. As McIntosh points out, the actual process by which some human beings are privileged over others, and in which a quiet form of cultural violence organizes the everyday lives of individuals, is often invisible to many people. Or it is taken as common sense to be obvious, necessary, or unavoidable. Nothing illustrates this ability to combine both the democratic promise of equality and the realities of privilege and hierarchy better than our system of public education.

Schooling and the Unmet Promise of Equality

School is the primary vehicle through which society produces and legitimates inequality. This is perhaps the most important consequence of educational institutions. From the time children first enroll in school they are being subjected to a process that sorts and selects them. Schooling produces winners and losers. As David Purpel suggests,[9] public education might more accurately be called public *evaluation*. It is hard to think about our system of education without considering the whole regime of testing, grading, and tracking that channels kids in the direction of future success, mediocrity, or outright failure. This is why the "hidden curriculum" of the classroom is so much about competition between students and the reason that schooling is such an anxiety-generating experience for young people. Of course, the sorting process must give the appearance of fairness and objectivity. As McIntosh and other observers note,[10] the way that privilege and advantage are distributed must maintain the illusion that success is equally open to all. School must seem to be a place that offers everyone an equal shot at success. Educational researchers have known for a long time that nothing could be further from the truth regarding the way our educational institutions function. In reality, our schools legitimate much of the social and economic inequality that kids bring with them from their homes and communities. We know that schools themselves tend to reflect the affluence or poverty of the surrounding communities. This is reflected in the quality of buildings, adequacy of resources, and experience and qualifications of teachers. In a recent essay review Alison Lurie[11] notes that schools in expensive suburbs are big, handsome and well kept, in contrast to the rundown old buildings common in rundown urban areas. Students in poor schools are overwhelmingly poor, Black, or Latino. Lurie continues:

> Inside the building, the contrast may be even greater. The upscale suburban public school is clean and well lit and spacious; it has an attractive cafeteria with good food, and its library is full of new books, and its magazines and computer terminals that always work. When students from a crowded inner-city school realize what they are missing, the result is apt to be some mix of depression or rage, which can lead to vandalism or violence. (It may be partly for this reason that most intra-mural high school sports and debating teams tend to play schools from similar demographic areas.) Disadvantaged students who somehow get a look at an expensive private boarding school and its country-club campus may become even more angry or dejected.

We know, too, that schools reward or recognize children who bring with them the language, vocabulary, and experiences that are available to middle and upper middle class children. Children's misbehavior in school is treated in vastly different ways depending on their racial or ethnic background. And children's success in school is highly correlated with the jobs, incomes, and educational attainments of parents.

And these latter qualities also shape children's expectations about how far they will travel in their educational journey. The aspiration of an education that "leaves no child behind" is a laudable one. Sadly, it flies in the face of so much that we know about how schooling "reproduces" success or failure dependent on the social background and identity of a student. For every $10,000 more income a family receives, a child's SAT scores rise by 30 points. Rich kids are 25 times more likely to attend the nation's best colleges than poor kids.

The biggest challenge of a society like ours is how to reconcile the democratic promise of equal opportunity for all with the realities of deep and pervasive social inequalities. The most persuasive way is through the claim that we are a *meritocratic* society. This means that while the outcomes in our society may be significantly unequal in terms of individuals' incomes, status, health, and well-being, everyone at least has a fair chance at being successful. And achieving success, it is believed, is the result of whether individuals are smart enough and diligent enough to make something of themselves. The world is open to all to succeed if they work hard and put their intelligence to good use. In this sense, school, especially public school, is regarded as the great arena within which individuals are invited to achieve through the combination of work and intelligence. Meritocratic ideology invites us to believe that we live in an open society in which significant social and economic mobility is possible if one is determined and able enough. In this view, whatever inequalities may initially exist, they do not limit the possibilities of individuals to move beyond their original circumstances. This view draws heavily on the quintessential American myth of a society in which every individual is capable of making it by sheer will and application. It carries echoes of the "rugged individualist" legend of the pioneers going west and making their own lives through persistence, courage, and initiative. This is, in short, the legend that underpins the American dream.

Meritocratic ideology is a powerful means by which a society can both recognize existing inequality and minimize its actual significance. The inequalities of race, class, gender, and ethnicity may exist in an abstract kind of way, but they really do not need to be a hindrance to those with "the right stuff" who are determined to achieve. Alas, however, things are not that simple. Success does not come with that kind of certainty, even to those who ardently desire it. However many extraordinary exceptions there are to this fact, we cannot eliminate the powerful effects of economic inequality on intergenerational social mobility. We cannot rest comfortably in the belief that success comes to those who deserve it (and that failure, too, is something

JUSTICE THEN PEACE

earned). The belief in a "deserving" society might allow us to rest easy in our moral universe, but it flies in the face of a reality in which the deep injustices in our society are not really so readily overcome. There is what Jonathan Kozol[12] describes as an *apartheid divide* in our nation's public school systems—one in which poor and overwhelmingly Black and brown children attend schools in which the buildings are decrepit, resources are depleted, classes are too large, teachers are overwhelmed, and rates of attendance and graduation are minimal. The children in these schools come from places where decent jobs are few, incarceration rates are high, violence is pervasive, and the likelihood of attending college is small. To talk about meritocracy in the face of such deep social injustice is to deny the stark and shocking reality of our nation's inequalities. *It is to ignore or overlook the violence of both body and soul that is inflicted on poor children day in and day out as they must cope with a world in which their intelligence is invalidated, their knowledge is ignored, their bodies are wasted through poor health and violent rampages, and their spirits are destroyed in the warehouse environments that are urban schools.*

MYSTIFICATION, DENIAL, AND REPRESSION

One of the most common responses to the evidence of deep inequality in any society is to simply deny the evidence. The facts of social injustice must, say the non-believers, be made up by those with some radical or self-serving agenda. Those asserting that there are deep injustices in the society must be manipulating or manufacturing the information. To believe that things really are so would call into question deeply held beliefs about the society's fairness and the way some people may be benefiting from how things operate. To accept their assertions may demand some serious interrogation of how advantage and disadvantage are distributed in society. How do white people benefit from racism? Are there hidden privileges to be gained from being white, say, for example, in how one is treated by the police or in making a job application, or in the way a teacher might view your ability, in applying for a mortgage, or in simply the ease with which one may stroll a shopping mall? It can be more comfortable denying the power of social class in determining one's likelihood of going to an elite college, one's access to political or economic power, or even how long one is likely to live. The discomfort that one will feel, if indeed the dice are loaded in this way, means that one may have to seriously reconsider the comforting myths about the society in which one has grown up. And then we may be confronted with the moral choice of questioning who really does benefit from the way things work? Whose interests does society serve? This is the case, too, when we are asked to think about how we benefit from the cheap, exploited labor of those in underdeveloped countries whose products help to maintain our high-consuming culture with its extraordinary abundance of choices. What would it mean for us if those who make our clothes, electronic goods, furniture, and housewares were paid fair market wages and worked in safe, clean, and dignified environments? It is much easier to ignore or deny the horrendous working conditions that millions of women and children endure in order to produce the things that sustain our high material standard of living.[13]

One of the ways that persisting inequalities can be maintained is by claiming that there is something remiss about the group that persistently loses in society's race for success or achievement. Various forms of racist ideology provide ammunition to those who wish to pin the fault not on the way that society functions to maintain inequality, but on the suffering group itself. So, for example, African-American children are said to grow up in families that are culturally dysfunctional. There is, it is claimed, something pathological about Black families with their propensity towards single parenting and economic instability, high rates of criminal behavior, and large numbers of inadequately cared for children. Such views work by looking at the African-American family as if it exists in some kind of isolation from the larger economic and social reality. There is a refusal to connect the problems of the family to the decrepit conditions found in many urban centers: lack of jobs that pay a living wage, rundown housing, blighted neighborhoods, and inadequate schools. Urban poverty may indeed generate a dysfunctional and self-destructive culture in which crime and violence are rampant, drugs are pervasive, unemployment is high, kids leave school without qualifications, and there are high numbers of teenage parents. Yet none of this should be viewed outside the context of the debilitating environment that is the legacy of a history of discrimination, racism, and inadequate or punitive public policies. We cannot ignore the catastrophic decline of employment opportunities in the inner city with all of the dependency and hopelessness this produces. Or the well-documented "red-lining" by banks in these areas, which has made support for home ownership and improvement prohibitive to many residents. We have already referred to the existence of what Jonathan Kozol has called the "apartheid system of education" in this country that makes many of our urban schools little more than debilitating warehouses for Black and brown kids. Accusing the residents of our inner cities for their failure to live up to the middle class norms of the American dream is too often a manifestation of what William Ryan called "blaming the victim."

Behind the denial is ultimately fear—apprehension rooted in the psychology of scarcity. Where there is a belief that the opportunities, resources, or money available in society are limited and scarce, any challenge by one group to the fairness of the existing distribution of these things is seen as deeply threatening to what other people already have. Those with power and wealth, in particular, will typically deploy all their resources to beat back any insurgency that demands a change in the way things are working. It is continually seen how elites are willing to use their control over information, knowledge, and culture to persuade ordinary people that any change to the way things are would be harmful to their lives and is not in their interests. Failing this we also see how ruling groups are willing to mobilize physical force and violence to maintain their grip on power, wealth, and privilege. There are very few places in the world where, at one time or another, such groups have not used military or police force to deter or resist groups demanding a greater level of social justice. This may be seen in the form of resisting unionization of workers who demand better pay and work conditions. It may be seen in the arrest, torture, or murder of those working for human rights among exploited and abused groups. It may be seen in the violent overthrow of democratically elected governments of the left by those whose economic and social interests compel them to resist changes in how wealth and power are currently allocated. It may take the form of rape and abuse of women as a way of deterring insurrections against the oppression of one ethnic group by another. Or the forced militarization of children compelled to support the oppressor's army or militia.

The tragedy of violent oppression, torture, abuse, and even genocide in order to ensure the continuation of one group's power over another is the continuing and tragic saga of the human race. It can plausibly be argued that this has been the reality of human relations since the beginning of recorded history. The will, often brutally imposed, to maintain one's privilege at the expense of others is the bloody thread that runs throughout history. But whether this is the *inevitable* condition of being human is quite another question. *Whether this violent history foretells our inevitable future is perhaps the single most important question that confronts us as citizens, parents, and educators.* It is not surprising that the violence used in the cause of maintaining the power and privilege of the few is typically met with violence directed against those attempting to resist change. The history of the twentieth century is a history of anti-colonial struggles that have typically become violent insurrections as empires and elites refused to revoke their control of a territory. It is argued by those engaged in the liberation struggle that only these kinds of acts have any chance of ending the rule of rich and powerful minorities. This is a difficult and complex argument that, unfortunately, cannot easily be dismissed. It is certainly difficult to imagine some of these struggles having succeeded without the use of arms. I am, however, persuaded that the use of violence in liberation struggles usually leaves a terrible legacy of dehumanization and callousness towards life that imprints itself on the new society. The culture of the gun, militarism, and rule by force too often becomes part of the culture of the liberated territory. In many parts of Africa, for example, post-colonial states degenerate into new forms of violent rule in which weapons and brutal force shape everyday life. In too many struggles for liberation and change, the medium becomes the message. How we make change will often shape what kind of new world we are bringing into being. And too often the "new" world looks sickeningly like the old.

What makes the issue of resisting change so much more complicated is the fact that this resistance is frequently not limited to those who would be the most obvious losers in any significant change of power or privilege. Those who are themselves vulnerable, and certainly not a part of the ruling class or elite, can often be found at the forefront of defending the existing inequitable system. Why is this? In the United States, for example, there appears to be a strong need to defend or justify those who "have made it." There is certainly a good deal of adulation for the rich and the famous. Perhaps this is because our culture constantly promises us the opportunity to join this group—if we work hard enough, are talented enough, or are enterprising enough. "One day," it is said, "I, too, might be a part of this group so why should I attempt to reduce the value of success?" In this sense those who most definitely are not part of the privileged groups may still identify with them. Those who aspire to wealth, status, or power want to be able to hold on to all their "winnings" when they make it without having to share or give up any of it to others who remain lower down the social hierarchy. This was surely the meaning of the much ballyhooed "Joe the plumber" incident during the 2008 presidential election—a man who condemned the idea of the well-off paying more in taxes because *one day he himself hoped to be a part of this group*! It represented the same appeal to middle class groups that any idea of redistributing wealth was not in their best interests. The fear of "socialism" was invoked against those who were accused of wanting to deprive individuals of what they had earned and achieved in order to give to others who were less deserving. Perhaps the same attitudes are at work in the middle class resistance to giving mortgage relief or adjustments to those whose homes are being foreclosed. In this worldview there is no problem of "social injustice," only individuals who have, or have not, taken advantage of the possibility of success through their own hard work and talent. Yet despite whatever means of denial, mystification, or deceit are employed to distract people from the gross inequalities that bear down on their lives, the reality cannot in the end be hidden. A recent 20-year study by the OECD (Organisation for Economic Cooperation and Development) showed that inequality increased in 27 out of 30 member countries. The report noted that although incomes at the top level continued to soar, the majority's stagnated, driving more and more people into poverty. The recent debacle on Wall Street revealed the extraordinary wealth accruing to executives and managers with annual take-home incomes running into the millions of dollars. All of this while millions of ordinary people were losing homes to foreclosures and more than nine million children don't have health insurance. Around the world the United Nations reports that 60 million children have signs of acute malnutrition and 40,000 children die each day from want of basic medicines and clean drinking water. Violence and the assault on our bodies and well-being comes in many forms.

Ethnic Minorities and the Politics of Hatred

At other times, groups on the lower or middle rungs of the ladder are led to vent their fears and frustrations at those they see as their rivals on the ladder of upward mobility. This venting frequently becomes a potent vehicle for rage directed at racial, national, or ethnic groups that are perceived as threats to the limited opportunities or security currently available to these working and middle class groups. So affirmative action, which is intended to ensure opportunities for historically discriminated against minorities, are vehemently opposed by whites who fear the loss of their long-time advantages in job hiring and access to educational institutions and programs. Immigrants become the focus of hate propaganda as they are regarded as depriving native groups of jobs. This animus is usually accompanied by prejudiced assertions about other groups as behaving in ways that are culturally abnormal and defying "acceptable norms" of behavior. There may be claims that such behavior is the result of some kind of genetic deficiency or cultural pathology. This animosity usually becomes much more intense as economic conditions worsen and jobs become harder to find. Historically, it is well known that employers and other powerful groups have sometimes fomented these conflicts among workers as a means of redirecting the anger and frustration of working and middle class people away from those groups that hold real economic power.

Time and again we have seen how fears and anger among the most vulnerable groups can be refocused into violent forms of racism and ethnic hatred. We see this phenomenon in many countries around the world.[14] For example, economic liberalization in Russia has unleashed widespread anti-Semitism in which Jews are seen as the principal beneficiaries in the growth of the new capitalism there. Jews are accused of being the new system's main architects. It is seen in hostility towards the Indian community in Kenya, where it is claimed that a tiny handful of Asians control the entire economy. Hostility in that country is also tribal, in which the Kikuyu tribe are seen as the main beneficiary of success and were the focus of the recent unrest and violence. In Rwanda, as in many places in Africa, the seeds of the brutal civil war were laid during the time of colonial rule. Here, the Belgian colonists openly favored the "more intelligent, more active" Tutsis, giving them superior education and assigning them all the best administrative and political positions[15]:

> The Hutu majority were reduced to a humiliated pool of forced labor, required to toil en masse under their Tutsi taskmasters. Over the years... "an aggressively resentful inferiority complex" deepened and festered among the Hutus. By the time independence rolled around, the Tutsi were a starkly privileged "arrogant" economically dominant ethnic minority. And the Hutu political activists who were calling for "majority rule" and "democratic revolution" were seeking not equality—but revenge.

In other parts of Africa there is a similar process in which market success and economic inequality become defined in growing tribal animosity. Members of the Ibo tribe, for example, are known as the "Jews of Nigeria" for their unusually successful entrepreneurial activity. Non-Ibo groups in Nigeria will attribute Ibo success to corruption and crime. In 1966, tens of thousands of Ibo were slaughtered indiscriminately by angry mobs. In Ethiopia, the relatively prosperous Eritreans were expelled from the country. In many parts of Asia such as Vietnam, Laos, Thailand, Philippines, Indonesia, and Malaysia, ethnic Chinese minorities have figured prominently in the newly emergent market economies, bringing with it animosity and violence against this group. In several of these countries there have been periodic bloody riots, leaving hundreds or thousands dead. In Western Europe continuous migration of immigrant groups from the underdeveloped world has resulted in upsurges of nationalism and racism directed against ethnic minorities such as the Turks in Germany, Pakistanis in Britain, and Muslims in Holland and France. Such hostility has, in turn, ignited radical movements among immigrants, especially the young, to resist discrimination and exclusion and to assert the superiority of their own religious and ethnic identity.

Sometimes, as in places like the Congo and Sierra Leone, ethnic politics become mixed with the brutality of corrupt rebel groups attempting to take over the mineral wealth, such as the diamonds, oil, and gold reserves, of countries. Ethnic hatred can be mobilized and manipulated to support groups whose only real interest is their control of a nation's wealth. The entanglement of ethnicity and race with economic inequality is a dangerous brew. Racism and ethnic hatred is certainly used to obfuscate and redirect people's fears and anger against vulnerable targets, and against people who have had no role in creating the real difficulties that are the consequence of unequal, exploitative, and destabilizing social and economic conditions. Where ethnic groups do, in fact, represent a successful minority within a society, the call for a more democratic and equitable distribution of wealth can easily turn into a vicious racist form of politics in which one group becomes demonized and persecuted, sometimes ending in the forced expulsion of the group or even genocide. Such was the case with the expulsion of the ethnic Indian minority in Uganda during the regime of Idi Amin. The most notorious example of this was the Nazi genocide of the Jewish people, which mobilized the fear and frustration of working class and middle class Germans around the myth of creating a *Juden rein* German homeland and resulted in the extermination of 6 million Jews.

At other times despair and hopelessness can be mobilized into dangerous delusions that produce indiscriminate terror attacks against innocent civilians in the name of a God-inspired crusade. Although the emergence of fanatical and militant Islamic movements around the world has complex roots (which we will look at in the next chapter), it is a phenomenon that cannot be separated from the terrible economic inequalities that exist in the world. In a world in which one-half of the population lives on less than $2 dollars a day, one out of every five people in the world survive on less than $1 dollar a day, and one-third of the world's children are undernourished;

in which 10 million people die each year from malnutrition, lack of clean water, and basic medicines, and a third of the world's population has a life expectancy of less than 40 years, it is not exactly surprising that the consequences are often fury and resistance to such inequities. Militant, religiously inspired movements have emerged following the failure of previous secular nationalist and socialist regimes that emerged from the anti-colonial struggles to make good on their promise of a radical improvement in the life of the masses. Instead, in many places what emerged were corrupt regimes that succeeded in lining their own pockets at the expense of the poor, the peasantry and working classes. The political and business elites in such regimes were often seen as working hand in glove with powerful business and military interests in the West and were the real beneficiaries of the new corporately dominated global order. These governments were ready to use torture and repression to maintain their power and their privilege, and usually resisted the introduction of real democracy and free political expression. In addition, technology made it possible for ordinary people to see how those in more affluent parts of the world lived and offered tantalizing images of what was available to those who could afford it. All of this, along with the huge expansion of young people who saw no realistic way out of their present impoverished condition, even with increased education, produced the conditions for movements that inspired hope for social transformation. Such movements often carried with them a fanatical, indiscriminate rage at those they defined as the source of their woes—other ethnic, national, or religious groups that did not share their particular view of religious orthodoxy. And the method of their redress, to the hopelessness and despair of so many people's lives, was sometimes the indiscriminate death and destruction of innocent men, women, and children. I write this during the terrible and indiscriminate massacre of hundreds of innocent lives in Mumbai, India, by Islamic Kashmiri militants—one more savage episode of violent and sadly misdirected rage by those who feel humiliated, ignored, or whose suffering has not been redressed. The larger origins of this rage are well summed up by the Indian activist and scholar Vandana Shiva, who points to the real forms of social injustice that underlay the sense of unmet grievances:

> The privatization of public goods and services and the commoditization of the life support systems of the poor is a double theft which robs people of both economic and cultural security. Millions, deprived of a secure living and identity, are driven towards extremist, terrorist,

fundamentalist movements. These movements simultaneously identify the other as enemy and construct exclusivist identities to separate themselves from those with whom, in fact, they are ecologically, culturally, and economically connected.[16]

LESSONS FOR PEACE FROM A WORLD OF INEQUALITY

I want to suggest five lessons around which the issue of social injustice and its relationship to peace education may be focused:

- *Inequality and Human Inferiority?*

Long ago I learned that the liberation of the Israelites from their enslavement in Egypt did not take place at the moment of their fleeing from Pharaoh and escaping across the Red Sea. This was only a part of the liberation. The whole process actually took 40 years during the time this tribal people trekked through the desert. Why, one may ask, did it continue for such a long time? One answer is that we must understand liberation from oppression to be a process that involves changing both our *outer* circumstances as well as our *inner* consciousness. Ending the overt forms of domination and exploitation are, of course, necessary to a people struggling to be free. But oppression often becomes a part of the inner mentality of people who have suffered unequal and oppressive treatment. There is an "internalization of oppression" by people who, because of their suffering at the hands of others, come to doubt their own value, worth, beauty, and intelligence. They have taken inside them the oppressor's distorted and limited view of the humanity of this group. These biblical narrators, it appears, knew something about the human condition and the deep consequences of social injustice on human beings. For these commentators, depriving the body of the material conditions that would allow it to thrive can never fully be separated from the emotional and spiritual deprivation that always accompanies deep social inequalities—a deprivation that represented a much more enduring condition.

As I write this, a new report notes that almost 700,000 children went hungry in America during 2007.[17] (A situation that has significantly worsened in the succeeding two years.) These are individuals who "didn't have enough money for food or access to enough aid to maintain active healthy lives." We know that currently in this world one person in seven goes to bed hungry each night.[18] As terrible as this food deprivation might be, something else is also at work here.

We are not just inflicting grave physical suffering on these lives. We are also conveying a message about how we view the worth of some of those who coexist with us in our nation and our world. The message is one that denies the full value of these individuals. The fact that we allow them to go hungry says that they may be invisible to us, their presence goes unnoticed, or that, for whatever reason, they have a lesser claim on our collective wealth and resources. This is always the terrible message that accompanies significant inequality. The hurt and pain of injustice is always felt twice over: the first time in terms of lack of income, legal residence or citizenship, access to work, food, housing, or care of one's health. But, secondly, each of these communicates a statement about one's lack of worth, value, or recognition from those who surround us. Not to be recognized in the fullness of our humanity is the ultimate pain or humiliation. *It is the ultimate violation of human beings.* I will return to this problem of human "invisibility" in the next chapter. The injustices of social class, the divisions in the world between the affluent north and the impoverished south, racism, patriarchy, ethnic or national domination, homophobia, and religious exclusion all share the sense that inequality signifies being thought of as less than others. Such denial is a violence inflicted on the soul of our neighbors who are cast as "other" in this system of unequal treatment. Not surprisingly, such violence finds its echo or response in the anger of those who are humiliated, excluded, or deprived. *Peace requires, in the first place, that we recognize as fully and as consciously as we are able what we are doing to so many of those who share our world, both to their bodies and their spirit; to understand as fully as we can the way in which inequality and injustice damages, and sometimes destroys, the lives of so many of our fellow human beings.*

- *Individualism or Solidarity?*

There is a reason why those who are concerned with the dehumanizing effects of inequality talk about the struggle for "social justice." When people are treated in ways that undermine their worth, well-being, and opportunities, the consequences are seen as contradictions to our cherished beliefs about the dignity and value of all human beings. Deep and enduring inequality contradicts our fundamental moral and spiritual commitments. More than this, such inequality is to be understood not as an idiosyncratic phenomenon affecting random individuals, but as a systematic bias built into the social system itself that ensures the continuation and reproduction of the disadvantaged treatment of one class or group of human beings.

Commitment to bringing about a world of greater social justice—and with it the greater likelihood of peaceful relationships between human beings—requires that we question and resist those ideologies that lead us to blame individuals for their "failures" or their "losses." When we see the world through the lens of individual failure, not systematically produced inequality, we find fault with the person, not the society. We blame the victim, not those who have caused the suffering or the system that perpetuates it.

Moving away from an individualistic worldview means brushing against the grain of our socialization. It means refusing to see the rape of a woman as the woman inviting and causing her own violation, rather than the result of a culture of machismo that has instilled a violent and dominating attitude as part of what it means to be a "real" man. It means refusing to see unemployment or low income as being the result of some personal inadequacy or failure on the part of a worker, rather than the result of economic interests that resist raising the minimum wage to ensure an adequate or living income, or the result of companies that would rather sell out and move to third-world countries in order to pay workers a fiftieth of what they may pay in this country. It means resisting racist attacks on Mexican workers for "undermining" wage rates while failing to see how NAFTA has resulted in the widespread destruction of small farming in Mexico that has forced millions off the land and onto the road to look for employment.[19] It means refusing to see that the failure of Black kids in our schools has nothing to do with some innate deficiency in intelligence or as being the result of poor and disinterested parenting, and has everything to do with rundown and inadequately financed schools, and communities in which the prospect of decent and reliable employment has disappeared. It means understanding that the gross discrepancies of income and living standards in the world are the legacy of generations of economic exploitation by the most powerful nations and the well-documented continuing and systematic inequities in the rules that govern trade between rich and poor nations.[20]

The lesson of all this is that widespread inequality cannot be blamed on the lack of others' personal resourcefulness, intelligence, or motivation, or some other personal dimension of who they are. To take this attitude is a convenient way to avoid or deny our ethical responsibility for others' lives. *It is a way of saying, "This is their problem, not mine. They need to change how they behave or act. I myself need to do little." It removes from oneself any responsibility to challenge or contest the way our social, cultural, political, or economic systems function.* In religious terms we may say there is only personal sin but no social transgressions. From an ethical standpoint we may say, "I am not my sister or my brother's keeper. They alone are responsible for their fate in the world." Yet peace without some degree of social justice is unlikely. And to wish for peace means to work to overcome how human exploitation, degradation, and insecurity is often built into the very structures that govern our lives as workers, citizens, consumers, and students. It means to question the very way our identities are socially constructed—as men or women; migrant worker or citizen; gay or lesbian; young or old; black, brown, or white; member of a wealthy elite or member of a poor community. As Cornel West suggests, *identity is who we are in relationship.* And too many of our relationships have built into them ways in which we learn to see human inequality as an inevitable, unchanging part of the human condition. *We need to see the issue of human suffering and injustice in the world not as someone else's problem. We are all complicit in some way in perpetuating our world, and we are all responsible for challenging and changing it.*

- *Who Deserves to Live Well?*

So far the process of understanding and challenging inequality and seeing its connection to conflict and violence has been a pretty cerebral one: understanding, analyzing, and deconstructing assumptions and beliefs. Yet what moves us to demand and work for change in the relationships between human beings depends on something much more visceral or "embodied." There must be a *felt connection* between those who are advantaged or privileged in some way and those who are treated as if their lives matter less. To be concerned about inequality depends on a sense of compassion and empathy between human beings—to see in the face of someone else, as the French-Jewish philosopher Emmanuel Levinas says, a fellow traveler who cries out to us for support, concern, and human solidarity. The politics of our emerging postmodern world rightly places increased focus on long ignored or submerged differences between human beings in matters of ethnicity, nationality, religion, sexuality, and so on. *Yet for there to be a widespread contesting of the social, economic, and political inequities that ravage our world, there must exist a sense of outrage and horror that our fellow human beings can be treated and acted upon in that way. Hunger among children, sexual slavery, jobs that exploit and abuse people, environmental conditions that lead to deadly illnesses, and so on, must be experienced by those not directly affected by them as if they happened to members of one's own family.* They must produce the horror and outrage we would feel if those nearest and dearest to us suffered in this way.

One of the ways I have found useful in my classroom to prompt this deep reflection on our concern for others is by asking the question, "Who deserves to live well?" On the face of it this is appears to be a rather simple question. Some in the class will perseverate on the word "well" and argue that this is such a relative term that it makes consideration of the question impossible. I tell them that while there is some truth to their confusion, this should not become a means to our avoiding dealing with the question. Others will state quite simply that everyone deserves to live well. As much as I might like this response, I am always a bit wary of the speed or ease with which they answer (perhaps they know what would make the teacher happy!). I ask them to think about how others they know might respond to this question. Of course, what I am really seeking here is some serious reflection on what I believe is our culture's schizophrenic response to this question. Typically, I find that my students believe that every person has the right to live a life as fully and as happily as is possible, and society is responsible for ensuring the best conditions and opportunities for making this happen. On the other hand, they also usually believe that the world is a competitive place, that no one is guaranteed a good life, and they will have to "earn" their well-being. I like to complicate things for them by asking whether all of us (especially children) deserve to have enough food, shelter, and health care, regardless of whether they have "earned" them. The issue of health insurance is an especially pertinent one because it makes clear the current conflicts in our society's approach to human well-being—whether we do what most other developed countries do, which is guarantee insurance for all citizens regardless of who they are, or whether we allow the allocation of health care to depend on the good fortune of our income or employment. At the end of all this discussion, something becomes clear to many of my students. It is the question of whether we are committed to the belief that all deserve, and have the right to, a decent and secure life, regardless of who one is and what our circumstances are. Or whether we believe that human well-being should be allocated in an unequal manner, guaranteeing this to only the fortunate minority? The dilemma, I like to say to my students, is certainly a matter of politics and social policy, but it is also a deeply moral and spiritual question that goes to the heart of what it means to say we are our brother's and sister's keeper. The question of who deserves to live well is one that confronts us ever more seriously as we look at our responsibility to ensure a decent life not just for the citizens of this country, but also for the millions of human beings ravaged by hunger, disease, and poverty throughout the world. And, as we increasingly recognize, we cannot hope for a more peaceful world unless we really try to guarantee to all people a life free from such want and the pain of gross deprivation.

- *Fatalism or Agency?*

The vast social and economic inequities that exist in our world can easily lead to a sense of fatalism—a belief that things are so vastly unfair that nothing can really be done to change things. Indeed, the scale of suffering is so great that it is best if we simply turn inward and take care of ourselves—the only thing over which we can really exert any control. It is one of the hazards of teaching for greater awareness of the levels of poverty, injustice, and inequity in the world that students are often quickly overwhelmed by the sheer facts. In my experience, students will often declare that this kind of education is very depressing. This response is certainly understandable. I sometimes remark to them (half-jokingly) that Mondays and Wednesdays I share their despair, while during the rest of the week I'm energized about the possibility of change! One thing that seems very important in attempting to lift individuals out of a sense of hopelessness is knowledge of history, not in the typical tired sense of memorizing dates and disconnected bits of information, but through recognizing how history represents the continuing struggles of humankind to create a world of greater justice, peace, and dignity. And, being far from futile, these struggles do sometimes bear fruit. Progress happens. Colonized people win freedom from empires; women gain greater social, political, and economic rights; workers become politically organized to fight for better lives; the environmental movement gradually impacts our laws and the way we live; ethnic minorities achieve greater equality, opportunity, and recognition of their rights; indigenous peoples take political power in places where they were downtrodden for generations; sexual minorities win greater acceptance. It must be made clear, however, that while there are victories and successes, the struggles are still incomplete. There is always much more to do. There are those who want to reverse the progress and place more obstacles in the path of moral and social change. It is necessary to hold in our hand "both ends of the chain"; we need to see and appreciate how much has been done to overcome social inequity and injustice, but also recognize that there is still much, much more that awaits us to accomplish.

In the effort to lift students out of a sense of hopelessness, they need, I believe, not just an awareness of what has happened in the past to change the world, but the sense that they, too, can participate in this process of making history. Through this participation they acquire a sense of empowerment and agency that combats resignation and fatalism. Fortunately, we are beneficiaries of the current unprecedented power of technology to provide us with immediate access to the extraordinary range of efforts—locally, nationally, and globally—concerned with advancing equity and social justice and developing a more compassionate and connected human community. For many students, I have found, awareness of the range of organizations, groups, and institutions focused around these issues is in itself an inspiring and empowering experience—one that awakens them to the level of energy and creativity that exists around making our world more just and peaceful. It is for this reason that I have included in this short book an appendix that lists some of the organizations and groups engaged in this work, and how they may be contacted. Participation in any of these efforts is a sure way to combat fatalism, cynicism, and hopelessness.

- *Rethinking the Dominator Paradigm*
Finally, it is important to encourage students to envisage a world in which the "dominator" paradigm of human relationships is replaced by what Riane Eisler has called a "partnership" or cooperative model. Human relationships that are organized around domination and control are incapable of producing peace. They inevitably mean that some human beings are not viewed in the fullness of their being; they become vehicles for other people's interests and demands. Those who are dominated experience themselves as less than human. They exist in a world in which they are instruments of others' desires and concerns, existing as things or objects to be manipulated or used by those with more power. In whatever circumstance these dominating relationships exist—families, classrooms, workplaces, places of worship, the political regimes of a nation—the result is nearly always the same. In all these situations individuals feel diminished, reduced, and negated in their being. *This negation of who we are is a violence that stifles and constricts our value and capabilities as human beings.* And history, as well as our own experience, tells us that this form of denial of our full human value is a certain recipe for resistance and conflict directed at those who would place us in this dehumanized condition.

Our educational task here is a simple one. It is to encourage the re-imaging of human relationships. To nurture among our students a willingness and a capacity to envisage all our relations with others as ones in which each of us is seen and treated in the fullness of our lives. It means, in the first place, asking questions about all the ways we relate and interact with others; the way that gender relations are conducted; how workers are treated by their bosses; how the lives of children and youth are ordered in schools; how government agencies deal with the poor or migrants; how differences of race and ethnicity influence and shape our interactions; how those of us who live in affluent nations depend on the work of those who live in the world's poor nations. We must also consider the abuse and pain inflicted on animals through our factory farming methods and product testing in the laboratory. The goal is always to recognize the possibilities for harm when people are placed in situations of domination or exploitation. But beyond this the goal is to imagine the ways in which human relations and behavior can become more life giving and life affirming when we radically change how we connect with and relate to others who share our world. What does it mean when domination gives way to human relations that are reciprocal, empathic, empowering? How would this change the way we perceive and treat one another? What changes would be required in the nature of our institutions to make these changes possible? As with all exercises concerned with imagination and possibility, thinking must involve what Henry Giroux terms a "utopian realism." It must demand from us those flights of imagination and creativity that allow us to be free of the everyday forces of convention, expediency, and ingrained habit. But it must also not represent something so free-floating that it is disconnected from all possible realities. There must be the will to transcend what we are used to as reality, as well as an awareness of the way other societies, other institutions, and other people have constructed and created ways of living and acting that reduce or eliminate domination and the exercise of "power over" others, and in their place manage to produce human relationships that are a good deal more compassionate, affirming, inclusive, and democratic than the ones that currently surround us. Without moving away from institutions and social systems that perpetuate relationships of domination there can be no end to violence. The first step in moving beyond the tyranny and stifling oppressiveness of dominating relationships is to free our minds from their seeming inevitability and "see" the world in ways that take us beyond what is given—to imagine what is not yet so that we might understand what might be.

Postscript: Justice or Peace?

My six-month stay in South Africa allowed me to see that the paths toward a world of justice and peace do not always run smoothly or harmoniously together. Indeed, there are times when the two seem to be in clear conflict. They talk in Africa of "transitional justice," meaning that "principled compromises" might be necessary to ensure that the pursuit of justice does not lead to more conflict and violence (something so clearly present in many post-colonial nations). So, for example, the much celebrated Truth and Reconciliation Commission (TRC) that was set up following the end of apartheid in South Africa offered amnesty to those who had committed crimes while attempting to maintain the system of racial oppression if they would acknowledge, and show contrition, regarding their violent or brutal acts. This was a hard pill to swallow for those who had suffered so much at the hands of this vicious regime. Yet the wider thinking behind the TRC was that pursuit and punishment of all those who had perpetrated crimes of this sort would likely only help to create a new regime of oppression and pain in the country, making any future reconciliation or national cohesion impossible (it is sometimes said that "an eye for an eye leaves everyone blind"). Of course this meant that "retributive" justice—justice requiring punishment for all those who perpetrated crimes—would be cut short or limited. Individuals would be allowed to go free without, seemingly, any real cost to their lives. (Many of these appeared to be the "foot soldiers" of the regime who lacked great political or economic power and who carried out the daily tasks of policing and surveillance, rather than those who had designed, instigated, and been the major beneficiaries of the exploitative system.) Yet the new leaders of South Africa believed that this magnanimity was needed if a new democratic society could emerge from the years of bloodshed and suffering and be able to provide a better life for the majority of its inhabitants. The larger goal of those behind the TRC, such as Archbishop Desmond Tutu, was that of "restorative" justice in which punishment of and revenge against perpetrators would be less important than the vision of a healed society in which there could be renewed recognition of the humanity, dignity, and worth of all citizens. This would require ways to reconcile former adversaries rather than doing things that would further separate and inflame an already deeply divided society. Still, the reality for many in South Africa is that too few paid any penalty for their brutal acts, and that reconciliation still requires reparations to be paid to those who have for so long been oppressed and deprived of social and economic justice. The latter remains an enormous problem as the legacy of apartheid is one of continued deep social, educational, and economic inequities. However much peace may be a desired goal, understandably there is anger that remains with those whose lives were, and continue to be, so blighted by systematic injustice. *It is difficult to deny the deep human need to punish those responsible for creating and maintaining so much suffering and indignity. It is not easy to forgive when we cannot forget what has taken place. Yet wisdom tells us that without some forgiveness, societies are locked into an endless cycle of retributive acts.*

In the classroom, too, acknowledgment of how some have benefited from the injustice inflicted on others is a necessary part of the healing process. But for any of us who have engaged our students in an exploration of the way racial, class, gender, or other forms of inequality work, we know that the process can be an emotional and painful one. Guilt among those who may come to recognize their own advantages at the price of others' lives can be a burden that blocks the desire for further understanding—a feeling that "I don't want to hear anymore about this, it just makes me feel bad!" The pain that comes with recognition of one's complicity might lead to a refusal to accept any responsibility—"I'm not a racist and its not my fault that there was slavery or segregation." Rather than healing the divide and recognizing our common humanity, such pedagogy can lead to more, not less, anger and frustration. It can lead to a rejection or refusal to see one's continuing part in the process of social injustice. Yet such work must be done. Without an honest exploration of the way we demean and violate one another, we are left in a world of denial and irresponsibility. Still, the best teachers I have seen are the ones who manage to do this work in ways that ensure an environment of compassion and community and teach with great love and gentleness towards all. They may even inject humor into the situation, so that the pain of understanding is always accompanied by the joy of hope and liberation.

Chapter Five

THE VIOLENCE OF INVISIBILITY

The trip to Auschwitz served as a kind of initiation. The freight cars, each carrying about 100 people, came from as far as Bordeaux and Rome and Salonika, voyages of a week or more, stifling in summer, arctic in winter. Sometimes the trains were shunted onto sidings for days on end, nights on end. The prisoners' cries for food and water went unheeded. When they banged their fists on the doors, their guards usually ignored them. Occasionally, they answered by banging the outsides of the doors with their gun butts. Sometimes, by the time the sealed trains finally reached southern Poland, the dead outnumbered the living.... Once the selection was finished, the prisoners chosen for the gas chambers were taken by truck to two neat little farmhouses, with thatched roofs and whitewashed walls, surrounded by fruit trees and shrubbery. Teams of Jewish prisoners who had been assigned to the Sonderkommando, or "special command" shepherded the victims onward, urging them to move along quietly into the shower rooms and to take off all their clothes.... Here, and later in the new crematoria at Birkenau, the Final Solution took place. What happened can best be described in the detached words of Rudolf Hoess, who was in command of all this: "The door would now be quickly screwed up and the gas discharged by the waiting disinfectors through vents in the ceilings of the gas chambers, down a shaft that led to the floor. This insured the rapid distribution of the gas. It could be observed through the peephole in the door that those who were standing nearest to the induction vents were killed at once. It can be said that about one-third died straight away. The remainder staggered about and began to scream and struggle for air. The screaming, however, soon changed to the death rattle and in a few minutes all lay still...The door was opened half an hour after the induction of the gas, and the ventilation switched on...The special detachment now set about removing the gold teeth and cutting the hair from the women. After this the bodies were taken up by elevator and laid in front of the ovens, which had meanwhile been stoked up. Depending on the size of the bodies, up to three corpses could be put into one oven at the same time. The time required for

cremation...took twenty minutes...about 2000 bodies in twenty-four hours, but a higher number was not possible without causing damage to the installations."
—From "Kingdom of Auschwitz" by Otto Friedrich in *The Atlantic*, September 1981

INVISIBILITY IN THE CLASSROOM: WHAT'S IN A NAME?

Some of the most shameful moments I have experienced in the classroom as a teacher have to do with the simple fact of not remembering, or not knowing, the name of a student. There are many times I have found myself taking a sneak look at the official roll in order to try to identify a student. Or sometimes holding my breath while taking a guess at the name of someone sitting in front of me. The problem gets more acute the longer the semester goes on. I emphasize in my pedagogy the importance of there being a personal connection between teacher and student instead of the often remote and depersonalized kind of relationship. Knowing the name of each person sitting for weeks in my class seems like a basic indicator of such a connection. This problem is compounded when race becomes a part of the equation. I am particularly sensitive to the possibility that not knowing the names of students of color will be taken as a symptom of white people's inability to adequately distinguish such students from one another—another dimension of our racist upbringing and socialization. Now, in my later years, I confess I use age as an excuse for not remembering students' names and as a justification for getting students to wear name tags. I guess I have some dislike for the latter as there seems to be something infantilizing about this method of identification.

So what is so terrible about forgetting a name, or never really knowing it in the first place? My gut instinct about this is that there is something in this failure that really hurts. The inability to properly refer to someone in your presence, with whom you promise a human connection, feels disrespectful and insulting. In the classroom I do not forget everyone's name—there are those, for whatever reason, who I easily remember and am able to clearly identify. In other words, some of those in front of me are recognized in their singular presence while others are not. For some students, their presence as distinguishable and identifiable individuals is made clear through my correctly naming them in front of their peers. For others, the lack of this public identification indicates a kind of anonymity and invisibility. Am I making too much of this? Is it really such a big deal that a teacher cannot remember the name of a student? My own belief is that it matters a lot. It matters because there is little that is more significant to any human being than the question of his or her recognition as a distinct, unique, and irreducible entity. Our names are the signature on our singular and irreplaceable presence in the world. To forget someone's name is to condemn the person to invisibility. *Such invisibility perpetrates a type of violence against them—a quiet, symbolic form of violence, but an assault on their being no less than more overt and physical forms of violence.* More than once I have noted the words of those forgotten students who will painfully assert that the teacher "didn't seem to know that I even existed." It should be no surprise that these individuals are often the ones who are most alienated and disengaged from the class. Lack of recognition becomes a source of frustration, resentment, and sometimes outright hostility to anything I, as a teacher, might want to do. The first rule of engaged pedagogy, I have learned, is the need to make clear that the presence of all those who are part of this learning community is acknowledged in that most primary way, through being called by our names.

In a moving reference to the importance of this, Allister Sparks in his book about the struggle to end the apartheid regime in South Africa[1] notes Nelson Mandela's extraordinary memory for names. He writes about the iconic leader of this great liberation movement:

> ...the incident revealed a personality trait that has astonished many who have met Mandela since his release [from jail], and that is his close attention to personal detail, his almost card-index memory for people, which enables him to recognize men and women he may have not seen for years or may have met only briefly in a crowd....I was the first journalist to interview Mandela after his release, and as we began talking in his sitting room in Soweto, we were interrupted by a family member who announced that some tribal elders from his home village in Transkei had arrived to pay their respects. The old men were shown into the room, and Mandela proceeded to ask them for news of their extended families, who had married whom and what children and grandchildren had been born in the twenty-seven years he had been away, and one could see him mentally card-indexing all the names. "This is no trick of political showmanship," Nadine Gordimer, the Nobel literature laureate, has written of the man she knows well. "Seemingly trivial, it is a sign of something profound: a remove from self-centeredness; the capacity to live for others that is central to his character."

More than Bread Alone

As I argue elsewhere in this book, the sense of unfairness in the distribution of resources and opportunities in a society is a powerful force in creating frustration and resentment among those who are disadvantaged. Material injustice, as Marxists and socialists have made clear, has been a potent source of struggle against ruling and privileged groups throughout history. Yet the past 60 years have also made clear that there are other powerful reasons that cause human beings to pursue change. Principal among these is the belief that one's presence, and the presence of those who share one's identity and experience, is denied by others. *The failure to fully appreciate and validate human presence has been a continuing catalyst for anger, resistance, and struggle by those who feel themselves devalued, invisible, or depersonalized by those who have the material and cultural power to control the process of recognition.* The issue is not material injustice, though this usually cannot be separated from the issue of recognition and affirmation. What is at stake is the belief that one's dignity and existential value are under assault. Here, human beings have been led to see their own worth and value as less than that of others. They are ignored, or become invisible, in the eyes of others. In the most extreme cases, the recognition of the very humanity of a group has been withdrawn or denied. We know of many times in history in which individuals have survived harsh bodily deprivation of hunger, cold, homelessness, and so on. But what enabled human survival in these conditions has been the dignity of spirit that people have managed to retain in spite of these most difficult conditions. At these times, an oppressed people have managed to confirm their own humanity in spite of how they are seen, *or more accurately, not seen,* by others.

We do, indeed, live by more than bread alone. Beyond the needs of our bodily sustenance is the urge towards being recognized in the fullness of our humanity. We must be *seen* by others, recognized as beings of *infinite* worth whose value must be acknowledged as no less than that of others in the world. I cannot say for sure whether the demand to be seen in this way is something that is imprinted into our genetic makeup, or whether it is the product of a particular historical moment and the spread of a particular cultural understanding about what it means to be human. All the great religious traditions seem, in some sense at least, to affirm the idea of the precious value of every human life (even while they have elaborated justifications for persecuting those who deviate from a particular understanding of faith). Democratic and liberal discourses have enshrined belief in *natural* and *human* rights that inhere in *all* people. Sadly, these noble and uplifting beliefs have often coexisted with deep class inequalities, vicious racism, sexism, demeaning behavior toward those with disabilities, anti-Semitism, homophobia, and other forms of human devaluation. Yet what is clear is that we are witness in our time to an unprecedented demand by all kinds of groups to be visible (to "come out of the closet!"), and to challenge the ways that they have been dismissed, patronized, dehumanized, and invalidated. *We have come to see how misrecognition of human beings represents another form of violence.* Coerced invisibility is another kind of death—one that destroys human agency and the capacity for fulfilled living.

The Politics of Identity

This is the age of the *politics of identity*—a politics that has made us become far more sensitive in our speech, humor, sporting symbols, history texts, and so on, to how we characterize others. "Political correctness," as it is called, is sometimes indicted or ridiculed for its compulsive insistence that we take much more care in how we refer to, name, or describe others. Yet beyond the (relatively small) inconvenience of becoming more sensitive in our language is something of much greater importance. Under the surface, questions of appropriate language and symbols are some of the most profound spiritual and ethical imperatives that face the human community. What is at stake is the question of whether we recognize the very humanity of those different from ourselves, or whether we continue to depersonalize and demean them.

I am writing this chapter while living, temporarily, in Cape Town, South Africa. This is a country in which less than 20 years ago, 80 percent of the people who live here were treated as inferior beings, deprived of those elementary rights to travel and live where they would like, to speak or to assemble, to have their voices heard in the legislatures and public media, to sit and associate freely with anyone they choose, including whom they might marry or with whom they may have sex. In this country, human beings were classified by their skin color and ethnicity into a rigid and hierarchical system of power and status. This system required that individuals designated as inferior carry passes at all times that showed their racial classification and restricted their places of residence and movement. It was a system in which three and a half million people were forcibly moved because of the pernicious doctrine that people were so fundamentally different that they could not be allowed to share the same residential space or social life. This was a monstrous system of legally and militarily enforced segregation that was widely condemned and shunned throughout the world. It produced a society that enriched and privileged a small section of the population while condemning the mass of people to the worst forms of exploitation, poverty, and injustice. Today, South Africa is a transformed country. It continues to face very serious problems, many of them the legacy of the apartheid era, especially around the profound differences in opportunity and well-being that still exist there. Yet one is also struck by the now easy and free movement and interaction of individuals who but a short time ago were barred from meeting except in the most exploitative and hierarchical ways. This is a country whose constitution now commits it to being a democratic, non-racial, non-sexist society and does not discriminate against gays and lesbians. Whatever the challenges it faces, it has ended for all time the culture that legally codified and enforced the inferiority and depersonalization of most of its citizens. There is now public recognition of the universal humanity of all men and women. All are worthy to be seen in the fullness of their individual presence, and as a consequence have an equal moral claim on the possibility of a decent life. Rather than having separate and irreconcilable destinies, the inhabitants of the "new" South Africa now have a shared fate as equal citizens of the society. The South African experience reveals that the tangible violence against the non-white citizens of the country in the form of harsh work conditions, miserable housing, restrictions on movement, and so on, were supported by the more intangible assault on the very human status of these citizens. From this we learn that violence begins when some human beings are classified as being less than fully recognized members of a society, and their humanity is less than fully visible and affirmed. Diminished in this way, any group of human beings is then positioned to become the victims of the most exploitative or cruel treatment. Before there is the violence that assaults the body, there is the violence directed against the spirit and dignity of a human being. In 1994, Black South Africans finally had their citizenship restored to them after so many years of being treated as if they were invisible non-citizens. An unemployed Black man standing in a long line to vote for the first time expressed simply what this change meant: "Now I am a human being," he said.[2]

Sadly, while I am writing this I am also listening to news about events in Gaza where the "hundred-year war" between Jews and Palestinians continues in all its bloody ferocity. It is one more round in the seemingly endless violence, bloodshed, and killing that marks the history of the peoples in this region. The fury of each side in this current round of combat adds to the accumulated poison of hatred and irreconcilability. Putting aside the question of who is really the culprit here, what I am struck by most at this time is how rage and frustration have produced utter contempt for the humanity of the other. Blinded by anger, each side finds legitimacy in strategies that inflict mutilation and death on the other. And the distinction between combatants and innocent civilians erodes in the apparent need for vengeance. For Hamas, all Israeli Jews are illegal usurpers of a land that is rightfully Arab and Islamic. They thus feel justified in firing their missiles into towns and settlements that kill civilians, regardless of whether the victims are children, women, or elderly people. For the Israeli army, Hamas terrorists use "human shields" to protect them and thus argue that there is justification for the bombs and shells that land in densely populated areas, killing and maiming children and innocent bystanders. Behind all these arguments it is not difficult to see how the poison of dehumanization seeps into the consciousness of these protagonists. Human beings have become enemy targets. The pain and suffering of children and the anguish of parents are lost in the language of strategic considerations or the intransigent demands of fanatical purists. The cries of human hearts cannot be heard in the depersonalized din of war and hate. Each side vows to teach the other side a lesson that will stop them for good. But instead, each step in the direction of dehumanizing the enemy further compounds the inability to see the precious worth of the other. Instead, what remains are the hateful and distorted caricatures of malevolent beings. The violence against bodies is preceded by the violence that makes the real human presence of the other invisible. Before the killing comes the callous misrecognition of the beings and lives that confront one another.

THE IRREDUCIBLE VALUE OF HUMAN LIFE

We live in a world that offers immense hope around our capacity to witness the other as no less human than ourselves. *Our era is one in which, for the first time in human history, we are asked to see all other human beings as persons of infinite value and precious worth.* According to the influential Jewish philosopher Emmanuel Levinas,[3] we are to see in the face of each person before us the presence of God. Whether or not we accept his religious metaphor, what he asks of us is that in our social relationships we make our decisions and choices according to the ethical imperative that each life is irreducible to some abstract formula of human value or a depersonalized system of judgment. *Each individual demands from us the respect and dignity that is the consequence of his or her sacred and unconditional worth.* To view human beings in this way is to see them as embodied creatures who cannot be adequately recognized unless we take fully account of their existence as flesh and blood beings—individuals who cannot simply be converted into numbers on an accounting sheet or ciphers for a sociological category. They cannot be robbed of their humanity. Their subjectivity must never be reduced to less than that of extraordinary and ineffable beings. Our mental categories always fall short of capturing the full preciousness and beauty of life. In this sense, to talk about the wonder and worth of the human person is not to separate our embodied selves from the nobility and dignity of the human spirit. Unlike the way so much of our monotheistic theology sees these as separate and opposing forces, body and spirit actually reinforce and enrich one another. Our material lives and the intangible qualities of being are inextricably joined. It is precisely by recognizing the depth and power of our feeling lives—our pain, joy, desires, ecstasies, hunger, suffering, and anguish, all of which are inseparable from our lives as sensuous and embodied beings—that we gain the immeasurably profound quality of being with all of its capacity for love, care, and compassion, as well as rage, despair, and alienation.

To recognize human beings as fully human means to recognize the rich complexity of each individual's intuitive, moral, cognitive, sensuous, and spiritual life. The deep and precious value of each life requires the acknowledgment of the interconnection of the tangible and the intangible in what Terry Eagleton refers to as the "body-subject."[4] We possess both that "swarming region of feeling" and emotion that Eagleton refers to and that mysterious spiritual self that demands recognition as the locus of dignity and unconditional worth. And the extraordinary capacity for reason and creativity found in human beings can never be fully separated from our selves as aesthetic and spiritual beings. All attempts to reduce us to thinking machines or computer-like intelligence distort our grounding in something beyond rational calculation and dispassionate objectivity. It obscures the awe, wonder, and mystery of life. Because of this we can only be wary of all the attempts, whether through science or political ideology, to "map" and "engineer" human life. As the social theorist Zygmunt Bauman has made clear, each attempt at this ends up with a theory, doctrine, or mythology that compresses, reduces, and truncates the essence of a human life.[5] At the opening of this chapter is one man's searing account of the process of mass murder at Auschwitz. Yet the murderous violence of Nazi genocide did not begin with the train journey to the extermination camp. The violent assault and destruction of the human body began much earlier with the assault against the very humanity of Jews and others. It began in the system of elaborate classification that resulted in the vilification of whole groups of people whose very claim on being human was vitiated by the Nazi ideology. The rich, infinitely complex, and ineffable beauty of each person was replaced by a system that reduced each individual to the abstract disfigurement of racist classification.

To look into the eyes of another person is to witness the mystery of the inexpressible and incomparable other. It is to bear witness to the infinite complexity of each and every individual that stands before us. Yet, despite this, history is the endless and catastrophic narrative of how incommensurable beings are reduced to a form in which their unique presence is obliterated. We continuously invent myths that compress the infinite complexity of human beings into a single, limited dimension of who we are. The multiple strands of our identity give way to one "privileged" aspect—the hue of one's skin, the language or dialect that we speak, the particular way we pray, a physical or mental "disability," the objects of our sexual desire, anatomical difference, a particular cognitive or expressive capacity. The significance of one real or imagined dimension of our being becomes elevated in the eyes of others—a process that not only sets limits to my own being, but reduces all those who may share this characteristic to a single depersonalized and distorted entity. In this process of compression and distortion we have all become less than our full humanity promises. And it should be understood that the distortion of our humanity belongs not just to those who are most obviously subordinated by this process. Over two centuries ago, the philosopher Hegel showed how slavery debases both master as well as slave. The jailer becomes a prisoner in his own jail; he, too, is a creature of this process, never fully free from this world of oppression and confinement.

Such a result is no accident. The reduction of human beings in this way to a single dimension with all of its exaggerations becomes a weapon in the hands of those who wish to degrade or subvert the humanity of the other. It becomes a vehicle through which one group can assert and legitimize its superior status, control, or privilege by creating a mythology of ontological difference. In other words, my advantaged position in the world is given moral credibility through my claim that the other is part of a larger group that shares a restricted, and restricting, form of humanity. Such beings are "handicapped," "abnormal," "unnatural," "depraved," "*untermenschen*," "savages," "animals," and so on. Always, in the use of these terms (and many, many others), is the inference that such people are less than fully human, and their individuality is reduced to that of an abstract and stereotypical category. The fullness of their humanness becomes occluded or invisible. And the violence of human invisibility typically precedes the physical violence that maims and murders, and exploits and enslaves. The tendency to diminish other human beings in this way is certainly not new. We can find plenty of evidence of how groups come to define others in this diminished way in pre-modern times. Tribal and ethnic warfare, religious conflict, and "the war against women" certainly predated the modern era. But the modern era—of capitalism, industrialism, and imperialism—has accentuated this process, bringing new and more powerful forms of human categorization and abstraction that have had, and continue to have, a deeply destructive and disfiguring effect on how we see much of the human family. In the next section, I will look a little more closely at some of the forms that this process takes and how it depersonalizes and dehumanizes human beings—the process through which violence is perpetrated against the human presence, dignity, and spirit.

Framing Invisibility

Around the time I wrote this, the British Foreign Secretary, David Miliband, acknowledged that the so-called "War on Terror" was inappropriately termed. Over the past few years, certainly since September 11, 2001, we have become used to this quick and convenient blanket reference that appears to describe, in one simple phrase, all those who would bring harm to us. It suggests a single homogeneous group whose common platform is to attack and kill civilians in any part of the world in order to achieve their political, ideological, or religious goals. Miliband's rethinking of this, I believe, has to do with his recognition that as convenient as the reference to the "War on Terror" may be, it obfuscates the complex and hugely different demands and struggles of many people in diverse parts of the world. It conjures up images of bloodthirsty, morally indifferent people who live by norms quite different from our own. Terrorists, by this definition, are seen as beings that are united through their commonly held, impaired moral sense and evil inclination. The term can blind us to the particular struggles and conditions that a group of human beings may face that drive them to extreme and violent forms of political behavior. Instead, we are faced only with images of irrational and demented people who share none of "our" concerns and sensitivities. Such people possess—or can be reduced to—a shared essential kind of being that marks them as different and deficient human beings. Their limited and demonic nature means that no response on the part of the "civilized world" is unwarranted, including torture, withholding of the usual procedures of judicial process (innocence until proven guilty, the need to know the charges brought against one and by whom, etc.), and the destruction of their sites of operation, even if this should mean the killing of children and other innocents in the same vicinity. The "War on Terror" conjures up images of those who are less than fully human, whose lust for innocent blood places them in a category that is quite different from the world of civilized people. Any kind of violent response aimed at them is now fully justifiable. We need not be bound by the hard-won humanitarian conventions of the democratic world.

Yet we know that one person's terrorist is another person's freedom fighter. The world can look quite different when a group struggling for their freedom or dignity is faced with the power of a modern, well-equipped military force. The latter's use of lethal force with all of its consequent bloodshed is described as carefully and precisely targeted (civilian casualties are described as "collateral damage" and weapons are termed "smart" because of their supposed accuracy). It is difficult, too, to separate our image of the terrorist from some despised and denigrated ethnic group. It is difficult to convince many Americans that someone whose middle name is Hussein could not be a Muslim—and by extension a terrorist or supporter of terrorists. Barack Obama's presidential campaign met the constant insinuation—and for some, the unshakeable belief—of his association with terrorism (even now, after being in office for more than a year there are many who want to deny his American citizenship). From the work of scholars like Edward Said,[6] and from those who have seen the depiction of Arabs and Muslims in Western media, we know just how this world was constructed in Western minds.[7] Cartoon-like caricatures replace human complexity. Instead of thoughtful, sensitive, intelligent, concerned human beings, we are confronted with devious, mendacious, manipulative, irrational, and bloodthirsty individuals. Such a depiction, with its imputations of the clash of the "advanced" West and the "backward" East,[8] conveniently ignores the extraordinary legacy of Arab contributions to Western culture, whether in philosophy, medicine, mathematics, or astronomy. It erases, too, how

Muslim, Christian, and Jewish cultures have engaged together in rich and vibrant ways during other historical periods.[9] This alternative historical narrative contradicts the current belief that we are locked into an inevitable conflict that pits European reason and tolerance against the moral and intellectual blindness of the Arab world. Such distorted and limiting views of any group of people encourages a mentality of violence against both the body and spirit of people in this group. It licenses an attitude of arrogance, dominance, and, ultimately, the necessity of war to contain this threatening "other."

This reduction of human beings to limited and stereotypical images of backwardness, ignorance, and stunted intelligence finds fertile soil in other parts of our social landscape. Immigrants to our shores have usually been depicted in these ways. Their "refusal" to adapt to our supposedly more civilized, respectful, and hygienic ways is part and parcel of how migrant workers are reduced to less than full human status. Any perusal of our history will reveal the similarity between contemporary accusations that are aimed at other immigrant groups and those found in past eras.[10] Lack of cleanliness or respect for property, laziness, stealing, a refusal to learn "our" language, clannishness, and intellectual defectiveness were, and are, the typical complaints. The most telling effect, however, in our view of these "surplus" populations is an inability to see that beyond the reality of menial, low paid, and typically grossly exploited laborers are human beings with lives, loves, desires, hopes, and concerns no less than our own.[11] It is this moral and spiritual blindness that licenses their work in abysmal conditions, threatens their health, and justifies poor or sometimes nonexistent wages, decrepit accommodations, and general obliviousness to their lives and welfare. The creation of vast pools of casual, and often illegal, labor living horribly at the very edge of survival is one of the hallmarks of this age of globalism.[12] General economic insecurity and the precariousness of jobs for the local population accentuates the apprehension towards these economic "invaders" who appear to be willing to live and work in ways far below the generally established social norms of Western society.[13] Their inability to speak the local language, unfamiliar religious practices, different appearance, and so on, add to the sense that these are people not like us. Instead of the richness, complexity, and depth of a human life, we see the depersonalized, de-individuated cipher for an indistinguishable mass. The real human being has become invisible, and instead we witness only an abstract category—field hand, poultry processing plant worker, road construction crew, or sex slave.

The Sex Trade and the Invisibility of Women

"Sex slavery" is a special case. Here there exists what might be called a double whammy of violence. In the first place, there is the depersonalization that comes from being an economic migrant of dubious or nonexistent legal status placed in an environment in which one is viewed as an outsider or alien with all of its humiliating dimensions. At the same time, women forced into prostitution and sexual exploitation experience the degradation that is the consequence of their becoming the dehumanized objects of male fantasy and gratification. They exist purely as the instruments of male pleasure. The global sex trade is a massive one that involves, at a recent count, somewhere around 50,000 to 2 million girls and women a year and generates somewhere between $7 and $12 billion per year.[14] It involves often forced removal of women from their homes and a brutal process of coerced employment in prostitution and sexual services. Such women, who end up in strange countries often without rudimentary knowledge of the local language or laws, are subject to a terrifying regime of captivity. Without any rights or choices they find themselves in situations of almost total subjection to the whims of their thuggish captors. They become little more than commodities to supply sexual pleasures in often the most degrading circumstances in which their bodies are at risk of disease, mutilation, or death. Such women lose any claims to make choices or exercise control over their lives. In the forced trading of their bodies and the reduction of their humanity to the exchange of cash for their services, they endure a sickeningly violent level of depersonalization. It is worth noting, too, that the use of girls and young women in this trade adds another level of barbarism to this process, involving as it does those whose human presence and identity are still in the most vulnerable stage of development and formation.

The human invisibility that is at the core of sexual slavery cannot be completely separated from other forms of gender-related depersonalization. The submergence of an authentic subjectivity is part of the process of female identity formation found even in more liberated social contexts. For many young women, growing up means substituting their own ineffable and unique presence as human beings for the abstracted and homogeneous vision of femalehood that inundates our culture. In this sense, girls come to replace their own incommensurable human presence with versions of who they are, or should be, constructed by powerful ideological forces and cultural institutions. A thousand times each day through TV, movies, advertizing, popular magazines, Internet, and video images, girls repeatedly learn to see themselves not through their own eyes, but through the vicarious, male vision of sexual allure and desire. These homogenized and predictable images of seductive femininity bear down powerfully on the imagination of young girls and women, urging them to replace their own singular human presence with a truncated and reductive idea of what it is to be a woman.[15] This is the process by which girls and women become objectified beings whose identity becomes a "stamped-out," interchangeable set of roles, appearances, and behavior. The ineffable beauty, sensibility, and uniqueness of the female subject is replaced by the made-to-order manufacturers of desire and sexuality. There is surely a connection in this process between the control and seizure of female identity and the violence against the female body that is so pervasive in our culture. The objectification of women means their invisibility as real, empowered, creative, thoughtful, and sensuous individuals. Instead, they become reductive, reified, manufactured creatures that invite male control and domination. In many parts of the world, this process of female invisibility cannot be separated from patriarchal structures that force women to enter limited social roles and have circumscribed expectations for their lives.[16] Limitations on schooling, work, marital, and reproductive choices all are part of the process of cultural and political invisibility that ultimately invites and legitimizes violence against their physical presence and being. It is also worth mentioning that violence against women is intensified by the way in which many men feel themselves to be invisible. Violence here becomes the perverse product of those whose own presence in the world is negated or diminished. It becomes the misguided outcome of those who attempt to make themselves visible through the abuse and physical control of others. In this sense, rape and other forms of violent sexual assault by men is not guided so much by sexual desire as by the effort to control and dominate—and through this make their own presence felt in the world. We may suppose, for example, that in the current economic crisis, as unemployment among men rises, their propensity to act violently towards women will also increase. It is apparent, too, among many of the soldiers returning from the war in Iraq who are suddenly deprived of the coercive power that comes with their armed roles as they return to the give and take of domestic life. Nor can we ignore the emerging awareness of the sexual abuse of so many young boys at the hands of priests in the Catholic Church. What, we must speculate, are the consequences on the psyches of men of such callous sexual exploitation and the painful violation of trust by those placed in positions of adult authority? For children of either sex, brutal disregard of their developing but still fragile humanity surely sows the seeds of new generations of wounded, angry, and mistrustful individuals.

Invisibility as the Weapon of the Oppressed

This attempt to overcome one's invisibility through control of others is seen not just in regard to issues of gender. Violence towards racial minorities is also often the outcome for those who try to rectify their own diminished place in the world through physical assault and brutality on others. Bullying of all kinds is most often the last refuge of those who feel themselves to have a diminished presence in the world—whether through lack of income, inferior social status, educational inability, or lack of social acceptance or popularity. And most likely the violence is aimed at those who themselves are vulnerable through their lack of visibility and regard for their own humanity. Racial and ethnic minorities are typically the ones who have historically been denied this kind of recognition. Instead of being seen through the lens of the ineffable beauty, dignity, and complex subjectivity that belongs to all people, they are depicted in the limited and stunted terms of racist or ethnic stereotyping. Blacks, it is asserted, are intellectually inferior, educationally unmotivated, indolent, and sexually irresponsible. Jews are devious, money-grubbing, overly ambitious, and lack loyalty to their nation. I have already noted how migrants from south of the border are viewed, or how Muslims are considered. Sadly, the human race is creative in its seemingly endless capacity to depict others in ways that are not just derogatory and demeaning, but reduce people to a limited set of fixed categories and attributes. We continuously see how it is possible to turn the rich and mysterious beauty of a human being into stunted and finite cartoon-like characters.

We witness in these times a continuing and inspiring struggle among those who have been so cruelly made invisible as real people to reclaim their rightful humanity. We see this in the battle by those who are named by our culture as "disabled" to not be reduced to this label. Disability is not destiny. Disability refers only to a part of one's humanness. It does not exhaust it. It speaks, usually, only to a limited aspect of one's being, one's attributes, and one's capabilities. People are not the wheelchair that transports them, a particular form of limited cognition, or the auditory or visual impairment that redefines how they interact with the world. *To speak now of the differently abled, as we have begun to do, is to refuse the violent reduction of people to a single defining condition.* It is to refuse to accept cruelly limited and demeaning assumptions about what another individual may do in his or her work or living situation. And it is to reject patronizing and pitying attitudes in regard to another's capacity to live as empowered and dignified human beings.

The struggle to overcome the violently imposed invisibility of gay, lesbian, and other sexual minorities is surrounded by even more drama and passion. Perhaps nothing in recent times more vividly expresses the oppressive nature of invisibility in our culture than the "don't ask don't tell" formula with its insistence that homosexuality remain officially unrecognized. The political battle to unlock this denial of one's full humanity is testimony to the powerful demand that we be recognized and seen by others in a way that does not distort or limit who we really are. At its core is the challenge of oppressive notions of "hetero-normativity," which assert that there is only one form of natural or normal human sexual behavior and desire. All other expressions of sexuality represent some kind of abnormal deviation. Although our sexuality does not exhaust the full richness and expansiveness of being, it is of such centrality to our lives that the attempt to limit and thwart the variety of ways that human beings manifest their sexual identities results in a painful denial or misrecognition of our humanity.

These forms of misrecognition and invisibility—whether through racism, sexism, disability, homophobia, or other types of limitation and stereotyping—share a violent disfigurement of who we really are. Their damage is, in the first place, to the human soul—to our dignity and sense of worth. We continually see how destructive its effects are on individuals' sense of well-being, confidence, and self-acceptance. The refusal to see and appreciate human beings in the fullness and richness of their being ensures that these persons are left to feel deep uncertainty about their value and worth. Guilt, self-doubt, and often self-loathing are its typical consequences. Beyond this the misrecognition of our fundamental humanity frequently undermines our capacity to live as empowered human beings as we constantly search instead for ways to be accepted and validated by others. This lack of confident agency is manifested in a self-censoring of ideas and creativity and a damagingly negative view of our own intellectual capabilities. Invisibility produces shame as well as a debilitating view of our abilities. However, this self-negation is only one side of a coin whose reverse is a forcibly imposed invisibility. Sexism, racism, homophobia, ethnocentrism, anti-Semitism, religious hatred, etc., are invariably accompanied by violence directed against the physical bodies of human beings. Rape, beating, lynching, bullying, murderous assault, ethnic cleansing, and in extreme situations, genocide are the inevitable culmination of situations in which the full humanity of another person is denied, questioned, or placed in doubt. The process of misrecognition and invisibility reaches its supreme folly in the way that military planners and political leaders can contemplate the wholesale destruction of millions of human beings through a nuclear war. In the scenario of a nuclear exchange between nations we are asked to coolly imagine the premeditated deaths of millions of strangers who become reduced to cold, abstract numbers in strategic warfare. The deaths of a vast number of human beings becomes part of a mathematical equation involving bombs with the equivalent explosive power of thousands of megatons of TNT. Its horrifying absurdity is captured in the acronym MAD, or Mutually Assured Destruction, in which the massive retaliation in the event of a nuclear attack would lead to the total annihilation of both sides in the conflict—and, in all probability, the end of human civilization itself. This is the ultimate effacement of real human lives by those who have wedded the power of dispassionate technical knowledge to the coldly calculated decimation of human beings.

Educating for a World of Human Visibility

In the final part of this chapter I will consider some the ways in which we can educate so as to overcome the worlds of invisibility and misrecognition that surround us. I think it is useful to start with the process that the social theorist Zygmunt Bauman calls *adiaphorization*.[17] This unusual term is Bauman's way of referring to the steady process of moral desensitization that characterizes our culture. It speaks to the gradual way we are eroding respect for the sanctity and value of human life and undermining reverence for the integrity and inviolability of human beings. It is surely not difficult to see how our media culture contributes to this process. It is hardly news to say that we are subjected to an endless stream of violent images through movies, TV shows, the Internet, and video games. Through the wonders of technology and special effects, these images become ever more intense and graphic. Indeed, producers of media culture are engaged in a constant process of ratcheting upward the shock level of screen violence. There is continuing debate over how much this influences the sensibility and values of individuals—especially the young.

Although it is probably impossible to provide an exact estimation of this, it is certainly reasonable to assume that a media environment that constantly exposes us to endless and increasingly graphic images of torture, murder, brutality, rape, and a world in which weapons and bombs are ubiquitous must affect human consciousness. It seems improbable, for example, that the constant placement of women in situations of terror, assault, and murder does not reinforce misogynistic cultural values and attitudes.

There is a peculiar resonance to the power of these images. On the one hand they provide an enticing adrenalin rush to those viewing them. To the young, especially, they offer an exciting thrill ride that, at least momentarily, lifts individuals out of the ennui of the everyday world of school, work, etc. Yet at the same time, the longer-term effect of these startling, but pervasive, images is to produce a dulling of human sensibility. Their endless content of blood, pain, and death inures us to the meaning of real violence and harm enacted on the human body. It has been pointed out by others that the carefully selected video images of war, whether in Iraq, Gaza, Chechnya, Afghanistan, or elsewhere, seems eerily similar to the images available on video games. The real consequences of missiles and bombs landing on houses and neighborhoods are lost in what seems to be just another electronic simulation. In a parallel way, the Internet's ever-expanding offerings of pornographic images with their undoubtedly powerful erotic draw occludes the often-violent reality and lives of female sex workers who live behind the video screen.

In an effort to cut through the desensitization process, it helps if students are better able to see what is "behind" the camera. How are images created? What kind of thinking goes into their construction? How are people's fantasies stroked and manipulated? How much money rests on this kind of exploitation? What are the different roles of women and men in this violent image making? Beyond this, educators have a responsibility to make clear just how different the simulated scenes of car crashes, bombs exploding, missiles landing, gun fights, and stabbings are from the terrible effects of *real life* bodily harm. What does it really do to people when they are shot or are victims of an exploding bomb or device? How do our images of military glory differ from the actual consequences for those whose bodies are torn apart because of war? It is not for nothing that the Bush administration placed severe restrictions on the return of bodies from the Iraq war, or that so little is seen of those who must contend with a lifetime of terrible wounds and disabilities and who must endure the never-ending pain of savage disabilities.[18] Educating for peace means asking students to confront the real effects of violence and compare these with the sanitized and simulated images that can momentarily thrill us, but allow us to walk away from them unharmed. We must also ask students to consider the Orwellian language we use that insulates us from the real pain and horror of organized killing. Such terms as "collateral damage," "kill rates," "extraordinary rendition," and "water boarding" are all ways to hide from or avoid the terrible pain and horror of state-supported violence.

Invisibility or Dignity for All

To educate so that we overcome the violence of invisibility means that educators must, in no uncertain terms, affirm human dignity for all. As discussed in this chapter, invisibility or misrecognition of other people implies that we see only a limited, usually stereotypical, view of others. Human dignity rests on appreciating and recognizing the full humanity of individuals, not a stunted, distorted, or limited image. This is a situation in which we must acknowledge that no education is, or can be, morally neutral. Education is always undergirded by human values and embodies a particular social, ethical, and spiritual worldview. Peace education embraces the belief that all human lives are of equal value and that all human beings deserve to be seen and treated in the full richness, beauty, and complexity of each life. Peace education is about helping students understand something about the spiritual, ethical, and political traditions upon which our views of human dignity and worth are built and the consequences of failing to live up to the deep significance of these traditions. This involves looking honestly at how all of our religious traditions have been vehicles that affirm the preciousness of every life, while also providing justifications for intolerance, persecution, and even war. It means also looking at our most noble statements of human dignity and human rights, such as the U.S. Constitution, the South African post-apartheid constitution, or the United Nations Declarations of Human Rights, and appreciating how each contributes to a strengthening of human dignity while also seeing how social, economic, and cultural reality falls far short of what they promise.

Equally important is for students to recognize in their own lives how being invisible or misrecognized is a painful and humiliating experience shared by us all. The classroom should offer a space in which individuals are able to openly acknowledge and share how invisibility and misrecognition have affected and shaped their own lives. How have racism, sexism, anti-Semitism, and prejudices towards others because of their language or dialect, religious preference, sexual orientation, disability, or ethnic and national origin caused suffering and pain in their lives? This is also the time to consider how social and institutional practices, such as those found in schools, create and maintain structures of invisibility and misrecognition.[19] How do institutions that are organized around differential rewards of human efforts and ability contribute towards the violence of negative human labels? This is also a place for students to consider what kinds of changes would be needed if we are to build a society in which all are visible in the fullness of their humanity. How would it affect what is taught in school? How would it influence who speaks in the classroom? And on what basis or criteria would we decide to reward or recognize students?

Capitalism and the Misrecognition of Humanity

It would be difficult to consider those things in a world that reduces human presence without looking critically at the consequences of capitalist culture. It is at the very core of the capitalist ethic to reduce all things human to the very limited criteria of profitability and efficiency. Capitalism encourages all of us to view our world through the monochromatic lens of commodification. The natural world—land, water, the oceans, forests, animals, air—are reduced to the most limited forms of calculation in which their value becomes entirely a matter of their monetary equivalence. Everything about them is a matter only of what Karl Marx once called the "cash nexus"—for how much can they be traded? What is their value in the marketplace? Within the capitalist consciousness the living matter of our world, which provide the vital and interrelated dimensions of our planetary home, are of value only in terms of how much profit can be wrung from them. In this crudely reductionist and simplistic calculus, the precious, life-enabling qualities of other living creatures, forests, oceans, air, and the soil have value only in so far as they can be made to turn a profit. In this reduction of our living environment to marketable commodities, it is easy to see the makings of our deep environmental crisis—a process now well documented with all of its threats to the future of an inhabitable earth. The consciousness that has brought the future of our planet itself into question has also jeopardized humanity itself. Increasingly we see how the global marketplace has dehumanized workers, treating them as interchangeable and disposable parts of the production process. With little regulation of global markets, companies are free to hire and fire workers at will, offer the least in the way of humane and decent working conditions, and as soon as greater profits can be made in other countries or regions, move to where labor is cheaper without concern for the individual and communal destruction they leave behind.

The results have been nothing less than catastrophic for the quality of human life. It has produced a "risk society"—one with increasing levels of human insecurity and a precarious and uncertain future for working and middle class people.[20] The era of guaranteed long-term employment and company responsibility for pensions and health care have disappeared. Human beings have become recognizable only as temporary employees, and their value as committed members of a work community has been replaced by a mentality in which they are the readily expendable bottom line. The general feeling spreads that within this erratic and predatory economic context, the humanity of people disappears into a dark hole of invisibility. Real human lives have become unrecognizable in this viciously dispassionate environment. As teachers, it is incumbent on us to alert students to the deeply dehumanizing course our global economy is set upon. Our responsibility is to help them understand something about the enormous dilemma that faces human beings in the twenty-first century, which is to continue to improve the living standards of the world's people without reducing people to faceless, dehumanized, and depersonalized parts of an industrial machine. We must courageously share with our students the terrible dangers of an economic system that counts efficiency and value only in terms of money and profit[21] and forgets that behind the decisions of the corporate power brokers and politicians are real human lives. Violence occurs when human beings are treated as nothing but a factor of the productive process, as if they are little more than expendable and disposable raw materials. We must also affirm, as teachers, that to recognize the precious and incommensurable nature of human beings need not be separated from the larger awareness of the precious quality of all life—both human and non-human. The consciousness that resists the violation of the dignity and value of workers is also one that resists the trampling and trashing of the earth. Both deserve our recognition and our active commitment to protect them from a predatory economic system that, as Oscar Wilde once noted, "knows the price of everything and the value of nothing."

Dehumanization and the Culture of Positivism

One dimension of this dehumanization process with which students in schools are intimately familiar is that of the pervasive quantification of human activity. Just as it is in the broader market system, so it is in schools—everything that that is considered significant must be turned into a measurable number. The origins of this "positivist" consciousness are complex, but it includes both the system of capitalism, with its concern for efficiency and profit, and the scientific method, with its focus on the empirical and the search for relationships between phenomena that are predictable and causal. What is clear is that contemporary schooling in almost every country is increasingly dominated by quantifiable and demonstrable measures of "outcomes." Students are deeply sensitive to the oppressive consequences of this process: the relentless and stressful focus on testing; education that is all about measuring individuals for their position in a hierarchy of success and failure; and the narrowing of the curriculum and what is considered educationally worthwhile. At some level all students experience the depersonalizing effects of this obsession with measurement and quantifiable outcomes. Usually, its effects—however oppressive to the lives of students—are not something that can be treated as the object of critical discussion. Yet here is a powerful vehicle through which individuals can, with the encouragement and insights of a critically minded teacher, see how the full richness, passion, curiosity, and imagination of human beings is reduced to the flat homogeneity of a numerical value. Focusing on the positivist culture of schooling allows students to grasp what it means for people to be treated in ways that reduce their unique and incommensurable qualities to the bland sameness of a grade or other similar forms of limited assessment. And allows them to understand how this facilitates the primary purpose of schools, which is to compare and rank students against one another. This is the quiet violence that compresses the wonder of human intelligence, creativity, and imagination to the stunted and stressful effects of a culture whose primary emphasis is on competition and measurable output.[22]

Education and the Disembodied Curriculum

There is another dimension of this educational process that teachers and educational leaders need to contest for the way it misrecognizes the fullness of human existence. For all the talk of educational change, the curriculum continues to be one that reflects a profound disembodiment of human cognition and awareness. Schooling reflects the dualistic mind/body consciousness that discounts or minimizes the dimensions of human growth and experience whose source is most clearly that of the sensuous body and sensitive feeling. This is most obviously seen in how subject matter that is dispassionate and detached from feeling is privileged in the hierarchy of learning. Analysis, logic, and abstract reasoning are the areas most highly valued and rewarded. Things that have to do with sensitive awareness of our lives and experience, or that emphasize feeling and connection to self and others, are of only secondary value. It is no surprise that subject matter that might cultivate the latter, such as art, dance, theater, and other forms of creative expression, are relegated to the margins of the curriculum. Other things that might add to an awareness of our embodied lives such as meditation and the development of our emotional and relational intelligence (especially as we progress through the school system) have almost no place in the curriculum. All of this means that schools encourage a distorted vision of our lives as human beings—long on the capacity for detached and abstract thinking and short on our capacity as feeling, aware, and sensitive beings alert to our lives as embodied creatures and to that of others who share our world.

Why this is so has much to do, I believe, with the power and privileging of masculine values in our culture with its separation and subordination of feeling, sensitivity, and the sensuous. The masculine has typically overvalued rationality and control, emotional detachment, and dispassionate calculation. The argument here is not to eradicate these attributes, which obviously play a crucial role in the development and maintenance of a technologically based and complex advanced industrial society, but for a *rebalancing* of what we value in human subjectivity. Education can play a critical role in this quest for individuals who are developed in the full richness of their being rather than in distorted and limited ways. Obviously, too, this rebalancing in the human attributes we value also speaks to the way our culture denigrates those qualities typically associated with women—nurturance, relational sensitivity, compassion and care, vulnerability, and feeling.[23] I do not believe it is too difficult to imagine a curriculum that expands our vision for what it means to be a fully developed human being. Such a curriculum—one that includes both the formal subject matter as well as the informal dimensions of the school and classroom—would emphasize not just the *head* but also the *heart*, not just academic intelligence but the capacity for caring, compassionate, and responsible relationships towards others as well to the whole of the natural world.

Educating students to become citizens who embrace the goals of a peaceful culture means attempting to create individuals who develop as more than the limited beings that can fill slots in our workplace organizations, become consumers in the capitalist marketplace, or act as compliant and unquestioning members of civil society and the military. Our educational goals need to reflect the recognition of human beings in the fullness of their being, which includes intellectual, emotional, moral, *and* spiritual qualities. I will have more to say about this in the final chapter, but suffice it to say here that the latter, in particular, means being aware of and nurturing that mysterious and ineffable dimension of humanness we call the *spirit*. Although, by its very nature, the spirit references something non-empirical and demonstratively elusive, this does not mean I am talking gibberish. Here, we know something not by its presence as a thing we can see or touch, but by the fact that we as humans simply recognize that something in the universe calls out to us and demands our respect and our attention. The Talmudic saying, "When you destroy one life you destroy a whole world," conveys the immense power and significance that is attached to human life. To educate against human invisibility and misrecognition means, ultimately, to affirm the extraordinary and precious value of a life—an idea that is the legacy of so many of our wisdom traditions. It is to acknowledge that men and women are much more than an assembly of cells and physiological processes, but each is a unique and incommensurable presence in the world. This presence calls out to us—demands from us respect, care, justice, and dignity. However we may wish to refer to this presence—whether as the human spirit, human dignity, or the unconditional value of human life—its mysterious power demands that we behave in ways that nourish and sustain rather destroy it. And in this sense, to educate for peace is always in some way the work of spiritual affirmation, connection, and care.

So, to return to the question that began this chapter, do our names matter? They do to the Argentinian mothers who have for years protested the disappearance of the bodies and the identities of their children during the brutal military dictatorship of that country. They do also to the contemporary African-American descendants of slaves who pour over genealogical histories trying to identify the exact names of ancestors who were forced to endure the horrific voyages that took them to slavery in America. And they do to the children and grandchildren of the victims of Nazi genocide who seek to regain the living presence of those who disappeared in the black smoke of the crematoria at Auschwitz and elsewhere.

Their names were the unique signature of their too short presence on this earth.

Chapter Six

VIOLENCE AND THE CRISIS OF MEANING

> The potency of myth is that it allows us to make sense of mayhem and violent death. It gives a justification to what is often nothing more than gross human cruelty and stupidity. It allows us to believe we have achieved our place in human society because of a long chain of heroic endeavors, rather than accept the sad reality that we stumble along a dimly lit corridor of disasters. It hides from view our own impotence and the ordinariness of our own leaders. By turning history into myth we transform random events into a chain of events directed by a will greater than our own, one that is determined and preordained. We are elevated above the multitude. We march towards nobility. And no society is immune.
> —From *War Is a Force That Gives Us Meaning*, by Chris Hedges

THE IMPORTANCE OF MEANING

Jean-Paul Sartre, the French philosopher of existentialism, famously noted that "man is condemned to meaning." Very succinctly this statement alerts us to the fact that human beings are impelled by needs that go beyond simply material desires. Sartre's assertion denies the crude versions of Marxist philosophy that reduce the human quest for social change and improvement to being only about the struggle for power and material interests. In place of this the struggle over purpose and meaning in our lives looms large in the quest for a worthwhile and satisfying existence. The need to find overarching purpose to our lives is as central to our being as the demand for food and shelter. Meaning is as essential to human well-being as the satisfaction of bodily needs. Sartre's words points us towards recognizing that a world that is without symbolic value and coherence constitutes a deep crisis in human existence and a profound indictment of a society. To live in such a world means to live an animal-like existence dependent on habit and repetition rather than being impelled by any sense of transcendent purpose, direction, or reason for our presence in the world. Such individuals are, in the words of philosopher Maxine Greene, "sunken in everydayness,"[1] merely going through the motions and routines of their lives without connection to something beyond the self that provides significance or value to our efforts and energies. The underside of such a life quickly becomes one of despair and emotional emptiness, frequently degenerating into depression, rage, or violence.

Today, in a part of the world in which many live in historically unprecedented levels of affluence, there looms another kind of crisis of scarcity—a scarcity of any kind of compelling meaning in people's lives. It is a world in which many people, especially the young, feel adrift in a sea of purposelessness. Such a crisis of meaning provides significant opportunity for those who would mobilize around hate, war, and xenophobia as a way to fill the widespread emotional emptiness felt by so many individuals. And in the part of the world in which multitudes of people struggle for even a modest subsistence, symbols that provide existential purpose take on extraordinary importance. In this latter world, frustration and the urge to find consolation for deprivation and injustice combine to produce ferocious counter-narratives that can provide individuals meaning to their lives through militant religious beliefs or aggressive assertions of ethnic or national identity. But in both worlds—the worlds of affluence *and* of material hardship—human beings find themselves "condemned" to search for meaning in order to counter the pain of purposeless suffering and to find the symbols and narratives that might make life livable and worthwhile again. Whether in conditions of deprivation or of material surfeit, our world is one in which there is a growing and desperate need to give purpose to lives of gnawing human pain—whether the pain of empty stomachs or of empty spirits. It is a search that too often comes with increasing costs in violence, killing, and destruction.

Human beings, as has been said many times, require more than bread to live satisfying lives. Without structures of meaning that offer purpose and coherence to our lives, existence becomes miserable at best and a source of emotional pathology at worst. Bereft of meaning, life quickly becomes a nightmarish journey into despair. And despair offers fertile soil not just for the internalized anger of depression, but for outwardly directed rage at a world that seems to offer frustration without consolation. *One can say that any society concerned with its emotional health and the expectations of a worthwhile future must ensure that its young, in particular, are socialized into a culture of authentic meaning and purposefulness.* The epidemic levels of depression and attempted suicide among the young in this country, or the endless distractions of video displays and digital technology, surely points to such a crisis of meaning in the lives of many children and adolescents. While schools have become more and more focused on preparing young people for college or the job market, and there are loud and persistent demands about teaching basic skills to our students, few voices are raised concerning education's role as a vehicle through which purposeful identities and meaningful lives can be explored and acquired. Schooling becomes entirely an instrumental vehicle for transporting individuals along the tracks of the credentializing society. Its all about the grades, test scores, exam results, and diplomas that allow one to ultimately claim some niche, however precarious, in the hierarchy of the marketplace.

Schooling and the Crisis of Meaning

In a previous chapter I talked about how the environment of school alienates individuals from one another through the relentless emphasis on competition and invidious comparison. Here I need to emphasize how education has become a process that estranges students from themselves—from their passions, interests, creativity, and imagination. Schooling has become a process that alienates young people from their authentic voices and the significance of their own experience. Human agency—the power to question, challenge, and change social reality—has been reduced to little more than teaching students to mindlessly follow directions and conform to what is required of them in order to pass a test or complete an assignment. There is no room here for what Maxine Greene calls the "ache" for meaning ,without which, she says, no purposeful education exists. In the world of contemporary schooling in which students spend a great deal of time filling in bubbles on test sheets, there is little space for young people to explore and pursue the questions that speak to the purpose of their lives. Why are they here? What are the pressing questions and concerns that confront them within this culture and this world? How does one live a life of meaning in a society in which so much rings hollow and fake? In the arid and sanitized landscape of the American school the pressing dilemmas and concerns of an endangered and dangerous world have no place in the curriculum. And attempts to put questions of meaning on the curriculum will likely threaten a teacher's future career. It is no wonder that so many young people complain about the boredom and pointlessness of schooling—apart from the fact that it provides the ticket that allows one to move on to college or a job.

I often tell undergraduates about how much their education is about *extrinsic*, not *intrinsic*, value. In other words, I joke, their attitude towards school is one in which the *less* education they receive the *better*. If they could receive a passing grade without ever attending a class or cracking a book, that would be just fine with them. This perverse and hostile relationship to their own education, I explain, is a manifestation of what it means to be alienated from one's own being. It means that one can go through the motions and satisfy the institution's demands (and thereby get the extrinsic reward that is needed), but do so while being thoroughly disinterested and estranged from one's own activity and presence. What we actually do, learn, or study represents nothing but the labor required in order to satisfy a distant authority. In this sense school might be said to be "good" preparation for a society in which authentic meaning and purpose to our lives becomes increasingly scarce. It is paradoxical when so many, especially parents, express anguish about the negative effects of culture on their children's lives and that school is thoroughly dominated by the goals of efficiency, effectiveness, and behavioral measurability. School has become less and less a place that enables young people to explore and discern the wisdom of what might constitute a purposeful life. As in the culture as a whole, a "technical rationality" dominates life in this institution, which means that "how" rather than "why" questions shape our concerns and practices: How do we get kids to read more fluently? Know more math? Achieve higher results on the tests? How do we reduce drop-outs and increase college attendance? And the list goes on. The goals are always about doing more, remembering more, covering more, and achieving more. None of this speaks in any way to the deep and pressing concerns about living lives of deep meaning and significance. That would take a very different kind of education. The failure in our schools is only part of a larger crisis of meaning that afflicts American society, and I will look at other dimensions of it in this chapter. It is a crisis that opens the door to other forces that seek to exploit and capitalize on the widespread existential emptiness in ways that offer to fill it with authoritarian, jingoistic, and militaristic beliefs and values. God, flag, and country, with all their aggressive, Manichean, and dogmatic certainties, will fill the void of lives desperate for compelling purpose and meaning.

School, just like work for many, is purely an instrumental chore that enables us to survive and move on (and, for some, move up) in the world. Yet at the end of the day one is left emotionally and psychologically empty from the experience. There is little in school that nourishes our human need for spiritual sustenance. In other words, what we are offered is a very thin gruel of purpose—something that might speak to that quintessentially human desire for connection to things that gives significance to our lives beyond mere existence or survival. In his moving book, *The Left Hand of God*, Michael Lerner[2] reports on his research with working people about the importance of non-economic issues in their lives. His report is a riposte to those on the Left who define political allegiances and decisions *only* in terms of economic issues. Far from this being the important factor in how individuals decide their political preferences, Lerner argues that questions of meaning (or meaninglessness) loom increasingly large in people's lives[3]:

> The vast majority of the thousands of Reagan supporters we got to know through our research were ordinary, sane, and reasonably smart people, as in general, are the Bush supporters we have interviewed over the past five years. Nor can the people who fill the mega-churches of the Religious Right be dismissed as uneducated fools or illiterate fanatics; they are as often working people who have completed college and whose income puts them close to the middle of the economic range in America.
>
> Far from being fools, we discovered, these people have needs that go beyond a narrow focus on the economy. People earning close to the median income in the United States told us that they wondered what their life was really about, what the purpose of living was, what they could tell their children they had achieved while living on the planet.
>
> Many complained that their work did not offer them an opportunity to contribute in some way to the well-being of the human race. They told us they wanted to feel that their work was about something more than just making a living, that it served some higher purpose. Some asked us, the group leaders, to tell them how we saw our own lives. Were we oriented towards serving something more than ourselves?
>
> When people talked about "meaning" in their lives, they frequently specified that they felt their lives should have a spiritual goal, a focus that would provide what some called "justification for being on this planet." They saw it as quite peculiar that we would need to ask them to explain what they meant for their desire for a "meaningful life," and at least several thought that perhaps something had been missing in our education.

The Meaning of Life

Should it be puzzling that the question of purpose and meaning looms so large in our lives? The very idea of what constitutes meaning may be an elusive one. My belief about this is that our compulsion to find meaning is rooted in the precariousness of the human condition itself. Painfully aware of our own brief stay upon the earth, and confronted with the insignificance of our own presence against the enormous magnitude of what exists outside of us, we are driven to find, or create, significance for our own finite and limited lives. Whether or not this significance is seen as rooted in a divinely impelled purpose for human beings, or whether it is understood as a sheer act of imagination and creative storytelling, there is a powerful need to construct a narrative that overcomes the painful limitations of a human life. Such a narrative creates meaning for us by showing how a single life represents something much more than a precariously assembled, thoroughly contingent, depressingly short-lived phenomenon or presence. Meaning in this sense is the way we can overcome our own very brief and temporary existence by connecting us to a much larger "chain of being"—one that links us to the multitude of other lives, both in the generations gone by and in the future generations who will follow us. Meaning thus gives our lives historicity—life becomes much more than a flickering moment of presence through its links to an unfolding narrative set against time and place. Contemporaneously, meaning represents those connections that bind us to what Benedict Anderson calls "imaginary communities,"[4] whether these are communities of religious belief, ethnicity, tribe, or nationality. Each of them powerfully offers us ways to enlarge our presence in the world. They provide the means to locate ourselves in a much bigger story than one that a single, solitary life could possible supply. To understand religious narratives in this way, as a response to the human quest for existential purpose, is certainly not meant to belittle the extraordinary contribution that religious traditions have made to the store of humanity's moral and spiritual wisdom or to sensitizing men and women to the awesome wonder of existence and the universe. Nor does it deny their importance in speaking to the ultimately ineffable mystery of life itself.

Not surprisingly, the power of the narrative is deepened and becomes more emotionally compelling through the way it embodies the heroism of survival, or through the manner in which it might claim some special chosenness of purpose or mission, or through its claim to represent nobility of spirit, creative genius, or high intelligence. Whatever is associated with each of our own particular stories, its special power and resonance resides in its capacity to contribute to some larger human narrative of purpose and meaning. I ask the reader to understand that my take on meaning as a socially constructed web of belief is not meant in any way to trivialize or ridicule this quintessentially human process. As I like to tell my own students, it's really all we have got! A single human life is a pretty insignificant event when viewed against 15 million years of human history, or when seen in the context of a universe that contains literally hundreds of billions of stars or against the background of an earth that today contains about six billion human beings. The truth is that after seven or eight decades (if we are among the lucky ones) we shuffle off this mortal coil knowing that few people, if anyone, will know or remember us or our deeds within a generation or two. It is hardly surprising that we have a strong desire to expand the significance of these short years through the construction of an identity that connects us to a much greater and compelling narrative of purpose and presence. This is especially so given the difficult, vexing, and too often painful journey that constitutes any human life. Certainly life itself contains the almost inevitable suffering of loss, illness, aging, and disappointments in our relationships or what we achieve. But beyond this is what Herbert Marcuse called the "unnecessary suffering" that besets so many lives. He is referring to the consequences of a particular set of social, economic, and political arrangements that can add immense suffering to people's lives through war and violence, social injustice, dehumanization and exploitation, discrimination and repression, and so on. Although these have blighted and destroyed countless human lives, none of them are the *inevitable* fate of humankind. Even if the search for meaning is eternal, the meanings that we do construct usually represent a response, not just to the inevitable forms of pain we experience, but also to the particular social reality we must confront.

Jurgen Habermas,[5] the distinguished German philosopher and social theorist, noted several years ago that in our kind of modern society, cultural meanings seem less and less like they are firmly rooted in tradition. Values and beliefs are no longer experienced as having the solidity and permanence of something that is grounded in antiquity, or something that appears to extend beyond the vicissitudes of change and the mutability of history. In the pre-modern world, meaning had an unquestioned legitimacy and inviolability. It offered individuals the enormous reassurance of living in a world that was securely grounded in purpose. Human beings could feel assured that their identities were firmly established through the dense network of relationships, obligations, and expectations that regulated their lives. However harsh life might be, the security of knowing who they were, what was expected of them, and the significance of their lives provided a powerful source of consolation and reassurance for people. It is this kind of world that, Habermas argued, is gone for many of us. Living in a world without stable and coherent meaning to guide us is like living in a disorienting and unanchored psychological state. It is as if we are looking at a TV screen and can only see the lines or dots of light from which the picture on the screen is constituted. There are bright flashes and rapid movement of images, but nothing comes together in a way that gives some coherent sense to what we are looking at. Or we are looking at a newspaper photograph in which we can see the black and white markings that give the picture its form, but we can't see the overall connections that together provide a meaningful and recognizable image. To live in that kind of condition is immensely painful. It is to feel dislocated and disoriented and lacking an existential compass that gives one a secure sense of identity. It is as if, in the famous words of Karl Marx, "all that is solid melts into air." When meaning becomes elusive or ephemeral, human beings become agitated and anxious. The lack of a reliable path for life's journey produces despair and the inclination towards suicide. It also generates frustration, anger, and rage. When the solidity of meaning evaporates, it may be expected that violent behavior is not far behind.

Anger in a World of Change

If we are to understand something about violence both at home and abroad we must take seriously how such things as modernity, capitalism, consumerism, and liberal democracy undermine or erode the stability of meaning in people's lives. This is not meant to suggest that stability is, in and of itself, a good thing. The undermining of long-assumed forms of domination and inequity such as patriarchy, absolute monarchies, and racist regimes are welcome changes. But we must still recognize that the dissolution of long-established cultural frameworks through which people have come to know and understand their world is immensely stressful for individuals and societies. If we are to become better able to see the sources of violence around us, we must pay attention to the changes and conflicts that increasingly beset people and the erosion of the meanings by which they live. And we will have to consider the possibilities of alternative structures of meaning that are needed. Nowhere is this more apparent than when we consider the forms of militant fundamentalism that now play such a large role in the Middle East. We have been fed the idea that the angry forms of Islam that have emerged represent a rejection of "our values" of freedom and democracy. Such a view is far too simplistic and in no way provides an understanding of the forces and currents that are running through many societies producing rageful violence and terror directed against innocent civilians. Certainly it ignores the anger that is provoked by American and Western intervention in the affairs of many Middle Eastern and Muslim states. No one can make sense of the hostility of Iran toward the United States, for example, without knowing about how the United States and Britain colluded to overthrow the democratically elected regime of Mohammed Mosaddeg in 1953 because of that government's intention to nationalize Iranian oil and subsequently support the repressive regime of Shah Pahlavi (President Obama's speech in Egypt in May of 2009 was a long overdue, but courageous admission, of such wrongdoing). Nor can Muslim anger towards this country be understood without recognizing the pent-up frustration over the failure to find a just solution to the Palestinian problem and what is widely perceived to be the United States' one-sided support for Israel. In other countries like Egypt and Saudi Arabia there is anger at U.S. support for authoritarian and repressive regimes. And, of course, there is the invasion of Iraq with all of its destructive consequences, which reinforced the view of the United States as an imperial power bent on dominating the Middle East in order to secure a continued supply of cheap oil. In addition to all of this, there is pervasive corruption in many countries that allows elites to maintain their profligate lifestyles at the expense of the majority of people who barely manage to subsist.

But beyond American policies, which continue to create deep feelings of resentment among many in the Middle East, there are other, more systemic kinds of causes that foment instability, anger, and violence among many people who feel like their lives and world are being undermined by foreign influences and corrupting values. In his book *Jihad vs. McWorld*, Benjamin Barber[6] provides a powerful picture of how global capitalism has assaulted and torn apart the cultural tissues that provide the meaning maps of so many societies. The free-market ideology, he says, is a battering ram against every kind of parochial or traditional identity, whether that of nation, religion, or ethnicity. The new world of global corporate power is less about manufactured goods than about goods tied to telecommunications and information.

It is, he says, about the cultural software and images manufactured in advertizing agencies and film studios. He continues[7]:

> McWorld is a product above all of popular culture driven by expansionist commerce. Its template is American, its form is style, its goods are images. It is a new world of global franchises where, in place of the old cry, "Workers of the world unite! You have nothing to lose but your chains!" is heard the new cry, "Consumers of the world unite! We have everything you need in our chains!"

This new world of global capitalism with its extraordinary capacity to shape wants and needs is nothing less than an assault on our very identity as human beings. It seeks to transform every human desire into a market-supplied commodity. The soul's quest for the sacred and transcendent becomes, in the hands of capitalism, transformed into the desire for the material and the profane. Barber continues[8]:

> The new telecommunications and entertainment industries do not ignore or destroy, but rather absorb and deconstruct and then reassemble the soul. In their hands it becomes a more apt engine of consumption than the physically limited body.... When the soul is enlisted on behalf of plastic—even protean—bodily wants, it can guarantee a market without bounds.

This is a world in which consumption is the central human activity. In turn, consumption is converted "into meaning, meaning into fantasy, fantasy into reality, reality into virtual reality and completing the circle, virtual reality back into actual life again so that the distinction between reality and virtual reality vanishes."[9] In this world, Barber tells us, we are urged to see ourselves as individuals who are private and solitary beings who interact with others primarily through commercial transactions. It is a world that inculcates secularism, consumerism, materialism, immediate gratification, boundless sexual expression, hedonism, and limitless desire. Such a values system is in collision with the traditional values and beliefs of parochial religious culture. It is a collision that produces militant and sometimes violent forms of Jihad (as well as angry fundamentalist religious responses within other religious traditions including Christianity, Judaism, and Hinduism).

Benjamin Barber argues that the forces of Jihad are best understood as the actual consequence of *McWorld*. They are its dangerous stepchild. Its imagined political community is the invention of the agitated modern mind forced to deal with the dissolution of meaning and the virtual reality of consumer culture. Its quest for the durable self and an unchanging social reality are the result of the upheavals and psychic tumult of this world of endless novelty, unleashed desire, and ungrounded identity. Although the forces of Jihad may seem like a throwback to pre-modern times with its emphasis on "religious mysteries, hierarchical communities, and spellbinding traditions,"[10] it is really a response to the feeling of being overwhelmed by the corrosive influences of Western corporate interests and the culture of unbridled consumerism. Of course, it is not consumer values alone that dissolve the glue of traditional culture. The unabashed flaunting of sexuality associated with consumer values is joined to the assertion of a global feminism that demands women's equality in the political, economic, and social arenas. Together they present a profound challenge to the patriarchal values of traditional religious communities. In addition, scientific rationality and empiricism undermine the epistemological certainties of fundamentalist belief systems. They challenge the literal authority of the religious text and the unquestioned validity of religious faith. The reflexive mind-set that is at the heart of the scientific community calls into question the unexamined claims and beliefs of any tradition-rooted system of belief. It turns increasingly more of us into *provisional* believers of what is true. In other words, all of our beliefs are seen as only temporarily reliable or convincing. What we know is only as good as the latest experimental proof or the persuasiveness of current arguments. Scientific rationality calls into permanent question the unexamined, the conventional, and the traditionally accepted. The turn towards fundamentalism, whether among Muslims, Christians, Jews, or Hindus, must in some sense be seen as the consequence of this deep erosion of the authority of tradition and the turn towards more conditional and tentative views of what is or might be true.

Let me emphasize here that the corrosive effects of consumer values on traditional beliefs and behavior, the challenges of more open and reflexive ways of approaching truth, and the profound challenge towards patriarchal values do not inevitably lead to violent aggression. This is just one possible response to the shifting landscape of so many people's lives. It is simply wrong to assume that everyone responds to such stresses and challenges with hateful rage. And the belief that this is the case augments the view of those who see the world as locked into a Manichean struggle of good versus bad, evil versus unblemished virtue. Although no one can be immune from the seismic changes of consciousness under way in the world, there is a full range of responses to it from those who would turn the world into a battlefield against infidels or satanic forces to those who struggle to understand and integrate the best of these changes into their structures of meaning and belief.

The Struggle for Meaning at Home

Although I have focused on the Middle East as perhaps the most visible arena in which tradition and global values compete, this in no sense exhausts the spaces in which such conflict exists. Our own society is one in which, as writers like David Korten, Michael Lerner, Zygmunt Bauman, and Sharon Welch remind us, questions of meaning lie at the very heart of political struggle and discourse. The issues that seem to be so apparent in the Muslim world have their clear echoes in this society. We, too, suffer from enormous challenges and shifts in our beliefs, values, and meanings. And these challenges have their repercussions in the levels of anxiety and unease in people's lives. It is clear that for too many the response is a hateful brew of anger and a turn towards an aggressive nationalism or an intolerant and cataclysmic Christianity. We, too, live in the shadow of postmodern uncertainty. For many there is the sense of being assailed by a moral relativism that offers no sure guideposts to wrong and right behavior. It seems to undergird an egoistic and irresponsible moral outlook in which any and all behaviors can be justified or rationalized. From this point of view, Wall Street greed and a more accepting view of the diverse forms of sexual expression and identity are lumped together as equal manifestations of unbridled desire and self-satisfaction. No distinction is made between the legitimate struggle to free oneself from historically repressive social norms that have blighted the lives of so many of our fellow citizens and the obviously selfish and socially irresponsible acts of greedy merchants and corporate traders. From the point of view of anxious and angry believers, all the world appears as a den of selfish iniquity, and politics and religion become fueled by an angry and resentful struggle to impose what is nostalgically seen as a prior world of individual responsibility, hierarchical authority, and unassailable truth.

Yet there is no avoiding the fact that our postmodern era is one that creates a profound dis-ease that fuels a vitriolic politics of meaning. For many, the sense of certainty about who we are, what we ought to believe, and the rightness of our national and religious narratives feel buffeted and besieged. Globalization is profoundly reshaping the contours of power and influence in the world. The short-lived unipolar world of American power that followed the demise of the Soviet Union is giving way to a world of multiple sites of economic power. There is good reason to believe that the new century will belong to the rising countries of China and India as well the European Union. Deregulation of finance and the resulting free and inadequately controlled flows of capital have plunged U.S. capitalism into an era of enormous economic instability. And the huge and ever-expanding U.S. national debt has made this country increasingly vulnerable to the economic largesse of others. The ruling of the globe of unrestricted capital markets means that goods are increasingly manufactured elsewhere, usually in places that offer the cheapest and most easily exploitable workers. The result is increasing insecurity for workers in this country who watch their jobs disappear to other countries that will pay far lower wages to their employees. The unrestricted flow of labor across our national boundaries and the provision of cheap labor upon which so much of our standard of living depends bring huge numbers of foreign workers into the country, not only depressing pay for local workers, but altering the long-established cultural makeup of communities who must deal with unfamiliar languages and ways of life. All of this represents an enormous challenge to the belief that the United States embodies unassailable power in the world and convictions about our national purpose and role. It represents a profound crisis around the deep assumptions about the meaning of American identity and values. One commentator on this crisis, the eminent scholar Robert Jay Lifton,[11] has argued that the calamity of September 11, 2001, and subsequent events have eroded the sense of invulnerability that has accompanied America's role as a superpower. At the heart of what Lifton terms the "superpower syndrome" is the need to maintain this nation's belief in its omnipotence. Although other nations, he says, have experiences in the world that render them and their citizens all too aware of the essential vulnerability of life on earth, "no such reality can be accepted by those clinging to a sense of omnipotence."[12] Fueled by apocalyptic religious beliefs, our unilateral military exercise of power is justified by our special responsibility to rid the world of evil and to protect our God-anointed role to be the dominant nation on earth. He notes[13]:

> It is almost un-American to be vulnerable. As a people, we pride ourselves on being able to stand up to anything, solve all problems. We have long had a national self-image that involves an ability to call forth reservoirs of strength when we need it, and a sense of protected existence peculiar to America in an otherwise precarious world.

Yet after the eight years of the Bush presidency such a view of who we are lies in shambles. We have witnessed the limits of our vaunted military power. Assertions about the need to continue the wars in Iraq or Afghanistan until we achieve some absolute victory are no longer plausible. The costs in lives, money, and military capacity are simply unbearable. The assertion of unilateral military power has deeply eroded respect for this country throughout the world. The catastrophic financial crisis in 2008 highlighted the vulnerability of this nation's economic strength and its reliance on the finances of other nations. Other events like Hurricane Katrina underlined the deep inadequacies in the way we protect and support a large portion of the American citizenry. As I write this in the spring of 2010, the deep antipathy that Americans feel for the instruments of their government and of those who control their economy indicates a profound loss of conviction in the legitimacy of our national purpose. As this sense of loss deepens we can expect, at some point, a return to a politics of meaning centered on re-establishing national purpose around the ideology of American power and supremacy. The discourse of such a politics will likely center again around the view of a Manichean world of good and evil and America's historic mission of safeguarding the world from evil. The consequences of this are a politics that emphasizes patriotic zeal, unquestioning affirmation of America's chosen role, and a fierce reassertion of military values.

In this kind of worldview, war and militarism have a special role in giving meaning and purpose to the lives of citizens. It harnesses a theology of what Michael Lerner calls the "Right Hand of God" in which a wrathful and coercive divine power legitimizes America's special and chosen role in the world to quell the "evil ones"—those who appear to oppose or threaten us. The sense of loss and vulnerability is also a catalyst for hatred and intolerance towards those who are seen as outsiders to our national culture (such as Muslims, immigrants, minorities, Jews, gays, and lesbians). Such "outsiders" can be defined as fomenting and exacerbating our national decline. *Without ensuring a widely held alternative paradigm regarding our values and beliefs as a nation, this angry, imperialist, uncompromising, and dogmatic vision will again be able to grow and hold sway.* Such an alternative paradigm will require us to educate our kids to see themselves as part of an interdependent, mutually responsible community of nations in which power is widely shared and no one country is able to define itself as the true voice of all that is right and certain, and in which military force is the very last instrument to be called upon to resolve any conflict or disagreement. We will need to ensure that our children understand just how dangerous and destructive it is when we seek to address our crisis of values through a vision of global domination, unilateral power, and a belief in one nation being selected to fulfill a God-inspired purpose. Or they learn that those defined as "other" come to be regarded as the cause of national decline or the symptom of this crisis. It will require us to educate our young so that war and militarism no longer appear as the privileged expression of patriotism and national purpose or the means through which a culture in disarray may be cemented into cohesion and solidity.

The Confusion of Having and Being

The crisis of meaning we and especially our children face is not just about national purpose. It is also about how we have been taught to seek purpose in our individual lives. However much Americans profess a religious faith (certainly much more so than people in other Western democracies), it is arguable that our true faith lies not in the direction of our churches and other religious institutions, but in the shopping mall. As one group of writers asserts, the mega-malls today are our version of the gothic cathedrals.[14] This same group of writers notes that 70 percent of us visit malls each week, more than attend houses of worship. Our true religious passion is about consuming. It is about the desire to own and have more. Our true zeal is the quest to purchase and acquire as much as we possibly can in the belief that this is the way to achieve satisfaction and happiness in our lives. It is no accident that the mark of passage to adulthood today is not in receiving a voter registration card in order to be a fully active citizen, but in possessing a credit card that allows one to shop and buy far in excess of the wealth one actually has. It came as no surprise to many that one of the causes of the recession of 2008 was the hugely excessive levels of debt incurred by consumers that was masked by constantly inflating house values.

The bumper sticker that tells us that "I shop therefore I am" reveals much. Humorously, but accurately, it represents the widespread reality that the act of consuming has become the central human phenomenon, and the primary focus of meaning, in our culture. At its core is the endless desire for more things—a desire that is never satiated or fulfilled. We spend nearly two-thirds of our $11 trillion economy on consumer goods. Americans spend on average six hours a week on shopping and only 40 minutes playing with our kids. We are encouraged to spend as much as possible through our dependence on credit cards. The average American possesses 6.5 credit cards for a national total of 1.2 billion. This way, Americans are urged to give immediate gratification to their wants even though this has meant increasing debt for millions of us. The waves of housing foreclosures that have now engulfed the country has made painfully clear just how overextended in our purchases we have become as a nation. The more that incomes have risen, the less we have saved, and the more indebted we have become (and as we see, banks and investment companies irresponsibly pinned their economic fortunes to consumers who, in many cases, were stretched to the breaking point). We have become convinced that the more we are buying, the more we are saving! Or that shopping provides us with a therapy that rewards us in our stress-filled lives. The huge increases in our consumption are reflected in the increasing size of houses. We are told that the average size of new homes is now more than double what it was in the 1950s. Even with smaller families and larger houses, there is an increasing problem of storage for family possessions. (I laughed recently on my way to work as I passed a new housing complex with a giant sign by the roadside that said simply, "Huge Closets.") We need more garages to store the overflow of goods that by now have become outdated and unwanted. And commercial storage companies have become growth industries.

The desire to have increasingly more is urged on by the unrealistic way we construct our needs. Sociologist Juliet Schor[15] studied people's attitudes towards consumption and found that most Americans compare themselves with the living standards of television characters or with higher paid coworkers when deciding what they need. She writes[16]:

> People on television tend to be upper middle class or even rich, and people who watch a lot of TV have highly inflated views of what the average American has. For example, people who are heavy TV watchers vastly exaggerate the number of Americans with swimming pools, tennis courts, maids and planes.

Since how people think about their standard of living tends to be in relative terms, there is a paradox that as people own increasingly more, have bigger houses, drive more luxurious cars, and so on, they tend to feel no happier about their lives. Although much advertising urges us to compare ourselves to others, the more we have bears little on how satisfied we feel. We continue to see ourselves as worse off than others around us. John De Graaf and his colleagues noted that in 1957 the percentage of Americans describing themselves as happy reached a plateau that has never been exceeded since then. Certainly in order to buy all of the things we feel we need means we are compelled to work more days and longer hours. Americans have fallen far behind European nations in the number of days of vacation they receive. As Schor notes, while productivity in the United States has doubled since World War II, working hours have increased substantially. Unlike the Europeans, who traded their increased productivity for time (to socialize, have vacations, and so on), Americans sunk their gains into increased consumption. In fact, she says, they work nearly nine weeks more per year! De Graaf and his co-writers note[17]:

> America's 111 million households...contain and consume more stuff than all other households throughout history, put together. Behind closed doors, we churn through manufactured goods and piped-in entertainment as if life were a stuff-eating contest. Despite tangible indications of indigestion, we keep consuming, partly because we're convinced its normal. Writes columnist Ellen Goodman, "Normal is getting dressed in clothes that you buy for work, driving through traffic in a car that you are still paying for, in order to get to the job that you need so you can pay for the clothes, car and the house that you leave empty all day in order to afford to live in it."

Our so-called normal way of life provides a recipe for a deep crisis of meaning. We are taught to believe that having more will lead to a life of greater satisfaction. Yet the opposite seems to be the case. In any given year, nearly half of American adults suffers from clinical depression, anxiety disorders, or other mental illnesses. Over and above a reasonable level of material satisfaction, greater gains in what we acquire produces little real gain in the quality of our inner lives. The endless pursuit of material things does not result in more fulfilled lives. Indeed, the opposite is the case. Living our lives so focused on getting and having more leaves us with a deep ache for meaning. The narrative of all advertising follows the same pattern in which a human need or problem is resolved through the promise of something we can buy. Yet it is a promise that is rarely redeemed in any deep and sustained way. Advertisers spend millions of dollars to connect human needs—sexual appeal, beauty, health, popularity, novelty and excitement, security and peace of mind, the capacity to impress others—to what we buy. Yet the result is rarely quite what is expected. Excitement is perfunctory, satisfaction is temporary, the sense of security is only fleeting. Consuming is *not* intended to leave one in a state of deep contentment—far from it. The corporate interest is in stimulating addictive behavior around material desire, of creating an itch for buying things that can never be fully ameliorated. The goal is to keep the customer restless and perpetually dissatisfied so that he or she will keep coming back for more. Paradoxically, the fuller our closets and storage spaces become the emptier we feel. The more we invest our life energies into this futile quest for meaning and contentment the more we feel a lack of real satisfaction in our lives. The truth is that dissatisfaction is built into the very nature of consumer culture. However much we seem to have, it never feels like it is enough. We are always wanting more—the "more" that promises to leave us feeling satisfied but doesn't. The current financial crisis has its roots in the greed of those who direct our banks and our financial institutions. Such individuals, with their astronomical salaries and other forms of remuneration, wanted still more. And to achieve this they shamelessly constructed a financial house of cards that finally plunged this country and many other countries into an economic disaster. Yet, however much we excoriate these individuals, in one sense they represent all of us in our shared voracious quest to always have more in the mistaken belief that it will provide real, purposeful satisfaction in our lives. More is always better; bigger is always more desirable. There is in this quest the confusion Erich Fromm referred to as that between "having" and "being."[18] There is the mistaken idea that human fulfillment comes from what we own instead of who we are and how we live. Consumer culture systematically confuses for us these two things. As De Graaf and his co-authors put it, "The products and the media distract us from the soul's cry for truly meaningful activities."[19]

The Culture of Buying Starts Young

Consumer culture puts us on a treadmill of increasing desire for commodities paid for by increasing debt with all of its stresses and anxieties. It forces us to commit ourselves to ever more working hours in order to pay for our purchases and the resulting loss of social time and time with our loved ones. It produces in us moments of delight with our new purchases followed by the ennui and boredom that quickly follows as our newest possession turns into "yesterday's" thrill. It seeks to convince us that having more means greater meaning and satisfaction in our lives instead of a restless sense of unfulfilled desire and the sense that someone else has it better than we do. The consumer culture emphasizes the private over the public, the individualistic over the shared or collective. It is easy to see this in America where private wealth has long coexisted with public lack and sometimes squalor. The market is concerned with what can be sold at a profit to the individual, not what raises the standard of living of the greatest number. And our consciousness is one that measures the good life in terms of what we, or our families, have or own, not what improves the well-being of everyone. Consumer culture, in short, encourages a selfish, me-oriented approach to life with little interest in the broader ramifications for what we can get or buy. We see this in the sub-prime mortgage crisis. We see it in the disastrous consequences of this culture's effects on the environment. We see it in our inequitable and wasteful health insurance system. We see it in the dilapidated inner city schools and decrepit bridges and decaying infrastructure.

The selfishness inherent in consumerism is also propelled by a nagging sense that someone has more than we do. Advertising's subtext is always one that encourages a comparing of what is our experience to the experience of another. "Someone seems happier than I; looks better, healthier, sexier than I am; has a more attractive or spacious house or car than I do; or has a more exciting and adventurous life than I have." The process of continuous evaluation of one's life through comparison to someone else is sure to promote a great deal of dissatisfaction and a nagging degree of self-criticism. It also produces a culture rife with envy and jealousy. Increasingly consumer culture is about what Zygmunt Bauman[20] refers to as the promise of living *optimally*. It is no longer enough just to live comfortably. Advertising urges us to live life to the maximum. Every experience needs to be of surpassing value—an ecstatic and orgiastic thrill ride! There is always another TV, video game, computer, cell phone, or iPhone that offers a more amazing service or set of functions. The tension between this and the essentially prosaic nature of everyday is one that must, in the end, produce intense boredom with our actual experiences and circumstances. As critics of our "egoic culture" point out, consumer culture promotes an instrumental view of one's life. In other words, we are preoccupied with how we can reach our destination. Life is to be lived somewhere else—when I have the right job, enough money, the perfect partner, the best products, and so on. Never right now. Our goal is to maximize the attainment of extrinsic goals (money, appearance, fame) in order to provide satisfactions that we can only ultimately find through the quality of how we actually live, work, and play, and in our relationships with others. Yet it is the energies demanded in pursuit of the former that occupies so much of our lives, depriving us of the opportunity to live fully in the moment rather than at some future time when we have acquired the things the consumer world tells us are needed if we are to live optimally.

It is important to bear in mind that inculcation into this culture of buying starts early. Young children are targeted as easily manipulated consumers or as goads to their parents' decisions about what to buy. From 1980 to 2004 the amount spent on children's advertising in America grew from $100 million to $15 billion a year. As John De Graaf and his colleagues note[21]:

> For the first time in human history, children are getting most of their information from entities whose goal is to sell them something.... The average twelve year old in the United States spends forty-eight hours a week exposed to commercial messages.

Following the deregulation of children's television by the Federal Trade Commission, the average child sees nearly 40,000 commercials a year—about 110 a day! Consumer values permeate not just the lives of young children. Observers like Alex Molnar and Henry Giroux have documented the degree to which advertising and the selling of products shape the culture of schools. There is a relentless tie-in of curriculum materials, reading programs, competitive events, and school fundraising to the marketing of pizzas, snacks, soft drinks, electronic gadgets, sportswear, and equipment. Commercialism increasingly shapes the culture and ambience of our schools. School hallways, books, and dining facilities all bear the marks of the penetration of consumer values into the education of our kids. Schools become one more site in which kids become an audience—a captive audience—for the transmission of the values and meanings of a consumer culture. Schools have become one more place where young people are taught the values of instant gratification, materialism, an insatiable desire for things, a restless need for novelty and entertainment, and a constant concern with whether they are "keeping up" with others. The latter concern, we know, fuels the insecurities of youth and the obsessive fears about whether one has the "right" gear or possesses a "cool" appearance to enable one to fit in and be socially accepted. At times, the focus on what we and others have is a marker of difference and conflict: violence occurs as rival groups of young people associate the things they own, wear, or drive with the right to belong and be recognized. The constant focus on the need to "keep up" with the ever-changing marketplace becomes the source of enormous stress and tension in young people's lives. Added to the competitive emphasis of the classroom, it is no wonder that depression and anxiety disorders have reached record numbers among young people.

Finding Meaning through War

Faced with a culture that generates so much dissatisfaction, restlessness, and emptiness, it should be no surprise that other beliefs and values become powerful alternatives, or consolations, to this culture. Chris Hedges[22] in his book on war articulates the seductiveness of patriotism and militarism to the spiritual and emotional vacuousness of so many lives. In contrast to the self-interest and materialism of consumerism, patriotism or nationalism offers the possibility of investing in something that feels greater and nobler than the former's shallow individualism. Such patriotism is typically understood in the context of a world that opposes or threatens who "we" are and what "we" believe. In this sense it is possible to see oneself as standing up against a dangerous or evil force on the side of a collective good. Hedges writes: "Patriotism, often a thinly veiled form of collective self-worship, celebrates our goodness, our ideals, our mercy and bemoans the perfidiousness of those who hate us." He continues: "The goal of such nationalist rhetoric is to invoke pity for one's own. The goal is to show the community that what they hold sacred is under threat. The enemy, we are told, seeks to destroy religious and cultural life, the very identity of the group or state."[23]

This worldview gives grand meaning and purpose to one's life. It places our necessarily small efforts inside a much larger narrative of history and collective mission. There is a high price to pay for this. Those who oppose us are usually stripped of their humanity; they become an evil or dangerous abstraction that must be stopped (as articulated so memorably, for example, in George W. Bush's "axis of evil" speech). We must do whatever it takes to maintain and safeguard our own nation. It also leads us to obfuscate or deny history. We might recall our support for the vicious regime of the Shah of Iran, which led to the Islamic revolution, or the role of the United States in supporting Saddam Hussein in his war against Iran. We could look at the United States' role in propping up numerous despotic, undemocratic, and repressive regimes in Africa and South and Central America. Or the huge arms sales to countries with appalling human rights records. The strong sense of purpose is augmented by seeing a world that is clearly, unambiguously divided into us and them, good versus evil.

It is but a short distance from this kind of thinking to the embrace of war. Hedges notes[24]:

> War makes the world understandable, a black and white tableau of them and us. It suspends thought, especially self-critical thought. All

bow before the supreme effort. We are one. Most of us willingly accept war as long as we can fold it into a belief system that paints the ensuing suffering as necessary for a higher good, for human beings seek not only happiness but also meaning. And tragically war is sometimes the most powerful way in human society to achieve meaning.

He continues:

> ...war forms its own culture. The rush of battle is a potent and often lethal addiction, for war is a drug, one I ingested for many years. It is peddled by mythmakers—historians, war correspondents, filmmakers, novelists, and the state—all of whom endow it with qualities it often does not possess: excitement, exoticism, power, chances to rise above our small stations in life, and a bizarre and fantastic universe that has a grotesque and dark beauty.

While consumer culture urges us to be preoccupied with the self and leaves society as a place of small-minded, competing egos, war urges us towards concern for the whole society, and sacrifice for the greater good becomes a valued calling. It is no wonder, in this kind of materialistic, greedy culture, that the military becomes lionized as the embodiment of something selfless and sacred. The uniform and the flag represent a higher purpose; they become emblematic of a community of shared meaning and collective responsibility. Consumer culture can offer only the most superficial, shallow, and vulgar form of meaning to our lives, and in this context patriotism and war fill the existential vacuum. As I have noted, in the United States such patriotic symbols frequently join together with a triumphalist "exceptionalist" myth about our perennial goodness as a country (one interested only in bringing the fruits of freedom and the free market to those deprived of them). And a distinctly American Christianity sanctions and blesses our military power and imperial involvements in other countries and decries as ungodly those who would question or criticize these adventures.

Consumerism as a way of life leaves in its wake a crisis of authentic meaning. It is a crisis for which war, militarism, and an aggressive patriotism is one particularly powerful response. It is a crisis that opens the door to dogmatic and fundamentalist religion, which offers belief and purpose that is free from ambiguity or doubt. It speaks to purpose as being more uplifting than the materialism, greed, and endless dissatisfaction of consumer culture, but, it must be remembered, at a heavy price. In this kind of religion there is no room for the questioning and critical mind that is the life blood of democracy.

Instead, authority must be believed and respected without reservation. Here the military mind and the authoritarian mind are easily twinned; each insists on the unquestioned correctness of those in control. While consumer consciousness is constantly in flux—always looking for what is new, exciting, or optimal—fundamentalist religion offers the assurance of a permanent, unchanging truth. And while the consumer culture creates lone buyers who restlessly seek to expand their world through what they can own, have, or experience, authoritarian religion offers the solace of a community of believers who support one another in their conviction of being right in a world filled with unbelievers and heretics. Such a community finds its strength in being both separate and incommensurable with the rest of the unbelieving world. It is a community that grows stronger by becoming more intolerant of and opposed to what is outside of it. It is, not surprisingly, a place in which the apocalyptic vision of an "end time" is preached and welcomed. A gigantic collision of the forces of good and evil fills the heads of believers. Armageddon is eagerly anticipated in the form of wars or a nuclear holocaust in which the earth will be purified of unbelievers. It is of little surprise how these beliefs mesh easily with an extreme right wing politics that categorizes the world in terms of good and evil, and in which military engagement and the sacrifice of blood is proof of a nation's high moral state. In which there is no higher calling than the readiness of the young to die for the cause of God and country.

Education has the extraordinary obligation of offering an alternative path for finding meaning in these dangerous and critical times. There can be no greater responsibility than the role of educators' in helping individuals recognize the crisis of meaning that engulfs us, while encouraging something other than the seductions of war, militarism, blind patriotism, and dogmatic belief as the antidote to this crisis. We must affirm to our students the deep "ache" for meaning that besets so many of our lives and the futility of the obsessive consumerism that offers to fill our time and energy with endless distractions and superficial novelties. Educators can help reveal the nature and dimensions of this spiritual crisis. They can deconstruct for students the mechanisms of the market that get us to endlessly want more. They can point to the dangerous and destructive ways societies can respond through the glorification of death and violence when there is an absence of compelling meaning. But most of all, they can help suggest other, more inclusive, life-affirming, and healing responses to our crisis that do not involve demonizing others or declaring or threatening others with war, and that do not assume that we are always perfect or right in our judgments as a nation. This demands a very different understanding of why and how we educate—one that unabashedly links education to moral and spiritual concerns. The classroom becomes a place in which young people are encouraged to pursue questions about the purpose and meaning of our lives. And these questions are set against the limits, shallowness, and ultimate emptiness of a consumer-driven life. Such an emphasis in education must be contrasted with today's limited focus on skills, competencies, and careers. The latter, of necessity, will form a part of preparing young people for our complex and technologically developed world. But it cannot be allowed to constitute all of our schooling. Education must not be severed from its deeper task of nurturing among the young a thoughtful and sensitive humanity and the wisdom to discern authentically worthwhile lives. Educators, parents, and citizens cannot stand by while those whose sole interest is to make our kids malleable consumers hold so much power to shape the identities of the young. Nor can military careers monopolize our nation's vision of selfless and public spirited service. Education's task is to challenge the limited imagination for what might constitute a purposeful life beyond either the peddlers of merchandise or the state-sanctioned machinery of violence and destruction. It is to this task that I will return in the final chapter of this book.

Chapter Seven

CRITICAL CITIZENSHIP

This conjunction of an immense military establishment and a large arms industry is new in the American experience.... In the councils of government, we must guard against the acquisition of unwarranted influence, whether sought or unsought, by the military-industrial complex. The potential for the disastrous rise of misplaced power exists and will persist. We must never let the weight of this combination endanger our liberties or our democratic processes. We should take nothing for granted.
—President Dwight D. Eisenhower,
Farewell Address, January 17, 1961

The central mystery of the modern state is this. The necessary resources both economic and political will always be found for the purpose of terminating life. The project of preserving it will always struggle. When did you last see a sponsored marathon raising money for nuclear weapons? But we must beg and cajole each other for funds whenever a hospital wants a new dialysis machine. If the money and determination expended on waging war with Iraq had been used to tackle climate change, our carbon emissions would already be in freefall. If as much money were spent on foreign aid as fighter planes, no one would ever go hungry.
—George Monbiot, winner of the United Nations Global 500 Award for Outstanding Environmental Achievement, November 7, 2006

You may not be interested in war, but war is interested in you.
—Leon Trotsky

CONTESTING WAR: TROUBLING AUTHORITY'S "TRUTH"

Deception, deceit and lies are the enemy of peace. We repeatedly see how it is possible to weave tales that see war as inevitable, the other as one's unalterable foe, and a military swollen by extraordinary expenditures that distort a nation's priorities and investments as absolutely needed. A sad truth of the human condition is that no story that legitimates violence and war has proven too difficult to sell to a believing public; no narrative that persuades people that killing is the only, or necessary, vehicle to resolve differences is beyond acceptance or belief. As I have argued elsewhere in this book, conflict is not the issue. Human beings will, in all likelihood, always find differences in how they view things and always have conflicts that have to be dealt with and resolved. Democracy as a system of governance has built into its core the belief that civilization depends on the people mediating and compromising different, even opposing, views. It is pure fantasy to believe that there may come a time when conflict will cease to exist and there will be a uniformity of views, perspectives, and beliefs. What is at issue, however, is the notion that differences and conflict must inevitably be resolved through force of arms and the violent imposition of one side's views and interests over another. The time has surely arrived when human beings can reject the long and horrifying history that has seen war as the inevitable outcome of human difference. With our knowledge of society, culture, and politics and our accumulated moral and spiritual wisdom, we are at last in a position to say that war has become an unacceptable and outmoded means to settle our conflicts.

Such a gigantic shift in human consciousness will not come easily. Conventional ideas and assumptions, and deep emotional investments and loyalties, together with basic interests in power, wealth, and resources, provide a powerful bulwark against such change. We only have to look at the past nine years in the United States to see how relatively easy it is to mobilize a nation and its leadership around the goal of fighting one more war. First comes the primal emotion of fear. There is a sense that our lives and all that we value are under threat of annihilation. This emotion is the great catalyst for mobilizing our resources and energies to strike back at whatever appears to threaten us. With fear as the lubricant, the familiar wheels of war begin to grind. Now comes the construction of an enemy. With support from the centers of ideological and cultural consensus—the mass media, think tanks, academics positioned to attain prestige and recognition—a narrative of an implacable enemy is woven that appears to make military intervention the absolutely necessary solution to the threat. As part of this narrative, those who try to provide an alternative reading of the situation are tagged as wimps, out of step with the mainstream and common sense, and unpatriotic. And, finally, in a time of stress, there is the invocation of national purpose and resolve embodied in the glory and power of the nation's military. Behind all this are far less noble interests and powers. The opening up of a foreign nation's natural resources (as one wit noted, if Iraq's main commodity was brussel sprouts, not oil, would we have even thought of invading the country?). There are the huge profits of corporations that supply the material for war—tanks, armored carriers, missiles and bombs, helicopters, planes—as well as all of the money to be earned by those who provide a huge army with the things that are needed for daily life.[1] And in the case of Iraq, there were the billions of dollars that were allocated to businesses for the purpose of rebuilding the country following its destruction through war and siege.[2] In addition were the vast sums expended to support the private militias that were hired to guard convoys, VIPs, etc.[3] A recent estimate by the Nobel prize winning economist Joseph Stiglitz was that the Iraq war has cost in the region of $3 trillion.[4] Of course, this is only the monetary cost. There was also the cost in human lives that ran into the hundreds of thousands (we include here Iraqi, American, British, and others) killed or maimed. And there are the more than 4 million Iraqi's who were made refugees because of the war.

Learning from Our Wars

Many other observers and analysts on both sides of the Atlantic have revealed the deceit, deceptions, and manipulations that underlay the whole of this war.[5] In Afghanistan, too, questions must be raised regarding the justification for this war—which continues to fuel resentment against the involvement of foreign powers in the ethnic and religious conflicts in that country. Questions are also raised about the relevance of this war to the wider problems of global terrorism, which are far more localized and disparate in their causes. These questions lead us to some sobering lessons about what it means when truth is distorted and repressed and a nation is misled into war. They remind us once again how important critical reason and intelligence are in deconstructing and troubling the narratives and tales spun by those in power. Although the embrace of armies and the glory of battle have deep roots in the human psyche—both emotional and cognitive—we must never underestimate the importance of the quintessential human capacity to question and contest what ordinary citizens are told by those in authority. In recent times we have seen the importance of the capacity of citizens "armed" with alternative explanations, interpretations, and understandings of events to provide another path that rejects war and violence as the only, or best, way to resolve human differences. There is nothing inevitable about this other path. But the resolve of millions of millions of people around the world to end the Vietnam War was a watershed in the refusal of ordinary people to passively accept the lies and misinformation of generals and politicians. There can be little doubt that this mass movement of people—citizens, students, military veterans, and others—shortened the duration of this war. Perhaps more importantly, the war empowered a whole generation with the belief that it was the right and responsibility of a citizen to resist the imposition of unjustified war. Years earlier, thousands of British citizens organized and marched against nuclear weapons and the threat of nuclear war and demanded nuclear disarmament. They argued there could be no winners in a nuclear exchange. After the Vietnam War, many people were drawn into the movement against America's involvement in the arming and training of right-wing military and paramilitary forces that were being used to prop up corrupt and reactionary regimes in Central America. And in the 1980s mass citizens' movements developed throughout Europe opposing the basing of a new generation of American missiles. Interestingly, this movement saw the coming together of independent civic groups in the communist states that also called for the end of the policy of nuclear confrontation with the West. Around these and many other issues, people were repeatedly drawn into questioning and contesting the policies and decisions of their governments. It was increasingly apparent that citizens who were aware and empowered were needed to call into question the arguments being made by those in authority who would justify wars and military interventions around the world, and with it the ever-increasing buildup of weapons and armies.

For a new generation the Iraq War provided a powerful lesson in the readiness of government to fabricate reasons for war and the ability to whip up patriotic fervor to support military intervention in another country. The extraordinary tale of government lies, deceptions, and flawed justifications that preceded the decision to go to war have been well documented. We know that there were no weapons of mass destruction, which was the original justification for the war. We know that the Bush administration (in collusion with Prime Minister Tony Blair in Britain) was set on going to war prior to the conclusion of the United Nations inspections and search for such weapons. We also know from members of the Bush cabinet itself that plans were being laid for the invasion of Iraq beginning shortly after the 2000 general election. We know that talk about bringing democracy to Iraq was always a far less credible reason for this hugely expensive war than the need to control the Iraqi oil fields, which are the second largest in the world. We know that talk about the evil deeds of Saddam Hussein did not preclude the former Bush administration from treating him as a friend and ally when it suited our national interests (which included supplying weapons to him during the terrible and bloody Iran-Iraq war). And it is well documented that Hussein had no connection with Al Qaida or the events of 9–11—even though the Bush administration continued to push this line while knowing it to be a falsehood. We know that lauding the bravery and sacrifice of our soldiers did not prevent the Bush administration from its shameful miserliness in ensuring decent and adequately resourced medical and rehabilitative facilities for returning vets. And we know about the no-bid contracts and vast sums paid to corporate interests who were supporting the war or were engaged in the reconstruction effort—much of which we have seen disappear into the hands of greedy and unscrupulous contractors. Perhaps saddest of all was the effort to contain the information about and images of those who died or were maimed in Iraq. No images of returning dead soldiers were permitted. There was little information on the huge numbers of returning troops with serious brain injuries or emotional traumas. And most shockingly, the hundreds of thousands of dead and wounded Iraqis rarely made it into the news at all.

With a few honorable exceptions, almost every member of the U.S. Senate voted for the war in Iraq. During the time leading up to the war and the subsequent invasion, by its own admission, the mainstream media abdicated its responsibility to act as a voice of skepticism and moderation—a key vehicle through which to speak truth to power. Instead, it largely became an echo chamber, and often a cheerleader, for the administration, and as embedded reporters, breathlessly excited participants in the military invasion. Yet in spite of this the spirit of a critical, informed, and resistant citizenry asserted itself against the submissive consensus on the need for war. Some of the largest demonstrations ever seen took place in many of the world's major cities. In the United States, millions organized and marched, held community meetings, and got their cities and towns to pass resolutions against the impending war.

From discussions in my own university classes, I realize how important it had become to present alternative perspectives on this conflict and to offer counter-information to what was being provided in the mainstream media. But above all, what was most important was the need to encourage a spirit of undeterred questioning among students and others. Teaching students who had, in many cases, come from conservative homes meant countering the notion that respect for authority meant a passive acceptance of a president's or government's words. It meant teaching that patriotism did not mean blind support for those who lead a nation. As I tried to make clear in these classes, the history of U.S. military involvements in many countries took place, too often, on the basis of lies, misinformation, and deception.[6] I suggested to my students that wars that could not be justified morally or politically were frequently being waged in our name. I emphasized that more than ever citizens of our country needed to develop the capacity and courage to contest where our leaders urged us to go. This is the responsibility and right of citizenship in a democracy. Our culture, which was so quick to resort to war and invested so much of our resources in the tools of war, needed a critical democracy in which we could seek other ways to deal with and resolve our differences than through killing and destruction.

The Banality of Evil

My passionate belief in the need for a citizenry that is able and willing to contest the words and justifications of those who govern was nurtured in my youth. While just a teenager, I came across Hannah Arendt's report of the Eichmann trial in Jerusalem in 1961. This distinguished political philosopher and commentator wrote her observations for *The New Yorker* magazine, which later became the book, *Eichmann in Jerusalem*.[7] As a Jew who had herself escaped from Nazi Europe, but lost much of her family who were murdered in the concentration camps, she was no dispassionate observer of this trial. Yet what was most paradoxical for her was that the man who was responsible for such inhumanity and the death of so many innocent children, women, and men appeared much like any other elderly individual in his later years. In spite of his terrible, imagination-defying deeds, there were no obvious signs that he was a sociopath or murderer. To the contrary, for Arendt the real terror of this man was in his ordinariness, his banality. What she reported then was something that haunts us to this day, as we note its appearance in too many instances of human barbarism. Eichmann, under interrogation, reported no particular passionate conviction regarding the task he was assigned. The assignment to exterminate 6 million Jews was to be fulfilled, he said, because these were simply his orders. He was, he said, just following what his superiors told him to do. He was, he added, a good German, by which he meant that he was taught by his family, his teachers, and his military officers to do what he was told. This was the mark of a good citizen and soldier, he believed. Whatever he was required to do by those in authority he would do to the best of his ability, without question and without hesitation. It was the sheer ordinariness of this man that shocked Arendt. His murderous deeds were not the product of fanatical and twisted passions so much as the result of a readiness to unthinkingly conform to the will of others. He was, indeed, the "successful" product of a cultural system that rewarded unthinking obedience and the freezing of one's own moral compass. His training had suppressed in him both *consciousness* and *conscience*. He had learned to empty himself of the capacity to question or challenge instructions that might lead to the violation of human rights and dignity, and instead to be a willing tool of the most shocking forms of inhumanity.

There are few classes in which I do not discuss Arendt's *banality of evil*. My concern is not the particular history of Nazi atrocities so much as the tendency for human beings to acquiesce submissively to authority and to act, or not act, without questioning the moral consequences of one's behavior. Eichmann's defense that he was "just following orders" has become a sadly repeated refrain among those charged with heinous actions. We heard it after the massacre at My Lai during the Vietnam War when hundreds of innocent men, women, and children were butchered. We heard it again at Abu Ghraib when American soldiers were charged with treating prisoners in sadistic and humiliating ways. And we heard it during the Truth and Reconciliation hearings following the fall of the apartheid regime in South Africa; after the Rwanda genocide; in Chile and Argentina; following the killing fields of Cambodia; and elsewhere. And each time we hear the echo of Adolf Eichmann as he defended himself against charges of genocide, blindly and unthinkingly following the inhumane orders of those in authority without question or protest against such detestable deeds. We surely have learned enough from these terrible events and the human behavior that allowed them to recognize that education must be a process that teaches the young the importance of thinking critically and approaching the truth of others' pronouncements and assertions with a healthy skepticism. A culture that will not fall blindly into war or organized violence depends on individuals who have been educated in the spirit of a fearless and penetrating readiness to question and contest the voices of authority. This is the radical meaning of civic literacy. Civic literacy means teaching young people the importance of engaging with the events, issues, and concerns that are shaping their world. It means that education must place at the center of its agenda the goal of individuals who see the connection between the quality of their own lives to the decisions and policies that shape their national and global communities. And crucial to this literacy is the capacity to go beyond a passive acceptance of whatever explanations and justifications are being presented by those in power. It demands the ability to critically interrogate the assumptions and values that are behind the decisions and actions of government or those who play a dominant role in setting the society's agenda.

Civically literate individuals are inseparable from a vital and functioning democracy. Experience teaches us the importance of citizens who are not cowed or bamboozled by the knowledge and expertise of those in authority or power. Left to the latter, there can be little hope of contesting a quick resort to war as a means of defending the nation's interests (or questioning what those interests truly are), or as a means to resolving conflict and difference.[8] Without the ability and willingness to question and contest the justifications of the powerful, there can be no possibility of resisting the priorities of a nation whose military expenditures now approximate a half of all the money spent on weapons and armies throughout the world. At the very least, standing up to what President Eisenhower called nearly 50 years ago the military-industrial complex (now, more accurately, the political-military-industrial complex) requires a people unafraid and determined to call into question the power of such a force.

Learning Critically

Civic literacy is more than a matter of information and knowledge, or even the capacity to be thoughtful and persistent interrogators of our nation and our world. It means teaching young people the importance of social responsibility, deep concern for our nation and our global community, an ethic of caring and compassion, the imperative of social justice to a humane and peaceful world, and, not least, a sense of agency and hope. Civic literacy means learning to be "border crossers"—comfortable with human difference and capable of seeing the world from the experience and perspective of others. We need young people who are taught to be courageous and confident in their readiness to hold and express a belief or opinion. And in the present world, civic literacy means teaching the young that they are more than citizens of the United States. They are global citizens who are part of a complex weave of interconnected communities. Poverty, disease, war, and ecological destruction, wherever they occur, are the responsibility of all of us and affect all of our lives. If civic literacy means a knowledgeable, concerned, and engaged citizenry, then education must be a process that teaches young people to think critically about their lives, their culture, and the broader world in which they live. We need thoughtful and aware human beings who are encouraged to question—and, where appropriate, challenge—the dominant or conventional assumptions about how we live our lives.

We are fortunate in that we have a rich tradition of radical educational thought and practice upon which to develop this kind of literacy. There is an extraordinary range of ideas and experience from which we can draw that connects the classroom to the struggle for a world of peace, social justice, and human dignity. We can find important contributions to this in the work of Paulo Freire, Henry Giroux, Peter McLaren, Bell Hooks, Jean Anyon, David Purpel, Maxine Greene, Cornel West, Parker Palmer, Riane Eisler, Sonia Nieto, and Donaldo Macedo, among many others.[9] Each points us in the direction of an education that emphasizes the power of critical thought to resisting our violent and predatory world, and the need to root this thought in a moral context that emphasizes community over competition, human dignity instead of dehumanization, and just social and economic relationships instead of exploitation and inequality. We find in all of these critical and liberating pedagogies an emphasis on reconstituting the classroom in ways that negate the authoritarian relationship between teacher and student and the competitive relationship between student and student. The traditional form of pedagogy encourages the kind of compliant passivity that produces the banality of evil. Students are urged to spend their energies searching for the single "correct" answer that meets the expectation of the teacher. Learning becomes a game of figuring out what pleases the person in authority and repeating information previously transmitted without seriously questioning what has been presented. In this kind of classroom the one-way transmission of knowledge stifles thoughtful interrogation and imaginative reinterpretation of information. The single correct truth reinforces the position of the teacher as the one and only voice of authority. Agency flows in one direction only, downward. The curriculum of the classroom cements authoritarian and hierarchical relationships.

If our concern is the development of questioning minds and assertive voices then a very different approach to learning must be practiced. The classroom must emphasize dialogue. The exchange of ideas and opinions must replace one way flow of information from the teacher. The search for the single correct answer must be replaced by the affirmation of multiple possible answers. Such a classroom has to encourage and celebrate a shared community of learners and the diverse perspectives, understandings, and interpretations that are unleashed in this space. Competition for the smartest and "rightest" answer must give way to an embrace of many potential "truths" and diverse creative possibilities. A critical pedagogy of peace is incompatible with top-down, hierarchical, and authoritarian relationships. Nor is it compatible with classrooms in which individuals fight to be "top dog." Such competition produces not creative non-conformity, but the struggle to satisfy those who control the flow of rewards. It socializes young people to try to impress others through their capacity to please or impress the person in authority.

Texts Are Not truth

We have learned, too, that the struggle against conformity and unthinking compliance is to be waged not just around human relations in the classroom, but in relationship to classroom texts. To encourage students to think critically about the words in front of them, they must be taught to read hermeneutically rather than treating a text as a document conveying a single absolute truth. The text has to be seen, always, as a product of the interpretive mind, providing a version of the world that reflects the assumptions, beliefs, values, and worldview of the writer. In addition to the hermeneutics or interpretation of what lies "behind the text" (the perspective of the writer), there is also the hermeneutic process that exists "in front of the text." There is, in other words, always a process of sense-making and decoding that involves the reader. This interpretive process reflects and is shaped by the assumptions, beliefs, and values of the reader. In my experience as a teacher, it comes as a shock to many students when I tell them that nothing they read in their classes should ever be called "The Truth," in which truth is some kind of final or absolute representation of something in the world. Whether in history or social studies, literature or science, nothing is ever more than the human attempt to provide some kind of *representation* of the world. What we know is no more than somebody's attempt to interpret and represent human experience. For many students, the news that we live in a "post-positivist" world in which nothing they read or hear should be seen as the truth is a stunning revelation. This is hardly surprising since schooling, with its emphasis on what is testable, measurable, and empirical, continues to leave young people with the impression that knowledge falls into a clear-cut divide between what is factual and true and what is fictional or a product of someone's point of view.

I try to make sure they understand how the whole edifice of testing and ranking students depends on the belief that individuals have, or do not have, the correct answer to any question. Any other view quickly reveals that our means of sifting and selecting students rests on slippery ground indeed. If, instead of the simple binary of true or false knowledge, we see that there are many possible answers to any question or problem, we have entered a very different pedagogic world. It is a world that invites and celebrates creativity, imagination, and intellectual possibility. Texts demand not passive acceptance, but active interrogation; the latter invites critical engagement not a submissive search for the "right" answer.

Pedagogy and Popular Culture

Educating against a blind submission to authority requires encouraging students to see any claim to the truth as only an assertion that demands questions and debate. Those who advocate for a critical pedagogy highlight the powerful influence of "out of school" texts—television, movies, videos, music, the Internet, and digitally transmitted images and information.[10] These popular cultural texts shape the meanings, understandings, and "truths" of young people's lives. Such texts construct more than knowledge; they constitute reality itself for people. As such, to interrogate these kinds of popular texts is more than a form of entertainment. It is central to understanding something about identity, belief, and values in the contemporary world. In this sense education becomes much more than an instrument of job training or social mobility. It is a means to make choices about how one would like to live and what kind of society one wants to live in. Critical interrogation of popular culture returns students to the recognition that knowledge of this world is the product of human creation, imagination, and interpretation. *Reality is always the result of a selection from a whole range of possibilities.* Which possibilities are heard, made visible, and influence who we are is always a consequence of how power is distributed in society. And this is a crucial point. What we understand about the world in which we live is not just an arbitrary construction of the human mind, but reflects the capacity of some in our society to make *their* particular version of truth hold sway, be heard, and shape how most of us see and understand things. In other words, power and knowledge are always connected. As a result, education always involves asking the most important question: In whose interest is it to get us to view and make sense of the world in this particular way? Who truly benefits when we accept that the world works in this way, or human nature has this particular character, or social relationships always follow this pattern of behavior? To understand that what we understand about the world is not just a matter of human construction, but reflects the way power is distributed, takes the purpose of education along new and important paths—ones that are crucial to those of us who have a concern for a less violent and more just world. It suggests a pedagogy in which we are encouraged to question the taken-for-granted beliefs about the necessity of the wars we fight, and indeed the necessity of war itself. It is a catalyst for questioning who our enemies are and how they have come to be seen in this way. It opens up space to question the reasons why there has been so much animosity towards the United States by those in other countries.

It is important to recognize that the forms of mental coercion that are exercised by those with power in the democratic world differ considerably from the totalitarian experience described by Hannah Arendt in her reports about Eichmann and the Nazi era. Today, at least in our part of the world, while direct forms of coercion to ensure conformity of thought do still exist (the threat of dismissal from a job, harassment of those who refuse to toe the line, even arrest and imprisonment), more often conformity and accommodation are the result of a much more subtle process of persuasion. Domination of our ideas, beliefs, etc., comes about through the effects of a *hegemonic culture*. In other words, our worldview is shaped far more insidiously through the way things seem to become a matter of *common sense*.[11] Everywhere we look we find language and images that reinforce a particular view of the world; this is the way things are and nothing else seems possible. For example, I discussed previously in this book the pervasiveness of competition. The daily impact of competitive relationships in every part of our lives—from school to work, to TV shows and sport—means that we come to accept competition as the inevitable way in which human beings relate to one another. The same might be said of war, which is taken to be an inevitable and unchangeable dimension of human behavior. It is precisely because of the insidious nature of cultural hegemony, which produces a consensus of belief through subtle persuasion and the inundation of our consciousness, that critical education demands the posing of questions that "pry open" our common sense understanding of the world. Maxine Greene, the educational philosopher, emphasizes the importance of questions that challenge the *taken-for-granted* dimensions of our world.[12] It is these questions about our daily lives, desires, assumptions, and practices that begin to uncover what we have blindly accepted or assumed about our situation. *Always, however, it must be recognized that our common sense assumptions function to support somebody's interests; they augment somebody's privilege and power.*

COMMUNITY AND THE COURAGE TO DISSENT

Critical pedagogy is more than a call to question in the mode of Talmudic study or academic debate. It is a call to question in order to challenge and change the prevailing social order, cultural beliefs, and individual behavior and consciousness. In the first place, it is a form of education that wishes to overcome a silent passivity in students. Silence is the product, at some level, of fear—fear of not being accepted because one thinks differently or simply stands out from the group. In this sense, teaching students to be critical is to nurture the courage to dissent, to refuse to go along in order to get along, and to be ready to articulate an alternative point of view. Beyond this the questions that are posed grow out of particular moral commitment. This is not about asking questions that will gain you some advantage in the academic game, but that reflect a commitment to a set of beliefs about what ought to be. These are questions that flow from the embrace of a definite human perspective that honors diversity and that values life and abhors violence of all kinds against human beings and, indeed, all creation. It is out of this moral consciousness that questions are posed and assumptions, beliefs, and knowledge are challenged. David Purpel refers to the prophetic consciousness articulated by Abraham Heschel in which our questions highlight the dissonance between what we in our world do and say (and justify) and the noble beliefs that represent the best of our society's moral commitments, which include social justice, human dignity, and the value of peace.[13] From this point of view our questions are concerned with showing where we fall short of living up to our life-giving and life-affirming human practices. The questions we want our students to ask are the ones that disrupt the culture of violence, death and inhumanity, and open consideration of other ways we may live and act.

Social change depends not on the solitary act or thought of an individual, but on the actions and consciousness of a community. In this regard a critical pedagogic classroom emphasizes the collective strengths of a group. Our society lionizes individual achievement and effort. But here the consciousness we aim to nurture is one that values what can only be achieved by human beings working together and supporting one another. Hope can best be sustained in the context of supportive human relationships. Going against the grain of how we have been taught to think, feel, and act is best maintained within a network of like-minded individuals. And the medium is the message. A world that values solidarity, caring, and respect instead of competition, violence, and domination must be nurtured through the very process of thinking about change. To paraphrase Gandhi, *the classroom must, in its actual dynamics, become the change we wish to see.* The very notion of the most prized American value, freedom, is now understood, not as the pursuit of the lone, unfettered individual, but as what is stirred when individuals come together to jointly seek another way to live our lives.

THE POWER OF IDEOLOGY

Despite what might be implied above, it would certainly be wrong to assume that we all act blindly without questioning what we read, see, or are told—whether in school or out. One only has to look around to realize how many people do *not* passively conform to what those in authority would like them to believe. We often see individuals resisting what is presented to them as fact or truth, or think about the great degree of skepticism that confronted the last Bush administration around its reasons for going to war or other aspects of its policies and decisions. Our media, especially the Internet, are full of views and perspectives that challenge the dominant arguments and justifications. We are not a nation of sheep unthinkingly going about our business. Among young people there has been, certainly since the 1960s, a deep and widespread cynicism towards authority that manifests itself in popular expression and underground culture.[14] Given the dire economic conditions millions of people have experienced in recent times, it is unlikely for this to not produce contrary beliefs and insights that contest the prevailing wisdom. Analysts of popular culture have made clear that whatever ostensible messages are transmitted through the media, this in no way guarantees a smooth acceptance of the intended text. Audiences are not simply passive receivers for the values and arguments of those who hold power or influence. Whether it is the pronouncements of political leaders; reports in the newspaper, TV, or on the Internet; advertising messages; or the words of the "experts," individuals appropriate and interpret things they see or hear in their own way. There is no automatic acceptance of what it is that "they" want us to believe or know. Throughout the culture there is a great deal of cynicism about anything ordinary people are told by authority. As a result, a generalized disbelief throws doubt on any and all beliefs. Is climate change really a threat or is it nothing but a passing fad? Is the bank bailout really needed to save our economy or is it just a way for rich bankers to get money at taxpayers' expense? Does any winning athlete today compete without drugs? Do any politicians really represent the interests of ordinary people?

Cynicism denies the possibility of any valid or convincing belief. It is the path to hopelessness about any real alternative to the present. *The critique of ideology is intended not to leave people with the sense that everything is a matter of lies and deceit, but with the capacity to see that how we are led to understand our world distorts and legitimates what we see, hear, and think.* To teach students to think critically about their world requires the ability to grasp how the dominant beliefs, values, and assumptions function—-not to become hopelessly cynical, but to become more empowered to challenge and change what is presented as unchangeable. At least within democratic societies, ideology, not physical coercion, is the cement that holds things to the present course. It is the power of ideology "to work beneath the radar" so that what we come to know or believe about the world is not part of our conscious awareness. It shapes our assumptions, values, and beliefs in ways that are often subtle and difficult to detect. Only by gaining some understanding of the manner in which ideology works can we really transcend the paralyzing grip of the present on future possibility.

IDEOLOGY AS NATURALIZATION

I have already mentioned how ideology *naturalizes* the world. To makes thing seem natural implies that they belong to an unalterable order of being; it defies how the universe works. To think of change flies in the face of the innate capabilities of human beings. There is no more powerful means through which to deny the possibility of something else than to say *it would deny nature*. It is the reason I begin many of my classes with the questions, is there such a thing as human nature? And if there is, what is it? Invariably these questions produce heated discussion and much frustration as I do my best to refute each attempt at stating just what human nature is by questioning whether this or that behavior can be found in *every* culture and society. The question of human nature has everything to do with the possibility of a nonviolent world. The lynchpin of the belief in the inevitability of war and violence between human beings is found in the acceptance, usually unquestioned, that this is the way we have been "programmed" to resolve our differences. No matter what we try to do or say, *man* is bound to the path of violent resolution of conflict. War has always been our history, and will remain so. It is not for nothing that I speak of "man's path"; when we talk about human nature and our destiny to be violent we are, after all, mostly referring to masculine behavior. It is men, not women, who have done and continue to do most of the killing in the world. So we must pose another question—is it *male nature* to kill and fight, or can men find other ways to resolve their differences, deal with their anger, and mediate their conflicts. Certainly not all men act violently. There is abundant evidence of men's capacity to live their lives lovingly, compassionately, and gently. The rise of the women's movement around the world has not only freed women from prescribed roles, but released men, too, from the deadly grip of masculinity defined as domination and emotional detachment. It has allowed great numbers of men to participate in the work of nurturing the young and the old and give far more expression to life-giving and life-sustaining values. The higher levels of testosterone in men, it would appear, does not represent destiny. We know, too, that history provides examples of cultures that were pacific and not war-like, and in which matriarchal values of gentleness, caring, and a sensuous valuing of the body and nature held sway.[15] Society, it appears, is not doomed to be centered on warrior values. And, as writers like Riane Eisler[16] have made brilliantly clear, there are important differences among contemporary societies as to their propensity for violence and their embrace of military solutions to problems.

The power to make something appear *natural*, and thus part of an unchangeable world, is found in many other things that bear on questions of peace. Nation states with their often zealous concern for borders, flags, anthems, and other trappings that distinguish them from other states and allow them to make claims to their superiority are themselves actually imagined communities whose reality is usually far more contingent than generally understood. National entities are creatures whose histories are usually much shorter than generally recognized; their borders are constantly shaped and reshaped; their identities are far more labile and shifting than typically claimed by the nationalists and patriots. Nation states are not part of a permanent cultural and physical geography. They are typically temporary, changing, and in process—splitting, dissolving, and being reconstituted and re-branded. Ideology's power persuades us to see the impermanent as permanent, the changeable as immovable, the socially constructed as part of a sacred and transcendent order. The job of critical education is precisely to trouble such rigidity; to see possibility where fixity reigns.

IDEOLOGY AS MYSTIFICATION

Ideology also *mystifies* how we see the world. We in the United States have repeatedly seen how the claims of bringing democracy and freedom to other parts of the world has licensed invasions, occupations, and interventions in so many countries. Beneath this story of military involvement is often a very different set of reasons for the policies that justify making or supporting wars. I have discussed in this book the reasons claimed for invading Iraq, which in retrospect we know now to be at variance with the true timing and purposes of the invasion.[17] We recall the justification for our covert support of military dictatorships in places like Chile where a democratically elected government was overthrown by a brutal and bloody coup in the name of fighting communism. Or our training and support for death squads in El Salvador, Guatemala, Honduras, and Colombia that killed workers, human rights advocates, and union organizers and helped maintain brutal and violent regimes in power. In Nicaragua, our government, in contravention of our own laws, trained and equipped an army that fomented a long civil war in that poor country against a popular government. We have forgotten our covert involvement in Iran that led to the overthrow of an elected government in the 1950s, and our support for the tyrannical regime of the Shah in the 1980s—involvements that have not been forgotten in Iran and are responsible for the continuing animus and suspicion towards the West. We have forgotten, too, the long U.S. support for bloody dictatorships in Panama, Indonesia, and the Philippines. In Vietnam, our long and costly war was fought to ostensibly end the worldwide onslaught of communism (refusing to recognize the desire of the Vietnamese people for national independence, free from decades of foreign interference). Millions died in a war that not only devastated that small and poor country, but was intentionally spread to surrounding countries such as Cambodia, which ultimately produced the horrifying and genocidal regime of the Khmer Rouge. More recently, our government has turned a blind eye to the continuing repression of the Palestinian people and the forcible expropriation of their land by Israeli settlers, while providing Israel with the latest military hardware with which to maintain this situation.[18]

For most people it is difficult to reconcile this litany of support and involvement with violent and undemocratic regimes with our nation's purported character as a free and democratic "light to the nations." This is hardly surprising given the bland panegyrics that fill the history textbooks in our schools. Writers like Howard Zinn and James Loewen[19] have helped us see how a great deal of what we learn about our nation obscures, distorts, or hides our real history, especially the violence with which we have conducted ourselves, not just in other countries, but in the United States itself. Beyond the registering of "formal" truths about slavery and segregation or the Indian wars and the westward expansion of the United States, there is little real engagement with the sheer horrors of enslavement with all its suffering, death, and brutality. The same can be said of the genocidal treatment and dehumanization of America's indigenous peoples. Sadly, we know that where there is a serious attempt in our education to convey something about America's history that gives a more adequate attention to its frequently callous disregard for democratic and humane values, the voices of right-wing protest are heard demanding we protect the "true" patriotic narrative of "our" history. This narrative of mystification insists that this nation's actions are always motivated by the best of impulses—the desire to bring freedom and democracy and to defeat the forces of evil in the world. It is one reason that Americans abroad are often so astonished to find far more malevolent views of the United States than anything we have heard at home. In Chalmer Johnson's book *Blowback*, he gives some explanation for how much hatred there is for the United States around the world. He says,

> The concept "blowback" does not just mean retaliation for things our government has done to and in foreign countries. It refers to retaliation for the numerous illegal operations we have carried out abroad that were kept totally secret from the American public. That means when the retaliation comes—as it did so spectacularly on September 11, 2001—the American public is unable to put the events in context. So they tend to support acts intended to lash out against the perpetrators, thereby most commonly preparing ground for yet another cycle of blowback.

Mystification succeeds in papering over the contradictions in our national values. For example, we learn to be blind to the conflict between democratic values and the imperative to treat people and resources as the means of profit. While the former leads us to see human beings as ends in themselves who must be treated with respect and whose rights include those that guarantee us secure and dignified lives, capitalism views human lives as expendable and useful only as long as they add to the profitability of business interests. It is this "hidden" contradiction that might explain how we come to live in a world in which 100 million children live on the street. We are taught not to question how our impulse for a world that ensures the well-being of all somehow coexists with the everyday economic violence that blights and destroys so many young lives. Similarly, the widely held desire for a world in which we live in community and in solidarity with others, ensuring that all are treated with compassion and kindness, somehow coexists with the acceptance that greed and selfishness are what makes the world go around. The power of mystification makes it possible to hold two such competing views of human existence together as if they are compatible. And around the desire for peace instead of war, there is widespread sentiment, enshrined in our religious and spiritual convictions, that supports the former. Yet amazingly, and in spite of such sentiment, wars continue to happen and nations such as our own arm themselves to the teeth readying themselves for the next spasm of killing and destruction.

Holding such contradictions together is no small feat for a species that prides itself on its faculty of rationality. On the one hand, one does not have to be a conspiracy theorist to recognize that it works in the favor of powerful interests for the great mass of people to be blinded to the utterly contradictory ways in which life proceeds. Obscuring our ideological contradictions is certainly one way that those who hold political and economic power can continue down their own path motivated by the desire for more—more power, wealth, control, etc. At the same time, for many others, ignoring the dissonance between what we say we believe and what we actually do may be the product of denial. It is, after all, painful to see and acknowledge just what one's country, gender, or race has done to others. Perhaps it is this that the historian Richard Hofstadter had in mind when he noted that Americans had a "'remarkable lack of memory' for violence. It was enough, he said, to blind the country to decades of bloody turmoil which had nevertheless left behind reminders for those who cared to look."[20] But perhaps it is more than just a lack of memory. It is perhaps something more willed—the desire not to face up to how we have brought so much unnecessary suffering to others. The effort to misrecognize the results of our own society and culture does offer an important sliver of hope. It speaks to the painfulness of acknowledging our own complicity in the hurt we have brought to others—even if that complicity involves remaining silent. For teachers, any efforts to overcome denial and shame as to our history as a nation cannot be dealt with lightly. It is bound to produce some resistance to this information, which may take the form of hostility to the teacher and resentment toward what is being taught. It may also produce a deep sadness as a hitherto veiled reality comes to be recognized. In either case, a pedagogy that seeks to overcome denial requires a classroom that offers a compassionate space in which both feelings and truths can unfold and reveal themselves in safety.

The Language of Rationalization

Appearing not to see is but one strategy for salving our own troubled conscience. We have many strategies by which we can fail to recognize how we participate or contribute to the continued suffering of others. Often this involves a language of *rationalization*. We may, for example, come to believe that one group or another are inherently violent, and therefore violent conflict or war is the inevitable outcome. How many times do we hear it said that it is in the nature of being Muslim to respond with violence to anything that appears to be a provocation? The same thing was said about other groups—Russians, Japanese, Germans, Chinese, Irish. "You have to stand up to them. It's the only thing they understand." We may justify or rationalize the grotesque inequities in the world as simply a reflection of who works hardest or who is most intelligent. In this way we come to see our own privileges as a matter of our deserving more than others. Domination and inequality are then fully justified. Redistributing wealth or power is seen as unfair to those who have worked hardest or are the smartest. Or we may come to believe that some people invite brutality or violence, for example, women are sometimes accused of inviting rape because of the way they dress. From this point of view, *we* are never the aggressor; we are only responding to someone else's behavior or provocation. "If only those in that group would change their behavior and learn to fit in better they wouldn't be harassed or threatened." As teachers, we have to teach students to listen carefully to what is being said—to detect this insidious language of rationalization.

24-Hour CNN Coherence

In the end, our ability to make sense of our world is heavily dependent on the information made available to us through our news media. We now know that the words uttered each night at the end of the CBS news by the famous TV anchor Walter Cronkite, "And that's the way it is," was far from being an accurate summation. All news is subject to some kind of "mobilization of bias"; everything we hear is the result of a process that sifts and selects, shapes and organizes from an endless variety of happenings and events. There is no news that simply tells it like it is. Whatever we hear is the result of a complex process in which human prejudice, corporate interests, political power, and ideological bias come together to shape what is called "the news." In the same way that much of what is most powerful about schooling is in the *hidden* dimensions of the curriculum—what is transmitted through the way knowledge is organized, shaped, and delivered—so it is with the news media. Although human beings, at least in developed countries like the United States, have never before been so inundated with news coverage, this should not be confused with a broad and cogent understanding of how our world functions. John Berger[21] is correct, I believe, when he describes a typical CNN news bulletin, or any mass media news commentary, as a space of incoherence and frenzy:

> There is no horizon there. There is no continuity between actions, there are no pauses, no paths, no pattern, no past and no future. There is only the clamour of the disparate, fragmentary present. Everywhere there are surprises and sensations, yet nowhere is there any outcome. Nothing flows through: everything interrupts. There is a kind of spatial delirium.

His meaning, I think, is clear. The world of 24-hour news mass media is frequently a breathless, frenzied show filled with dramatic highs and lows, of attention-shifting fragments of "breaking news" and the promise to be right where the action is, or will be (after the next commercial break). All of this is brought to us from the high-tech command centers of the digital age from which we are told that "we are in the situation room"—a place from which we are made to feel we are viewing the very forces that are shaping our world. Yet, paradoxically, what we actually feel is often the very opposite of this. In reality, we know very little about how things truly operate in our world. The excited fragments of information that follow one another do not provide a whole picture. They offer little that would allow us to place an item of news in a greater perspective, especially one that situates what we are viewing in the context of history—how did we get here? What events and processes led up to the present situation? This is certainly the case for this country's wars and other forms of violent involvements. Contrast the way the Columbine shootings (or school violence) was covered by the news media with the way that Michael Moore's film, *Bowling for Columbine*, attempted to situate this event. The former offered the usual wall-to-wall coverage, but offered little to explain the context for this or other similar eruptions of school violence. Moore provided a broader frame—one that showed that this kind of gun violence cannot be separated from a culture in which fear, suspicion, racism, militarism, and an economy in which weapons production is a major source of employment run together in ways that will inevitably produce such tragedies.

Mainstream media offers citizens little opportunity to grasp the scale and influence of war-making in the shaping of our national life—how much it directs our public policies and shapes our thinking about how to deal with world events. The *Bulletin of Atomic Scientists*[22] reported that the total bill for defense spending in 2008 would likely reach $660 billion. The proposed military budget in 2010 was around $800 billion! According to the *Bulletin*, since 9–11 the United States has spent a staggering $4 trillion. The National Priorities Project[23] reports that in 2007 over 40 percent of our tax dollars went to military spending (in Raleigh, North Carolina, where I live, of the $4,620 paid in taxes by a typical median-income family, $1,949 went to military spending). An extraordinary 60 percent of the discretionary spending in the current federal budget goes towards defense[24]—more than what is spent on education, public health, housing, employment, pensions, food aid, and welfare combined. The Department of Defense's own reports lists the United States having some 725 foreign military bases in 38 countries.[25] The Pentagon notes that these bases have a mind-boggling total replacement value of $118 billion. In addition to the more than half a million personnel—either in uniform or civilians who work for the Pentagon—there are private military companies that employ tens of thousands of personnel. Estimates of the revenues of these firms were calculated to be around $202 billion. This does not speak to the extraordinary scale of corporate involvement and influence in the allocation of our national budget and the "revolving door" that sees corporate executives take key political positions that direct military funding and retired military officers assume managerial positions in major suppliers and developers of military hardware. Chalmers Johnson[26] is worth quoting at length here. A hallmark of militarism, he says, is

> the preponderance of military officers or representatives of the arms industry in high government positions. During 2001, the administration of George W. Bush filled many of the chief American diplomatic posts with military men or militarists....At the Pentagon, President Bush appointed Peter B. Teets, the former president and chief operating officer of Lockheed Martin Corporation, as undersecretary of the

air force; former brigadier general and Enron executive Thomas E. White as secretary of the army;...Gordon England, a vice president of General Dynamics, as secretary of the navy; and James Roche, an executive with Northrup Grumman and a retired brigadier general, as secretary of the air force. It should be noted that Lockheed Martin is the world's largest arms manufacturer, selling $17.93 billion worth of military hardware in 1999. On October 26, 2001, the Pentagon awarded Lockheed Martin a $200 billion contract, the largest military contract in our history, to build the F-35 "joint-strike fighter," an aircraft that conceivably could have been useful during the Cold War but is irrelevant to the probable military problems of the twenty-first century.

Johnson notes that another hallmark of militarism is a devotion to policies in which military preparedness becomes the highest priority of the state. The Stockholm International Peace Research Institute reported that in the early years of the twenty-first century the United States accounted for 37 percent of the world's total military spending—by far the largest proportion of any country. Johnson also notes in his book *Nemesis*[27] that if all the Department of Defense and non-DOD but defense-related expenditures are added together with the cost of the wars in Iraq and Afghanistan, it would actually double what the Bush administration called the annual defense budget. *It is, he says, an amount larger than all the other defense budgets on earth combined!*

The United States was also the world's largest arms seller, being responsible for nearly 50 percent of all munitions sales. At the beginning of this century the United States' nuclear arsenal comprised 5,400 multiple megaton warheads atop intercontinental missiles, 1,750 nuclear bombs and cruise missiles ready to be launched from planes, and an additional 1,670 nuclear weapons classified as "tactical." Johnson concludes[28]:

> The staggering overkill in our nuclear arsenal—its ability to destroy the planet several times over—and the lack of any rational connection between nuclear means and nuclear ends is further evidence of the rise to power of a militarist mind-set.

The power of ideology to "mobilize bias" means that there is very little real discussion of the extraordinary influence of militarist thinking to shape how we think, how we utilize our wealth and resources, and how we approach issues and problems in the world. There is little discussion of what it might mean to us if we really shifted our productive and creative resources from things that produce death and destruction to materials that would sustain and improve our lives. How much such a shift would mean, not just for the lives of American citizens, but also for human beings around the world. Even in the change-oriented campaign of then-presidential-candidate Barack Obama, although there was strong criticism of the Iraq War, there was little stated to challenge the overall militarist emphasis in American society or the need to radically reduce military spending. Raising fundamental questions about this would quickly be denounced as unpatriotic, to say nothing about the potential threat to Congress's ability to award jobs and money to their home districts and support the interests that finance their election campaigns. Raising questions about the interlocking power of our military-corporate-political institutions would threaten the enormous, increasingly secretive process through which the priorities and agenda are of our nation is shaped and constructed. It would raise dangerous questions about the "national security state" in which much that affects the lives of citizens in this country is determined behind closed doors, unreported by the media, little understood by average citizens, and shaped by those who are most dependent on the continued cycle of war spending and arms manufacturing. There are increasing questions about the real meaning of our democracy when so much that shapes the priorities of this nation is made by those whose influence is unseen and invisible to the majority of citizens.

THE IDEOLOGY OF DISTRACTION

The greatest obstacle to getting students to think more critically and deeply about their world, and in particular about questions concerning war and peace, may not be about the power of ideology to *naturalize, mystify, rationalize,* or *obfuscate* our world. The greatest difficulty may be through the power of culture to distract or offer an escape from the real issues that confront the human race. As in no other time in history, young people are surrounded by, and inundated with, sources of entertainment and escape that pull them into a world apart. Cell phones, text messaging, and social networking provide a continuous medium of conversation that encourages an obsessive concern with the detailed goings on of our own personal lives. Digital games offer another form of endless and compulsive distraction. E-Channel—type TV programming focuses relentlessly on the often tawdry sexual and romantic intimacies of celebrities (as increasingly do even "serious" TV news channels). The death of singer Michael

Jackson and the sexual escapades of golfer Tiger Woods provide vivid examples of the blanket coverage that for days preempted all other news stories. Supermarket checkout line magazines, likewise, focus on the lives of the rich, beautiful, and famous, as well as offering a continuous recipe for how to look more attractive and enjoy an optimal sex life. The professional sports industry, through cable and satellite television, offers almost 24-hour coverage of sporting events. Sports such as wrestling provide men with an escape into a world of super-macho heroes—one more manifestation of the highly popular comic book hero characters. This is expanded into the hugely popular casino TV with its high-stakes poker games. And the massively expanded program offerings on digital TV provides endless hours of variations on the tried and true themes—sex, romance, greed, crime, etc. And there is the less acknowledged but huge audience that whiles away its time in front of pornographic computer screen images. This is only a part of the endlessly proliferating avenues for amusement, play, chat, and simulation that is provided by the Internet, which exercises a powerful pull away from the reality of political issues and public affairs and into a highly individualized, egoistic fantasy world with its pretence at human agency and control.

All of this, and much more, must be added to the culture of consumption that leads us to spend long hours shopping or thinking about shopping—at the mall, on TV, or on-line.[29] The result is a culture that increasingly pushes us into an escape from questions that can only be answered through civic concern and engagement. Instead of facing and struggling with questions about the life and death of our planet, war or peace, or a world of greed or one of justice and compassion, our children are urged to turn inward towards an escapist world of shock, thrills, simulated adventure, and excitement or voyeuristic pleasure. Any pedagogy that wants to engage young people around issues upon which life itself depends will have to confront this culture of distraction and escape. This is a difficult, but not hopeless, quest. We saw during the campaign to elect Barack Obama how much longing there was for a politics that could engage the hopes and dreams of young people wearied and disgusted by the years of war, corruption, and social and environmental indifference. Despite the excitement and seductiveness on the surface of much of our popular and mass media, there remains a desire to engage and participate in a serious way in things that might genuinely reshape our world. Education can "tap into" and nourish these impulses. But only of it allows students to seriously question and challenge the beliefs and assumptions that have so endangered and damaged life in our world.

Chapter Eight

A Pedagogy of Peace

Understanding is very concrete; it is the opposite of ignorance. When you suffer, you get angry, and you want to punish your beloved. You believe that by punishing him you will suffer less. That does not understand, that is ignorance. After you punish him, he will suffer a lot, and he will find ways to punish you back. When you are punished, you get angrier, and you try stronger ways to punish him. In this way, the cycle of anger and punishment continues...
You as a group of Palestinians and Israelis, have undergone a lot of suffering. Every time your people are hit by a bomb or a weapon you want to retaliate. The message is very clear, "if you attack us we will attack you back. A tooth for a tooth—that is politics. If you commit an act of terrorism, you will be terrorized." That message is aimed at dissuading the other side. You terrorize and threaten each other. But if you are enlightened, awakened, and have seen suffering and learned from suffering, then you know that the course of punishment has not brought any positive result.
—From "Peace Begins Here" by Thich Nhat Hanh

There's a lot of talk in this country about the federal deficit but I think we should talk more about our empathy deficit—the ability to put ourselves in someone else's shoes; to see the world through those who are different from us—the child who's hungry, the laid-off steelworker, the immigrant woman cleaning your dorm room.
—Presidential candidate Barack Obama speaking at Southern New Hampshire University

Introduction

There is much talk about a crisis of education. Yet what is pointed to as the cause of this crisis is confusing at best and misleading at worst. There is, for example, the argument that our economy is in trouble because of poor education. This seems preposterous when compared to the role of the banks in our current economic crisis; irresponsibility and short-term considerations, lack of governmental regulation, and a culture of greed on Wall Street seem to be much more salient to this situation than education might be. Or when our automobile industry fails, blaming schools is surely obfuscation; poor planning for an era of higher gas prices, lack of innovation for changing transportation needs, and poor and expensive management seem much more pertinent. Indeed, despite talk of an economy that demands higher skills and more educated workers, predictions are for an economy that will continue to employ high numbers of low- and semi-skilled workers. Jobs that had been performed by high school graduates are now increasingly filled by those with college degrees. Elsewhere there is much talk about an educational crisis that is the result of our kids performing poorly in comparison with students from other countries. Accurate comparisons are difficult to make given they way school populations in different countries are compared, the different focus of school systems (schools in Europe and Japan specialize at a much younger age), and many other factors. Although a number of educational researchers such as Gerald Bracey and David Berliner[1] have systematically and thoroughly demonstrated how these assertions distort, confuse, and exaggerate meaningful comparisons between American and foreign schools, this has made little difference to those in the media, or to politicians who love to cry wolf in regard to our public schools. Empirical evidence provided by careful and thoughtful researchers has little impact on those determined to expose new faults and failures in our public institutions. I, and many others, have written at length about the so-called crisis of accountability in our schools.[2] This "crisis" has resulted in the calamity of an education system that is increasingly enthralled with a culture of testing that has sapped imagination, creativity, curiosity, and critical intelligence from our classrooms. The crisis of accountability has become the springboard for rigid and mechanical forms of control over the learning and teaching process in our schools. Others have argued that the crisis in our schools reflects a lack of cultural literacy, by which they seem to mean that students have not managed to memorize a particular set of information—names, dates, events, etc.—that are claimed to qualify one to be a citizen of the United States. I will not pursue here who exactly decides what particular information makes one culturally literate, or how learning and knowing become misrepresented as memorizing information. Of course, there are other crises associated with education, such as the safety of kids in schools, problems of behavior, and retention and graduation rates. And schools still mirror the gross inequalities of our class- and race-divided societies and reflect the continuing depth of social injustice in the United States.

Yet in all of this talk of crisis there is little that speaks to the profound moral and spiritual responsibility that is carried—or should be carried—by education. In this book (as well as elsewhere in my writing) I have argued that beyond the usual focus and obsessions of schooling (grades, test results, graduation rates, etc.) is something of far greater significance. Education has the capability and the obligation, I believe, to speak to the very issue of what it means to be human, of how we as human beings live and relate to one another, and how we relate to, and care for, the natural world that we share with all life forms. I have argued in this book that these issues are not frills or add-ons to the more important agenda items of education. These issues rise to the very top of what is important to our very survival as a species. For us, and even more so for our children, what needs to be our concern is the very quality of human life on our planet. And central to this is the continuing problem of violent conflict and violent behavior among human beings. This, above all else, I have come to believe, is the real crisis of education today. While I in no way dismiss or belittle the everyday concerns of students and their parents for basic literacy, jobs, economic security, opportunity and access, and an education that can help ensure these things, we need, I believe, to look beyond these concerns at the bigger picture that confronts us and the conditions that are destructive to any form of continued human well-being. In its 2009 report, the Institute of Economic and Peace estimates that worldwide violence or the "lost peace" costs $4.8 trillion a year. Peace, it says, is a significant factor in the creation of wealth. In a world of dwindling resources, increasing population, greater inequalities of wealth, and more powerful technologies of destruction, how can we as a human community develop the knowledge, attitudes, and skills that will allow us to survive and flourish as a species rather than succumb to a world of accelerating insecurity, fear of the other, and the impulse to destroy those who share our world?

In the following pages I want to outline, if only briefly, a number of things that I believe represent essential dimensions of a pedagogy of peace. These will, I hope, provide a succinct and useful summary of much of what has previously been covered in this book, but will also add some new things. My intention is to describe the moral, social, and spiritual aspects of human behavior and dispositions that are needed in order to bring about a transformation towards peace in both our personal and shared lives. My hope is that these will form the anchor points for a curriculum of peace. I have intentionally drawn on multiple cultural traditions in naming these dimensions of the language of peace. This is important to me in emphasizing the universality of the aspiration for, and vision of, a loving, caring, and peaceful world.

TEN POINTS FOR A PEDAGOGY OF PEACE

1. *Ubuntu*

Cape Town Archbishop Desmond Tutu suggests that the African term *ubuntu* means that one cannot exist as a human being in isolation. It speaks, he says, about our interconnectedness, our belonging to a greater whole. You cannot be human by yourself. Contemporary culture teaches us to think of ourselves as individuals, separated from one another. Schools usually provide a powerful vehicle for this ideology of the separate self. Most of what is defined as success (or failure) is a matter of individual achievement and performance. And, of course, what individuals achieve is always in competitive comparison to the success or failure of others. Likewise, consumer culture is always about the promise of improving the quality of our lives or social status through what we as individuals own or can purchase. The emphasis is constantly on the individual—on "me" and "my", and on what is mine and belongs to me. It is not surprising that this culture produces a world of so much loneliness, disconnection from others, and conflict. It teaches us to see ourselves as alone in a sea of other lonely strivers after satisfaction, validation, or success. At its core it denies the simple reality of the oneness of human existence, and with it the recognition that it is through our connectedness to others that we experience the deepest and richest satisfactions and joys of life. Earlier I mentioned how the Hebrew word shalom, meaning peace, has the same etymological root as the word shalem, meaning wholeness or completeness. In this context peace cannot be distinguished from the circle of life that connects us one to another.

In our world it is not just the personalist ideology of individualism that that separates us from other human beings. It is the constant reinforcement of divisive imagery in which "my group" (team, race, ethnicity, nationality, faith, etc.) is pitted against another. In one sense, this kind of dualism provides a powerful vehicle for the sense of community and connection that is missing in our otherwise heavily individualistic culture. But it comes at a price. The connection to other human beings is predicated on there also being a division from those belonging to the "out" group. Solidarity and connectedness on the one hand is accompanied by separateness and enmity on the other. The sense of a fuller humanity that comes from seeing ourselves as part of a larger whole requires disparaging or diminishing the humanity of others. This is a flawed form of *Ubuntu* in which one's own sense of self-value and self-assurance requires that others be deemed less worthy. To say here that "I am because we are" implies a restricted and limited understanding of who is the "we."

To affirm the concept of *ubuntu* and to educate for its radical promise requires a very different focus on what we wish students to learn, morally, socially, and spiritually. In the first place it means that school and the classroom move away from a relentless focus on the success and failure of the individual that is inscribed in every aspect of schooling. It means that we come to see our achievements and failures as learners as being the shared product of our communal efforts and not as something earned and owned by lone students. The classroom emphasizes the community's achievements over individual success. The "culture of separated desks" in which each student is a lonely runner in the race for success gives way to a classroom ambience of communal support, the sharing of knowledge and information, and mutual respect for each person's contributions. Beyond this the message of education must run counter to the individualistic and competitive message of the consumer culture; human fulfillment is found in how we serve, support, and care for the well-being of all other human beings. And contrary to our dualist preferences and prejudices, our highest moral and social obligation is to serve humanity undivided by markers of nationality, race, sexuality, ethnicity, etc. Loyalty or support for one's team or social group must be balanced by learning to recognize the *universal* interconnectedness of all people—to see ourselves, ultimately, as part of a single global family. The educational message of *ubuntu* resists all those things that separate and isolate human beings from one another—that cause us to see others as disconnected from ourselves. It leads us to question the moral environment of the school, the social relationships of the classroom, and the messages found in our texts, as well as the broader messages of the culture within which we live. In each case we must ask, does what we learn from these things help us to recognize and realize our mutual connectedness and interdependence as human beings? Does it enable us to experience the profound fulfillment and joy that comes from human sociability and interaction? Or does it thwart, undermine, and deny them? And to what extent are we coming to see ourselves as part of a global community in which particular connections to ethnicity, nation, etc., are less important than the ties we have with the *whole* human family. Do our educational experiences nurture and encourage this sense of global human identity?

2. *Tikkun Olam*

The search for a life of meaning can never be far from the goal of educating for peace. Education has lost its most profound purpose—engagement with what it means to live meaningfully and purposefully. Instead, schooling has become the soil for an arid and soulless focus of human energy and ambition: better scores, higher grades, greater retention, raised SATs, EOGs, AYPs, etc. School has become like a black box in which inputs are measured against outputs: How many students graduate? How many go on to college? Is education producing enough engineers, teachers? Raising the nation's productivity? Little is heard of the intrinsic value or rewards of learning: Does it make us more thoughtful, questioning, imaginative, or concerned human beings? Does it enable us to think more deeply about living our lives in meaningful ways? Our obsession with numbers, output, and averages has led us to forget our responsibility to a younger generation to provide them with the opportunity for serious reflection on the nature of a purposeful life.

The absence of such opportunity is especially sad given the demonstrable crisis of meaning in our larger culture. It is a crisis that manifests itself in record levels of teenage suicides and emotional disorders; in widespread feelings of despair, loneliness, and emotional emptiness; and in the turn towards self-destructive and violent behavior. None of this is that surprising given the dehumanizing nature of so much of the wider culture through which young people are expected to discern their life goals and aspirations. It surrounds them with a world in which the most important things are celebrity, fame, being rich, having more, looking great, exploitative sex, and being a "winner." In such a world, time is reduced to the immediate experience or most recent episode, and satisfaction the "feel great" moment. And nothing is more important than the search for the next exhilarating and optimal high. As I and others have pointed out, it is but a short step from this kind of cultural exposure and socialization to the despair and anxiety that leads to violence and destruction—whether this is inflicted on others or on oneself.

Tikkun Olam speaks to the need among human beings for an authentic life of meaning and the responsibility of education to facilitate the quest for such meaning. It rests on the mythic Hebrew vision of a world that has overcome division and fragmentation and become whole and united as a single caring community. The struggle for such a world becomes, in this vision, the overriding moral responsibility of human beings in this life. More than this, it is through the act of trying to create a world of compassionate and loving connection in the face of all the divisions, injustices, conflicts, and suffering that beset human beings that we are able to find the most profound sense of meaning in our lives. Obviously the message of *Tikkun Olam* speaks out against the false and distorted "meanings" of the culture. And those who educate in its spirit mince no words in calling into question the dehumanizing, vulgar, and over-commercialized values that shape our lives, and especially those of the young.[3] Such educators are also clear that everything that separates and fragments our world—war, torture, social injustice, nationalism, tribalism, racism, sexism, homophobia, religious intolerance, and excessive competition, must be called into question and challenged.

Tikkun Olam means "the repairing of the world," and it is through our engagement in this act of repair work that human beings find the meaning that animates a purposeful life. It is an expression of a wisdom tradition that is found in many different cultures, but holds in common the belief that meaningful lives are found in the work of bettering the lives of others and leaving the world a more peaceful, harmonious, and just place than we found it. To educate in this spirit requires encouraging students to see their lives in terms of the contribution each might make to healing the brokenness of our world, and to see how they may act to redress intolerance, indignity, and injustice—all the things that fragment and split apart our world. The lesson is powerful but nonspecific. It offers students a counter-vision to the tawdry and self-interested message so relentlessly pounded out by the culture of capitalism and modernity. It suggests a broad moral, social, and spiritual framework for how students may think about the direction of their lives. But exactly how it may be expressed, whether through one's studies, work, professional commitments, faith activity, or political engagement, is a decision students must make on their own. It asserts only the wisdom that the most purposeful lives are lived in the struggle to make whole what has been broken through frustration, anger, indignity, and selfishness—to create *shalom* and *salaam* from the shards of a fragmented and divided world.

3. *Parrhesia*
The quest for *ubuntu's* interconnected community or *Tikkun's* vision of a world beyond fragmentation is inseparable from the education of a courageously articulate citizenry. Peace education always inhabits that in-between zone where the "what is" encounters the "what might be." Henry Giroux has referred to this as the voice that speaks

in both the language of critique and in the language of possibility. Others have referred to it as a "critical utopianism" in which the imagined world of human dignity, justice, and peace is held up against the realities of our torn and divided world.

The lesson of critical social theory is that separating our hopes and dreams of a better world from the kind of cultural and political analysis that illuminates the forces and interests that thwart these possibilities reduces the social imagination to impotent dreaming. Conversely, providing this kind of critical analysis detached from the utopian imagination offers a sterile form of academic discourse that lacks the power to inspire and ignite the possibilities of a radically different world. Prophetic speech combines both forms of discourse: it speaks with indignation about the awful dissonance between our current situation and how far it departs from the possibility of a world without pain, bloodshed, and violence. And it does so in the voice of *parrhesia*—the fearless voice that challenges and questions the world's unnecessary suffering.[4]

Few who are concerned with driving policy in public education concern themselves much with *parrhesia* and prophetic speech. Education today, as I and many other commentators have noted, is overwhelmingly concerned with things that have little to do with developing voices that can question and challenge what is in our world. What we see everywhere is a focus on a one-size-fits-all kind of education that is more about conformity in thinking than anything else. The focus on standardized tests and measures of "performance" in our classrooms has induced a kind of learning in which students and teachers can do little else but be concerned with getting the one correct answer on the test sheet. And classroom time is increasingly spent on rehearsing this process—practicing the art of figuring out what examiners are looking for and giving it back to them. There is precious little opportunity for the kind of unconventional thinking that questions the accepted understanding of how things are. There is little time for the bold and outrageous challenges to the accepted nature of things. The current "regime" in education is all about conformity of thought—finding somebody else's idea of the one right answer. This conformity is reinforced, not just through the medium of standardized forms of assessment, but also through the sterility of what constitutes the learning space. This space mostly excludes the very things that are most salient to the direction and quality of young people's lives: sexuality, spiritual and religious faith, the impact of the media and the content of popular culture, war and violence, race and cultural difference, politics. Remove these things and we are left with a classroom that offers no possibility of the kind of passionate engagement that stirs us to find our voices and speak our truth to others who share our world.

The exercise of *parrhesia* in the classroom is a practical matter. It requires transforming these spaces into ones in which the sound of students' voices is heard. It should be emphasized that these are not voices that nervously seek the approval of any teacher. These are the animated and assertive, though reflective, voices that are encouraged to express their understanding, or their "take," regarding the text, event, or experience that confronts them. They are the products of a classroom that values more than the words in a book or the pronouncements of the teacher. This is a classroom that cherishes student expression, student opinion, and student experience. This is a classroom that embodies the essential dimensions of democratic culture— the capacity to think, question, and challenge what has been accepted and unquestioned, and to bring into the common space the diverse perspectives, beliefs, and understandings of a young and emerging heterogeneous citizenry. In this space the goal is always an education that nurtures the independent mind and the insistent spirit of unfinished inquiry. We have been reminded in recent times of the importance of a civic culture that refuses to passively accede to voices of authority and expertise—whether in government, media, or business. We face unprecedented dangers and crises as a human race. The times demand an education that equips students with the capacity to speak up and speak out—to question and challenge what is, in many areas of our global community, a culture of human and environmental destruction, violence, and death.

4. *Es Muss Sein*
Philosopher Maxine Greene[5] refers to this German expression meaning "it must be" when she describes how the knowledge that is transmitted in our classrooms often conveys a fatalistic sense of permanence and inevitability. Her argument is that much of the time, curriculum is constructed and taught in such a way that there is little understanding of the fact that what we know about the world is only temporary, provisional, and uncertain. How we come to know about the world indicates to the learner whether things can be other than what they appear to be. Knowledge that is understood to represent with certainty how things are invites no second look—it offers a reality that seems fixed and absolute. It suggests a world that is the way it is, demanding only accommodation and acceptance of the social and natural landscape before us. Greene speaks from the passionate

conviction that our understanding of who we are and the nature of the world we inhabit are inevitably constructions of the human imagination, always open to alternative perspectives and variable interpretations. To learn about the world in this way, she argues, is the gateway to liberating ourselves from a stultifying consciousness that demands acceptance of only a single right way of understanding—one that is usually guarded and protected, and often manufactured, by those whose power and privilege depend on it. To educate against the inevitability of war, violence, and brutality requires us to refuse the consciousness that says *things must be this way.*

In this book I am arguing that human beings need a radical shift in consciousness that makes, as Herbert Marcuse suggested, the "strange become familiar."[6] It requires a breakthrough (or breakout) of thinking that makes war, violence, brutality, and intolerance no longer seem the inevitable fate of humankind. It requires a shift in the sense of possibility so that we are no longer dominated by a single belief that asserts that war and violence must forever *name our world.* The history of human struggles for a more just world of greater dignity and equality teaches us that what we can imagine is the compass for our real efforts and struggles. And these efforts and struggles, the original products of our imagination, eventually bear the fruit of change. Imagination raises new possibilities for how we might live, and even more crucially, how we conceive of what it means to be human. If we can imagine in our minds a world freed from needless death and destruction then we have begun the process of making this a reality.

Sadly, our schools do little to liberate the mind from subservience to fixity of thought. Few students are ever invited to recognize the power of interpretation in making so-called "truth." Instead, they are daily bombarded by the message of give "only the facts," the need for the single correct answer, and the certainty of the text. The larger culture provides strong doses of a one-dimensional ideology that admits of few possibilities that the world and our lives can be radically changed from its consumer-focused, competitive, hierarchical, and earth-destroying ways (look at current "reality" TV with its constant emphasis on a world of winners and losers, often vicious criticism, and thinly veiled hostility). We might ask what it would mean for our schools to nurture a creative and imaginative consciousness. We might expect to see the expressive and visual arts be given far more importance in the curriculum (though they must not be turned into another vehicle for measurable competencies and competitive performances!). In all areas of the curriculum the emphasis would be on knowledge and meaning that are actively produced out of the experience and reflection of students. Creativity and imagination would not to be ghettoized in a few subject areas, but would be the currency of all learning. Likewise, in this education, myth is something to be understood not as the relic of primitive civilizations but how all societies attempt to make meaning out of the initial formlessness of experience. In this sense, students are invited to see and examine the myths we currently live by ("men will always act aggressively," "the earth is inert matter," "national self-interest always takes preference over global concerns"). Then the challenge for them is to decide what kind of myths we need currently to ensure our survival as a species and as a planet. The great educator Paulo Freire showed us what it means when students recognize that the reality we live in and through is only one of several possibilities. There is nothing absolute and inevitable about a world that hurts and destroys the lives of so many. As a first step to change we must awaken from our sleep so that we might actually begin to dream.

5. *Hermes (Messenger of the Gods)*
Recognizing that what we know is always an act of interpretation has both liberating *and* troubling consequences. We have seen the way it can free us to re-envisage our lives and our world. But what is much more difficult to see is the fact that it also gives legitimacy to the conflicting ways we may see things. From this point of view there is no "God's-eye view" of reality, only the sometimes contradictory understanding that people have of events, situations, and human motives. Earlier in this book I talked about the decades-old conflict between Palestinians and Jews. In that blood-soaked region the inhabitants bring their own painful narratives to explain the need to fight and defend what they see as rightfully theirs. For the Jews it is the tortured history of exclusion, persecution, and genocide and the belief that their state is legitimated by ancient connection to the land and by moral claims rooted in their catastrophic history. Palestinians' claims come from the conviction that the Jews wrongfully expropriated their land and forcefully expelled its inhabitants. Supported by the West, successive wars have allowed Israel to take more of the land and facilitated a brutal occupation of remaining Palestinian territory. It is clear that, short of endless war, peace between these two warring communities will demand difficult compromises involving deeply held beliefs and convictions. We can see in other parts of the world, such as Ireland, Sri Lanka, and Kashmir, similar kinds of near-intractable conflicts rooted in fundamentally different accounts of history and current realities.

One can find much closer to home (often inside our homes) conflicts that usually involve us seeing things in ways that are different from those with whom we fight. We all know the exasperation we feel when we try, unsuccessfully, to convince others to simply agree to make sense of a situation in the same way we do. How often do therapists have to say to warring couples or family members, "Try to listen to what the other person is saying." For a moment we are asked to unblock our ears and hear—really hear—how the other individual sees things. In these situations of conflict, knowing what is true is not about rationally apprehending the facts. Truth here means "somebody's truth." It means recognizing that, whether you like it or not and whether you agree with it or not, this is how the other sees and understands his or her world. And this truth is not an abstract phenomenon. It is rooted in our individual as well as collective lives, our history, and our experience. What we take to be true cannot easily be separated from what Dan O'Meara[7] (in his discussion of South Africa) refers to as the nightmares of our different histories. We are haunted by the unresolved fears of our different pasts and what these might augur for our futures.

Nothing could be more important to the task of peace education than the capacity to understand something about how conflict is constructed out of the differing ways we come to see our lives and our world. And to learn from this something about the way conflict can be mediated. From a pedagogic standpoint it requires a number of things: (1) the ability and willingness to honestly articulate and communicate to others one's view of things; (2) the development of the capacity for active, nonjudgmental listening to the other, even when what is being communicated is painful or threatening to the listener; (3) the readiness, for each party, to "walk in the other's shoes"—to be empathic to the other's situation even as this requires confronting one's own fears, resentments, and anger about what is being expressed. The ability to communicate, hear, empathize, and to not be captured by our own need to deny or resist another's truth is more than a single-semester high school class! It is the challenge of a lifetime for all of us. It is a task that is always before us in our collective lives as we deal with conflicts and differences of perception around such things as race, sexuality, religious beliefs, and politics. And it is ever present in our personal and intimate lives as we wrestle with the challenges of friendships, work situations, marriages, and family life. No preparation in school can ever equip us adequately to deal with all of this. Yet we might at least find in our education some insights, recognitions, and skills that will help us as, with less violence or rage, we act and negotiate the inevitable struggles and challenges of life as social and political creatures condemned, as Camus noted, to make meaning from our disparate experiences.

6. *Koyaanissqatsy*

At the entrance to a photographic exhibit in Cape Town called "The Unbearable Lightness of Seeing" were these introductory comments: *We are propelled to excel, pushed to compete, to outdo one another. Our icons are Stars, Leaders, The Beautiful, The Powerful—those who have reached the pinnacle of society. Our worth is measured against our heroes, and may the strongest prevail. Bigger, better, faster, stronger, prettier, sexier, smarter... But where is the organic in the constructed collective conscious.* These words express concisely but penetratingly what it is that modern culture has come to value above all else. The word *koyaanissqatsy*, from Hopi Indian language, refers to "a world out of balance." I believe that no term better captures the harmful effects of our present culture on life than this. In every area of our world we see how we have become addicted to the culture of winning, competition, and success—sport, entertainment, education, science, jurisprudence, politics, and of course work and the economy. In every field beating others is the driving force of human activity. The goal of almost every area of our lives is to outshine the next person—to succeed or to be ahead of others. Life is increasingly experienced as a race in which only the winners really matter or deserve recognition and appreciation. Increasingly the marketplace has become the root metaphor for how we live, with its overwhelming emphasis on competition, self-interest, and self-aggrandizement.

Nothing does more to prepare us for this way of life and this consciousness than schooling. Schools are the great initiator for a younger generation of what it means to live in a world in which everything is measured by one ability—to compete with other human beings. It is here where we are introduced into the moral economy of scarcity; we learn that gold stars, smiley faces, good grades, and recognition can go only to a few. We learn that success and achievement for some demands that others be designated failures. We learn that to become "somebody" requires that others must count as "nobodies." The deep message (the "hidden curriculum," some call it) of schooling is that the only things that count are the things that can be counted because they allow us to be ranked and compared to others on a scale of winning and losing. Here, as elsewhere in the world, our focus is turned so resolutely to the winners that we lose little time in noticing the deeper moral, social, and emotional consequences of our choices. For example, how the relentless emphasis on success for some produces a culture with powerful currents of envy, resentment, and suspicion. Or how it separates and divides human beings. The culture of competition and winning means learning to see social relationships as akin to standing on a ladder with others struggling and pushing over you to ascend to a higher rung. For everyone this is a culture that cultivates a deep insecurity about our worth as we are constantly being judged and compared to others, and a culture in which success or achievement is likely to be a momentary phenomenon. It is a culture that breeds hostility and aggression.

The human impulse to compete is very deep (though it seems to be more embedded in males than females). It brings with it undoubted pleasures and (speaking as a passionate fan of English soccer) I am making no pitch to eliminate the excitement that goes along with contests of skill and ability. Yet we have produced a world out of balance—a world in which getting ahead matters much more than getting along, in which competition matters much more than community, and in which sorting people out is more important than social solidarity. A more peaceful world is certain to be one in which much greater attention is given to how we may cooperate with one another and learn to see one another first as fellow human beings with similar needs to our own (such as the need to be treated with dignity), rather than individuals who must be beaten or countries whose citizens must be seen as our competitors. Education can make a major contribution to this more balanced way of existence. We can try to change our classrooms and schools into places that are less ruled by competition (admittedly not an easy task in this time of intense focus on standardized tests). We can articulate and practice a philosophy in which individual grades and test results are not what we value most. We can facilitate more time for group and peer-supported activity. We can try cultivating a social ambience in our classroom or school in which caring, compassionate, and supportive relationships are important and social divisions are lessened. And we can ensure that our curriculum gives at least equal time to social movements and events that enhance community and solidarity in our nation and globally. Obviously we cannot eliminate the culture of competition and selfish individualism. But we can enable young people to at least experience what it means to spend time in a community that cares and supports all and emphasizes the importance of cooperative and reciprocal relationships. In this way education might contribute to the goal of how we might live, both individually and collectively, more balanced lives.

7. Social Justice

It is not difficult to see how the need to rebalance our society and our world towards an ethic of care and community and away from competition and self-interest is inextricably connected to the goal of greater social justice. In these difficult economic times we have all been reminded of what it means when the desire for more in the hands of a few shapes our world. We have been forced to wake up to what happens when a financial system is steered by the rich and powerful whose major concern is to increase their already huge and disproportionate wealth. We have seen and experienced what it means when unregulated greed is allowed to govern how money and resources are used to the detriment of the mass of ordinary people. The current recession did not create the huge disparities of wealth that structure our world. In 2005 the World Bank reported that there were 1.4 billion people living on less than $1.25 a day (with the current recession, that number will be much worse). According to the World Institute for Development Economics Research, in 2000 the top 1 percent of the world's population accounted for about 40 percent of global wealth; the bottom half of the world's population owned merely 1.1 percent (the United States, which accounts for 4.7 percent of the world's population, owned about a third of all wealth). Noted economist Jeffrey Sachs states that 10 million people die each year because of hunger and poverty.[8]

Our world of tremendous inequalities was not born yesterday. The prophetic texts of our great religious traditions continually made clear that a moral society was incompatible with great social injustice. Each generation was enjoined to teach its children that our ethical and spiritual responsibility was to ensure that no one would go hungry or lack shelter or other basic human needs. President Franklin Roosevelt said it well when he noted that a good society was measured not by how well its richest could live, but how its poorest were treated. We know, too, that social injustice is not only about having enough food for oneself and one's family, a decent place to live, or the availability of affordable medical care. It is also about the spirit of human beings—the sense that your life matters to others and that your voice counts. And it means that one has some influence in shaping a society's public policies and agenda. A socially just society accords dignity to all by ensuring that all members of the society have the resources to realize their human capacities in full.

Sadly, we inhabit a world in which exploitation, abuse, and dispowerment of human beings is rife. Global television and other forms of mass communication bring home daily to the world's poor just how inequitable things are. The extraordinary concentration of wealth and opportunity is flaunted by the rich and protected through their control of both armies and culture on the one hand, and through a politics that ensures a continuing flow of wealth into the pockets of the few at the expense of the many.

It is hardly surprising that such a situation breeds a world of conflict and war as national and global inequities generate resentment and fury at the way things work. Sometimes such emotions produce movements of change of a genuinely more democratic and equal nature. Elsewhere they are steered into dysfunctional carnage and brutality as groups of those with little or nothing turn their resentment on others similarly dispossessed.

There is, I believe, no more important focus for peace education than to teach for a transformative vision of the world rooted in the quest for greater equity and fairness in social and economic relationships. Without significant change in these relationships, there can be no hope of a more peaceful, less violent world. Such an education would be centered on a number of things:

- Recognizing the different ways we create and reproduce inequitable social relationships (through class domination, patriarchy, racism, unfair trading practices between rich and poor nations, etc.). Students might consider how their own school or school system works to reproduce social inequalities.
- Understanding how self-interest and the concentration of economic power in the hands of a few create an unbalanced world in which wealth and resources are unfairly distributed.
- Becoming aware of the extent of poverty in the United States as well as globally, and its effect on people's lives.
- Understanding the connection between social injustice and environmental destruction (through socially irresponsible exploitation of natural resources, conflicts, and wars over diminishing resources such as land and water).

Alongside students' growing awareness about the corrosive effects of social injustice at home and around the world there must be an alternative vision of a world in which "enough is as good as a feast," in which the basic needs of all people are satisfied and there is a commitment to share and trade earth's precious resources fairly and in an environmentally sustainable manner for the sake of future generations. Although for some, such an education may seem dangerously radical, I believe there is growing recognition that this is precisely what it means to educate for a world of greater human dignity, fairness, and peace.

8. B'tselem Elohim

In the end, questions about social justice, a more caring community, and the end of violence can be reduced, I believe, to the need to see the extraordinary and unconditional value of each human life. To affirm this is to oppose all those things that diminish, degrade, or destroy a life. It is to oppose genocide, killing, mutilation, torture, rape, abuse of children, slavery, or any form of economic exploitation, racism, or violence and dehumanization directed against women, gays, or minority groups. The concept of the beauty and ineffable value of human life is an ancient one. The Hebrew bible talks about *B'tselem Elohim*—the belief that human beings are made in the image of God. If one is uncomfortable with this religious formulation then other secular or naturalistic perspectives are available that arrive, broadly, at the same belief about the inherent worth of each life. Either way, it is a belief that underpins our notions of democracy, civil rights, and more recently, human rights. In each case what is asserted is the conviction that societies and institutions must exist for the sake of the realization and fulfillment of an individual's potentialities and capabilities; they must ensure conditions that honor the integrity and inviolability of each person. It goes without saying that the actual conditions that have faced human beings have always fallen far short of this noble aspiration. Yet this belief's power as a template for measuring the quality, fairness, and humanness of a society is undeniable, and it is a continuing catalyst for social, political, cultural, and economic change.

We have come to see how even our best intentions can sometimes negate the precious value of individual lives. Attempts at creating societies that are more socially just have, notoriously, sometimes accentuated the importance of collectivist values that have denied or vilified individual rights at great human cost. Sometimes also, universal declarations about human rights leave too little space to recognize human differences. Loving one's neighbor presupposes respect for what each person is, no matter their language, race, ethnicity, gender, and so on. Human rights cannot become a reference for a bland assertion of human sameness. We must honor our commonality while recognizing the salience of our differences to how we take pride in who we are in the world. And finally, our contemporary environmental crisis demands of us new ways to think about the extraordinary value of life, extending it from merely human life to the life of the whole planet and the "great chain of being" that makes all life interdependent and interconnected. It is time to move away from the anthropocentric formulations that cherish only human life (or even only male life) to ones that are more inclusive and honor and protect all forms of life.

In an essay I wrote shortly after 9–11 on the lessons we might draw from this sad event, I noted one thing in particular. When the first responders raced up the stairs of the World Trade Center buildings they were not concerned with whether the people they were trying to save were men or women, gay or straight, Black or white, Muslim, Christian or Jewish, American born or immigrants. They were concerned only, at great danger to themselves, with trying to save lives. Here in this moment of terrible tragedy was a ray of light—the brave, unquestioning insistence that all lives had inestimable value and were worth saving from this catastrophe. At this defining moment, a life was a life no matter what's its skin color, religious belief, gender or sexual orientation, or country of origin.

Can we teach for the sacred inviolability of life? Perhaps the lesson of 9–11 is that somewhere or other we do learn about life's great value. Through our religious education, our democratic creed, or the simple love that we receive from parents, family members, friends, teachers, etc., almost all of us know something about the importance of being held in the embrace of loving affirmation that tells us our lives are irreplaceably important. Yet the confusion happens because so much that surrounds us suggests something quite different. The competitive, nationalistic, manipulative, and divisive aspects of culture teaches a very different set of values that diminishes or degrades others who are seen as not truly part of the human family. Our work as teachers, as well as parents, must be to emphasize our shared humanity and the preciousness of every life while honestly and forthrightly pointing to the ways we think and act that contradict and conflict with this conviction. The institution of school itself provides a powerful space for highlighting such conflict with its pervasive hierarchical ranking, competitive individualism, tracking and the differentiation of individual worth, social cliques and social status, bullying, and demeaning of those who might not fit the cultural or gender norms. What would it mean, we may ask, for us to act in ways that ensure that the worth and dignity of every person in our school is recognized and respected? What would it mean for us to do that with every life on earth?

9. Hope

I have no doubt that hope is an essential ingredient of change. There is no automatic, determined process by which human society moves from one stage to another. Change requires not just some understanding or grasp of what ails a culture, but also a sense that something else is possible, that things do not have to stay as they are. There has to be a positive energy that says our efforts at changing the way the things are can really bear fruit. No one who lived through the election campaign for a new U.S. president in 2008 can forget the immense energies that were released as people sensed the possibility of a real shift in the leadership and direction of that society. There was a euphoric release of intense joy, excitement, and anxious anticipation as we sensed that something extraordinary could really happen. Obama referred to the *Audacity of Hope* as the title of one of his books.[9] And in this he named at least a part of what it takes to ignite a sense of hope—an unlikely, even outrageous feeling of possibility at making something happen against all odds. Of course, there is more to hope than only this. Hope seems to combine this sense of unlikely possibility with other things such as courage, imagination, faith, a sense of history, and the elusive quality called grace. Hope should not be confused with optimism, which is the disposition to *expect* things to turn out fine. The optimist sees good things around every corner. Walter Benjamin, the great cultural critic, understood this distinction when he noted that "hope is given for the sake of those who are without hope."[10] Benjamin was expressing his belief that hope is the unlikely quality that emerges when things seem most daunting and most obdurate. For Benjamin, one could not read off hope or possibility from the social situation that we face. There is a mysterious quality to hope; hope arises in those seemingly impossible situations as the will to transcend some horror or terrible situation in the belief that something else is really possible. This horror is not our inevitable fate. Who can fully grasp how slaves, living in a real-world nightmare, could believe that there was a river Jordan that would someday be crossed into a new world of freedom and dignity. Or how Jews in Auschwitz could celebrate Passover as the festival of freedom in which they told once again the story of how an all-powerful Pharaoh would be resisted and overcome. With war, violence, and abuse of both human beings and nature so pervasive in our world, can we really believe that a radical change is possible? Hope is the unlikely quality that allows us to believe that this suffering is not our necessary destiny or fate. Things can really be otherwise. A different kind of existence can come into being.

The question for us is can hope be taught? Can the feeling of possibility be nurtured and encouraged? My answer is a tentative yes. My personal experience, observation of change in the world, and my work as a teacher of social change encourages me to believe that there is a pedagogy of hope. And that certain things can nourish this quality. One of these is knowing something about history. Not in the dead and disconnected way we usually teach it in school, but as the living struggle by human beings, often against all odds, to win greater justice, freedom, or opportunity or to stop a war. When history is taught as the memory of these impossible struggles, students are opened to the recognition that people at other times struggled to make change when such change seemed entirely unlikely, when the forces arrayed against them made it seem as if change was a futile quest. In my pedagogy I attempt to make students see the "present as history"—to see our current struggles for social justice, an end to war, a world of fair trading, and a sustainable economy and climate as unlikely (or as likely) as other previous "impossible" quests.

One important way in which fatalism is overcome and hope is nourished is through active involvement in change movements and politics. We all have at our fingertips the extraordinary facility of the electronic web, which allows us, at the touch of a button, to connect to the myriad of global human efforts to change the direction of our society and world. Students can become aware of the extraordinary range of global networks, NGOs and civic and political associations that are engaged in human rights, social justice, environmental, and peace causes. I have seen how powerful the effect of young people "plugging in" and engaging with these movements of change is. Such engagement is life changing in the way it connects one individual to a whole community of like-minded others, nourishing a sense of community of resistance and hope. What seems futile when attempted by a lone individual becomes a worthwhile and hopeful existential act when joined to the efforts of thousands, or even millions, of others.

It is helpful when our education emphasizes the constructed nature of knowledge. In this sense we help breakdown the "tyranny of facts" that seems to make reality such an unmovable force. To see the way we know and understand the world is but one possibility among many that opens the door to questioning whose "reality" this is, and in whose interests it is for us to apprehend the world in this particular way. There is nothing fixed and unmovable about the world. We only need the imagination to reconceive it. Such thinking nourishes a sense of possibility among students. An invitation to see the world in new ways, a sense that history was about the struggles of men and women to change their world, plus active engagement in movements of social and environmental change can go a long way towards overcoming a sense of fatalism, cynicism, or apathy among young people and encouraging a powerful sense of hope.

There is one more thing I wish to add to this list—the elusive and mysterious quality we refer to as faith. Faith is neither rationally provable nor empirically verifiable. Yet who can deny its power in human efforts to change the world? When Martin Luther King stated that "the arc of history is long but it bends towards justice," he did not intended it as a scientific statement of fact. Yet it represented a powerful observation of the course of human history—a testimony of what could and indeed would happen. Each year when I read with family and friends the Passover saga about the liberation of the ancient Israelites from bondage in Egypt it matters little to me whether this story can be verified by archaeological exploration. It, too, is a narrative that reminds us about the powerful forces that we intuit are at work in the universe—forces that encourage and fortify us with the belief that our efforts belong to something much greater. Our work for peace and justice in the world connects us to something profound and enduring in the universe that began long before we appeared, and will continue into the unknowable future. It is here that education becomes concerned not just with knowledge, but with wisdom— the understanding that what we do matters far beyond our own small efforts. Faith is the hard-to-name place where meaning and action come together to provide our lives with deep and purposeful hope. Whether we call it religion, spirituality, or merely our wisdom traditions, I believe that a pedagogy of hope needs to place our individual presence in the world within the larger narrative or vision of transcending purpose and enduring resonance. Among other things, such a vision almost always promises us the possibility of renewal—that however bad the present is, we can be sure that this, too, will end and new horizons for human existence will open up.

10. *Sangha*

Finally, we must consider how it is possible to find harmony or peace after conflict and violence have produced their painful effects. Most commonly we talk about the need to forgive those who have hurt us. All the great spiritual traditions emphasize the importance of forgiveness as the way to move beyond the scars and unhappiness of human strife and conflict. While I believe in the great importance of forgiving those who have wounded us, I do not want to suggest in any way that this is something easily achieved. I do not think many of us, for example, are capable of fulfilling Jesus' admonition to "love one's enemy." This is probably a state beyond the ability of most of us. And certainly crimes are committed that seem to be so heinous that it may not be reasonable to expect victims to forgive the perpetrators. Nor may it be right for third parties to forgive those whose crimes they did not themselves suffer. Yet despite all of this, it seems that forgiveness is still an essential element in moving beyond the stored up pain and anger that produces the vicious cycle of hate and violence so often seen in our world. No one can fail to be moved by the extraordinary process of the Truth and Reconciliation Commission set up following the end of the apartheid regime in South Africa to help heal the wounds of so much injustice and suffering. The new leadership of that country decided that in order for the country to move forward on a peaceful path of change, there would have to be a process that could facilitate reconciliation through the freely expressed acknowledgment of the crimes that had been committed and then broad forgiveness for what had occurred. The alternative to this path, it seemed, would have been an endless process of retribution that would have deepened suspicions, fears, and hate in the country.

Although such attempts can, perhaps, be expected to heal only some of the wounds, they are, I believe, the only real alternative to an endless cycle of violence and conflict. In this I have been deeply influenced by the work of the Vietnamese Buddhist monk Thich Nhat Hanh, whose courageous ideas and practices are much celebrated around the world. For Hanh, it is important for past suffering and pain not to imprison us. We have to shed the illusion that our own suffering can be relieved by punishing and bringing suffering to others. Far from bringing any relief, attempts to pass on our pain to others only compounds the situation by inducing anger and suffering among those we punish, whose greatest wish is then to avenge their plight. Our anger and acts of retribution only spur the endless cycle of hate, fear, and rage, while we ourselves live lives distorted by the poison of hate that festers inside us. We produce a spiral of suffering with each side contributing to the deadly process. Anger exacerbates the pain and prolongs the conflict. Instead, Hanh proposes a process of healing through deep listening in which we try to hear the voice of suffering in the other—to hear the anguish, pain, fears, and anxieties that lay behind the anger. In doing this we not only change our perceptions of the other, but we also recognize in them the same human impulses and qualities that we ourselves have. He notes, "... our real enemies are not human beings—they are division, hatred, suspicion, anger, and despair. And as we recognize and identify them, we try to transform them and remove them from ourselves and others."[11] Indeed, as he suggests, the word "forgiveness" may not be appropriate, as we see that we all share these similar qualities and each of us is capable of both hurting and being hurt. We are engaged, instead, in a process of humanization and compassion for all those involved. Being open to others and listening deeply to their lives is a very difficult process that he believes cannot be done alone. It requires a community or *sangha* of compassionate listeners who can support and challenge one another in this process. In order, as he says, to become "an instrument of peace for ourselves, for our family, and for our society,"[12] we need the encouragement and support of others. Here, Thich Nhat Hanh talks about the conflict between Israel and Palestine[13]:

> Sometimes it is easier to be angry than to express your own suffering. The Israelis think they are not Arabs, but they are very similar to the Arabs. They are human beings. They don't want to die, and they want to live in safety. They want brotherhood, sisterhood and peace. We are separated by names like "Buddhist," "Christian," "Jew," "Muslim." When we hear one of these words, we see an image and we feel alienated, we don't feel connected. We have set up many structures in order to be separated from each other and make each other suffer. That is why it is very important to discover the human being in the other person, and to help the other person discover the human being in us.

Can we create in our classrooms the *sangha* or community that this spiritual and political activist advocates? It would mean making our classroom, at least for a while, a place where young people could speak of their fears, anxieties, pains, and suspicions, and the anger that often accompanies these things, and to do so in a setting of honesty, support, and encouragement. Such a space could then become a place where young people might learn to see beyond the divisions and distrust that permeate their lives as much as the rest of us. They could better understand how we all are capable of hurting and being hurt. How we all carry wounds to our sense of self. And how such wounds can fester into hatred, intolerance, and the desire to punish others. To see how the process of inflicting pain, violence, verbal abuse, harassment, and the bullying of others produces only an endless cycle of resentment, anger, and fear, but does little to bring the love or happiness that we all deeply crave in our lives. As I have suggested previously in this book, in order to address the culture of violence, harassment, and division that is so rampant in our schools, we may need to look far beyond the more usual language of "early warning signs" and weapons detectors to the *sangha* of communication, understanding, and compassionate awareness among young people.

Conclusions

Any attempt to transform schools in the direction outlined in the ten points above would undoubtedly meet fierce opposition. The notion that education should be a place for serious exploration of social injustice, the competitive culture, human exploitation and indignity, or an opportunity to develop hope and imagination for a world that is free from violence, nationalism, racism, and sexual oppression contradicts the prevailing and deeply entrenched ideas of education's role and purpose in society. The belief that the classroom can be a location for open and honest expression of students' fears, concerns, and anxieties about their lives and their world is certainly at odds with the current emphasis on what should be taught. And there is little opportunity to understand knowledge as something uncertain, provisional, and functioning in the interests of established interests. Even in this time of a relatively progressive new president, deep educational change will require a social movement that is thoughtful, imaginative, and courageous enough to demand such change. One question to answer is where will this movement come from? Certainly there are teachers out there who yearn for a new paradigm for educating kids away from this deadening regime of endless testing, and educational administrators who see the stultifying irrelevancy and unfairness of current policies and practices. There are parents who are aware of how little schooling seems to speak to the real challenges faced by their children in the twenty-first century. And there are many students who are dying from the sheer boredom and disconnection of the classroom who would want nothing more than an opportunity for their education to speak in meaningful ways to their lives. Somehow these disparate parties, and others who are clear about the immense human crises that now confront us, will have to find their voices to articulate the need for a new and very different vision for education. I am optimistic that such voices are emerging in these troubled times.

Even if these hopes can begin to be met, there is a need for some modesty in what education alone can achieve. Too often we are subjected to the expectation that education can provide a fix to all our problems, from changing the sexual behavior of young people to ensuring a far more equitable society. Certainly education can contribute to changing society and human behavior, but its role is a more limited one than is often thought. This is also the case with transforming violence in our society and in our world. No matter how effective our educational program is, it is unlikely to end the stored up rage of the lives whose hopes have been disrupted by loss of jobs and economic security or who feel deeply isolated and alienated from the changing culture around them. Nor can it do much to stop those who embrace violence as some kind of purifying political therapy or a religiously inspired redemptive act. Nor is likely to touch the individual whose paranoid fantasies produce a pathological desire to kill or hurt those who are identified as a threat. It is also unlikely to change individuals who are brought up in an environment of deep hate and intolerance for another because of a different skin color, ethnic identity, sexual orientation, or religion. Yet while we can acknowledge the likely limits of what we can achieve with our work as peace educators, none of this provides a reason to abandon such work. We can see the changes that have been brought about by greater consciousness and understanding in regard to a whole range of issues, from human rights to the environment and from global poverty to militarism. Despite all the obstacles, immense changes in human awareness are under way in regard to the unnecessary suffering, wasteful consumerism, environmental irresponsibility, and squandering of human energies and resources on wars in the world. And in this regard we must be aware of the extraordinary effect of new or more powerful modes of education now made possible through technology. These have allowed the dissemination of ideas and information on a scale, and in a popularly accessible format, undreamt of in previous times.

Profound change of the kind I have been talking about in this book demands a transformation across a whole spectrum of social institutions, values, and human practices of which education represents only one aspect. A culture of peace requires policies that ensure a far more socially just world. It requires changes in gender relations and the end of racism, anti-Semitism, and other forms of intolerance. It requires economies that work for the needs of people, not just the profits of big corporations. It requires institutions that encourage cooperation and support rather than competition and division, and a responsible relationship with nature. Yet in no sense does this infer that educational work is not a significant part of the struggle to bring about a culture of peace. As I pointed out earlier in this book, whatever the outcome of these efforts, we are ethically enjoined to add to, and participate in, these efforts. Without such a commitment, with all of its uncertainty, we would simply have abandoned our children to the current course of things in our nation and in our world. It would mean accepting the endless presence of nuclear weapons with their ability to destroy our world several times over. It would mean accepting war as the perennial answer to conflicts over land, resources, and cultural identity. It would mean acquiescing to the pervasive rape and violence against women in many countries. It would mean accepting the inevitability of violence and brutality against gays and lesbians. It would mean allowing the abuse, brutality, and bullying of children and their exploitation as child soldiers in many wars. It would mean passivity in the face of the slower violence of human degradation and poverty found among millions of exploited workers in our global economy. And it would mean allowing, unchallenged, the destruction of our natural home, the earth, as it is irresponsibly plundered for profit and the culture of unrestrained consumption.

However difficult the challenge is, however deep are the changes we seek, is there any morally acceptable alternative to this struggle for a more caring, harmonious, peaceful, and life-giving world? This is a moment in history when our destructive and irresponsible follies are perhaps clearer to us than ever before. And our possibilities as a species to create a world of joy, abundance, and community are more sharply apparent than ever before. It is a time, too, when we see many hopeful signs of global cooperation around issues of fighting disease, protecting our air and seas, limiting pollution and halting climate change, challenging human rights and labor abuses, ensuring gender equality, ending racism, and stopping genocide. For educators this is a time to question and challenge the tired preoccupations of our profession and demand a radically different purpose and vision for our work—a vision that seeks to connect what we do to the ancient quest for a world of peace, love, and justice. Many generations ago, the Hebrew prophet Isaiah envisaged a new and different world in which, he proclaimed, *they will hammer their swords into plowshares and their spears into pruning hooks. Nation shall not lift up sword against nation. Never again will they learn war.* This call remains unfulfilled, even while the number of those who suffer grows larger and even more are threatened. It may be unrealistic at this time to think that we can finally and fully respond to the challenge. We may, however, choose to be among those whose efforts can be counted to move things along, at least in a small way—to add our energies, however modest, to the great and pressing challenge we face as a human race. As Rabbi Abraham Heschel noted, "While we may not complete the task, neither are we free from the obligation to participate in it."

Nor should we forget that the struggle for a less violent world is one that joins our inner changes as human beings to changes in the external world. We cannot separate our struggles for a more peaceful world from the struggles within each of us to be more compassionate, gentle, and forgiving individuals, less driven by our ego needs for more things, power, or recognition than others. It is too easy to focus only on the larger social and political issues, forgetting that we ourselves (as Gandhi famously reminded us) must embody the change we seek in the world. There is reason for hope here, too. There is, I believe, a growing sense that social change must go hand in hand with a spiritual change. No longer can we believe that the world will change without us ourselves, in the deepest aspects of our being, changing along with it. Although this suggests that change, real change, is even more difficult to achieve, it also means that we need not depend on others to begin the process. As the Buddhist teacher likes to quip, wherever you are, you are already there. Change can and should begin with each of us right now. Let's not wait any longer to start the process!

Appendix: Peace Organizations

AMERICANS FOR PEACE NOW (APN) was founded in 1981 to support the activities of Shalom Achshav (Peace Now in Israel). The leading U.S. advocate for peace in the Middle East, APN's mission is to help Israel and the Shalom Achshav movement to achieve a comprehensive political settlement of the Arab-Israeli conflict consistent with Israel's long-term security needs and its Jewish and democratic values. APN has a wide array of educational programs that reach out to communities around the country, and is a powerful force for mobilizing grassroots support among U.S. citizens. By demonstrating this support, and by working directly with decision makers and government officials, APN promotes U.S. policies that further the peace process.
U.S. contact: 1101 14th Street NW, Sixth Floor, Washington, DC 20005
Tel: 202-728-1893
Fax: 202-728-1895
Email: apndc@peacenow.org
Website: http://www.peacenow.org

The AMERICAN FRIENDS SERVICE COMMITTEE (AFSC) carries out service, development, social justice, and peace programs throughout the world. Founded by Quakers in 1917 to provide conscientious objectors with an opportunity to aid civilian war victims, AFSC's work attracts the support and partnership of people of many races, religions, and cultures.
U.S. contact: 1501 Cherry Street, Philadelphia, PA 19102
Tel: 215-241-7000
Fax: 215-241-7275
Website: http://www.afsc.org/

BUDDHIST PEACE FELLOWSHIP (BPF) offers open-hearted engagement with the world expressed through expanding programs in the United States and Asia. Through BPF, Buddhists of many different traditions develop individual and group responses to socially conditioned suffering. Through its worldwide network of members, BPF strives to bring peace where there is conflict, to promote communication and cooperation among Buddhist sanghas, and to alleviate suffering wherever possible.

U.S. contact: PO Box 3470, Berkeley, CA 94703
Tel: 510-655-6169
Website: http://www.bpf.org/html/home.html

The CARTER CENTER PEACE PROGRAMS strengthen freedom and democracy in nations worldwide, securing for people the political and civil rights that are the foundation of just and peaceful societies. Amid the trend toward greater democracy, the Carter Center has become a pioneer in the field of election observation. Beyond elections, the Center seeks to deepen democracy by nurturing full citizen participation in public policy making and by helping to establish government institutions that bolster the rule of law, fair administration of justice, access to information, and government transparency. The Center supports the efforts of human rights activists at the grassroots level, while also working to advance national and international human rights laws that uphold the dignity and worth of each individual. The Center offers mediation expertise and has furthered avenues for peace in Africa, the Middle East, Latin America, and Asia.

Contact: One Copenhill, 453 Freedom Parkway, Atlanta, GA 30307
Tel: 404-420-5100 or 800-550-3560
E-mail: carterweb@emory.edu
Website: http://cartercenter.org/peace/index.html

CHRISTIAN PEACEMAKER TEAMS (CPT) arose from a call in 1984 for Christians to devote the same discipline and self-sacrifice to nonviolent peacemaking that armies devote to war. Enlisting the whole church in an organized, nonviolent alternative to war, CPT places violence-reduction teams in crisis situations and militarized areas around the world at the invitation of local peace and human rights workers. CPT embraces the vision of unarmed intervention waged by committed peacemakers ready to risk injury and death in bold attempts to transform lethal conflict through the nonviolent power of God's truth and love. Initiated by Mennonites, Brethren, and Quakers with broad ecumenical participation, CPT's ministry of biblically based and spiritually centered peacemaking emphasizes creative public witness, nonviolent direct action, and protection of human rights.

U.S. contact: PO Box 6508, Chicago, IL 60680-6508
Tel: 773-277-0253
Fax: 773-277-0291
Email: peacemakers@cpt.org
Website: http://www.cpt.org/

CONSCIENCE AND PEACE TAX INTERNATIONAL (CPTI) was founded in Hondarribia, Spain, on September 17, 1994. Incorporated as an international nonprofit association in Belgium, CPTI was granted "special consultative status" with the Economic and Social Council (ECOSOC) of the United Nations in July 1999. The aim of the association is to obtain recognition of the right to conscientious objection to paying for armaments and war preparation and war conduct through taxes. In furtherance of these objects the association lobbies international organizations, publicizes efforts to obtain recognition of the right to conscientious objection, and facilitates coordination of similar activities of national movements at the international level. While CPTI is not an umbrella organization of all War Tax Resistance and Peace Tax Campaigns (WTR-PTCs), it complements the work of the many national and regional campaigns.

Email: cpti@cpti.ws
Website: http://www.cpti.ws/index.html

EUROPEAN NETWORK OF CIVIL PEACE SERVICES (EN-CPS) is an international network of NGOs with the common goal of promoting Civil Peace Services (CPS) as an instrument of nonviolent conflict transformation, both on a national level as well as within Europe. It does this through a multinational cooperation of organizations carrying out research, information sharing and dissemination, lobbying (national and European institutions), and awareness raising activities as well as the recruitment, training, and deployment of qualified civilian professionals/volunteers. The network is run through voluntary contributions of participating organizations.

Email: contact@en-cps.org
Website: http://www.en-cps.org/Home

FRONT LINE is the International Foundation for the Protection of Human Rights Defenders. Founded in Dublin in 2001 with the specific aim of protecting people who work, nonviolently, for any or all of the rights enshrined in the Universal Declaration of Human Rights (UDHR), Front Line aims to address some of the needs identified by defenders themselves, including protection, networking, training, and access to international bodies that can take action on their behalf. Front Line seeks to provide rapid and practical support to at-risk human rights defenders, runs a small grants program to provide for the security needs of defenders, mobilizes campaigning and lobbying on behalf of defenders at immediate risk, and conducts research and publishes reports on the situation of human rights defenders in specific countries. Front Line seeks to promote respect for the UN Declaration on Human Rights Defenders. Front Line has Special Consultative Status with the Economic and Social Council of the United Nations.

Contact: Front Line, Main Street, Blackrock Co., Dublin, Ireland
Tel: +353-(0)1-212-3750
Fax: +353-(0)1-212-1001
Email: info@frontlinedefenders.org
Website: http://www.frontlinedefenders.org/

INTERNATIONAL FELLOWSHIP OF RECONCILIATION (IFOR) was founded in 1919 in response to the horrors of war in Europe. IFOR has taken a consistent stance against war and its preparation throughout its history. The founders of IFOR formulated a vision of the human community based upon the belief that love in action has the power to transform unjust political, social, and economic structures. Today IFOR has 82 branches, groups, and affiliates in 48 countries on all continents. Although organized on a national and regional basis, IFOR seeks to overcome the division of nation states, which are often the source of conflict and violence. Its membership includes adherents of all the major spiritual traditions as well as those who have other spiritual sources for their commitment to nonviolence.

Netherlands contact: Spoorstraat 38, 1815 BK Alkmaar, The Netherlands/Pays-Bas
Tel: +31-(0)72-512-3014
Fax: +31-(0)72-515-1102
U.S. email: for@forusa.org
Website: http://www.ifor.org/index.html

INTERNATIONAL PEACE BUREAU (IPB) is the world's oldest and most comprehensive international peace network with 188 member organizations in 53 countries. IPB acts as a clearing house for information, links peace activists across borders, has consultative status with the United Nations, and organizes meetings, conferences, and events. The International Peace Bureau is dedicated to the vision of a world without war. It is a Nobel Peace Laureate (1910); over the years, 13 of its officers have been recipients of the Nobel Peace Prize. It is funded by the the Catalan Agency for Development Cooperation (ACCD), Risso Kosei-Kai (Japanese Buddhist Organisation), Ministry of Foreign Affairs of Norway, Allan and Nesta Ferguson Trust (UK).

Contact: International Peace Bureau, 41 rue de Zurich, 1201 Geneva, Switzerland
Email: mailbox@ipb.org
Website: http://www.ipb.org

The INTERNATIONAL PEACE INSTITUTE (IPI) is an independent institution dedicated to promoting the prevention and settlement of armed conflict between and within states through policy research and development. Since its establishment in 1970, the International Peace Institute (IPI) (formerly International Peace Academy) has become a leading policy and research institution specializing in multilateral approaches to peace and security issues, working closely with the Secretariat and membership of the United Nations. IPI's primary objective is to promote effective international responses to new and emerging issues and crises through research, analysis, and policy development. Its research spans regional and thematic issues and strives to provide thoughtful analysis and insight for international policymakers, practitioners, and the broader research community.

Contact: International Peace Institute (IPI, formerly International Peace Academy), 777 United Nations Plaza, New York, NY 10017-3521
Tel: 212-687-4300
Fax: 212-983-8246
Email: ipi@ipinst.org
Website: http://www.ipinst.org

NATIONAL PEACE FOUNDATION is a nongovernmental membership organization concerned with the development and implementation of conflict resoluation education and training in the United States, and with peace- and democracy-building internationally. They work where the institutions of civil society (such as health, justice, education, safety) have failed or are no longer effective, and empower local citizens to improve their situation and reduce conflict. Projects around the world support grassroots efforts that provide access to networks of experts, related citizen groups in other countries, and the technical tools needed to establish, operate, and sustain citizen-led initiatives.

U.S. contact: 1100 G Street NW, Suite 202, Washington, DC 20005–3806
Tel: 202–783–7030
Fax: 202–783–7040
Email: npf@nationalpeace.org
Website: http://www.nationalpeace.org/

NETWORK OF SPIRITUAL PROGRESSIVES is a community that advocates for a new bottom line—institutions and social practices should be judged rational, efficient, and productive not only to the extent that they maximize money and power, but also to the extent that they maximize love and caring, ethical and ecological sensitivity and behavior, kindness and generosity, non-violence, and peace. Central to its mission is the Global Marshall Plan, which calls for the United States to donate 1–2 percent of its gross domestic product each year for the next 20 to end domestic and global poverty, and to repair the global environment.
Contact: Tikkun, 2342 Shattuck Avenue, Berkeley, CA 94704–9914
Tel: 510–644–1200
Website: http:/www.spiritualprogressives.org

PATHWAYS TO PEACE (PTP) is an international peacebuilding, educational, and consulting organization. "Peace," as it is defined by Pathways to Peace, is both an innate state of being and a dynamic, evolutionary process. Envisioned in 1945, Pathways to Peace initiated research and development in integrative decision making in 1962 and began its consulting in the early 1970s. Pathways to Peace has consultative status with the UN Economic and Social Council and works with the UN Centre for Human Rights, UN Centre for Human Settlements, UNESCO, UNICEF, and other agencies.
U.S. contact: PO Box 1057, Larkspur, CA 94977
Tel: 415–461–0500
Fax: 415–925–0330
E-mail: info@pathwaystopeace.org
Website: http://www.pathwaystopeace.org/index.html

PEACE BOAT is "a floating village" onboard a passenger vessel on which people worldwide gather to discuss global issues such as peace, human rights, the environment, and sustainable development. Peace Boat is a Japan-based international nongovernmental and nonprofit organization that works to promote peace, human rights, equal and sustainable development, and respect for the environment through the organization of global educational programs, responsible travel, cooperative projects, and advocacy activities. These activities are carried out on a partnership basis with other civil society organizations and communities in Japan, Northeast Asia, and around the world.

Contact: B1, 3-13-1 Takadanobaba, Shinjuku, Tokyo 169-0075, Japan
Tel: 03-3363-8047
Fax: 03-3363-7562
Email: pbglobal@peaceboat.gr.jp
Website: http://www.peaceboat.org/english/index.html

PHYSICIANS FOR SOCIAL RESPONSIBILITY (PSR) is a nonprofit advocacy organization that is the medical and public health voice for policies to stop nuclear war and proliferation and to slow, stop, and reverse global warming and toxic degradation of the environment. Founded in 1961, PSR led the campaign to end atmospheric nuclear testing; PSR's work to educate the public about the dangers of nuclear war grew into an international movement with the founding of International Physicians for the Prevention of Nuclear War (IPPNW). In 1985, PSR shared the Nobel Peace Price awarded to IPPNW for building public awareness and pressure to end the nuclear arms race.

Contact: Physicians for Social Responsibility, 1875 Connecticut Avenue NW, Suite 1012, Washington, DC 20009
Tel: 202-667-4260
Fax: 202-667-4201
Email: psrnatl@psr.org
Website: http://www.psr.org

SEEDS OF PEACE works to empower leaders of the next generation. Treaties are negotiated by governments. Peace is made by people. Seeds of Peace is doing what no government can. It is sowing the seeds of peace among the next generation of leaders, educating them to develop empathy, respect, and confidence; equipping them with communication and negotiation skills; and enabling them to see the human face of their enemies. By empowering them to emerge as tomorrow's leaders, Seeds of Peace is working to forge the personal relationships so critical to peacemaking and reconciliation.

U.S. contact: Seeds of Peace, 370 Lexington Avenue, Suite 401, New York, NY 10017
Tel: 212-573-8040
Fax: 212-573-8047
Email: info@seedsofpeace.org
Website: http://www.seedsofpeace.org/

Appendix

SERVAS is an international, nongovernmental, multicultural peace association run by volunteers in over 100 countries. Founded in 1949 as a peace movement, Servas International is a nonprofit organization working to build understanding, tolerance, and world peace. They operate through a network of Servas hosts around the world who are interested in opening their doors to travellers, and of Servas travellers who want to get to know the heart of the countries they visit. Servas International has consultative status as a nongovernmental organization with the UN Economic and Social Council, with representation at many of the UN's hubs of activity.

U.S. contact: 1125 16th Street, Suite 201, Arcata, CA 95521-5585
Tel: 707-825-1714
Fax: 707-825-1762
Email: info@usservas.org
Website: http://joomla.servas.org/

STUDENT PEACE ACTION NETWORK is a grassroots peace and justice organization working from schools across the United States. They organize for an end to the physical, social, and economic violence caused by U.S. militarism. They campaign for nuclear abolition, disarmament, and an end to weapons trafficking. They oppose the complex webs of corporate and military power that perpetuate racism, damage the environment, deprive people of basic needs, and violate human rights.

Contact: Peace Action National Office, 1100 Wayne Avenue, Suite 1020, Silver Spring, MD 20910
Tel: 301-565-4050 ext. 322 or 1-800-228-1228
Fax: 301-565-0850
Email: SPAN@peace-action.org
Webmail: http://www.studentpeaceaction.org

The UNION OF CONCERNED SCIENTISTS (UCS) is the leading science-based nonprofit working for a healthy environment and a safer world. UCS combines independent scientific research and citizen action to develop innovative, practical solutions and to secure responsible changes in government policy, corporate practices, and consumer choices. Established in 1969, they seek to ensure that all people have clean air, energy, and transportation, as well as food that is produced in a safe and sustainable manner. They strive for a future free from the threats of global warming and nuclear war, and a planet that supports a rich diversity of life. Sound science guides their efforts to secure changes in government policy, corporate practices, and consumer choices that will protect and improve the health of our environment globally, nationally, and in communities throughout the United States.

Contact: National Headquarters, Two Brattle Sq., Cambridge, MA 02238–9105
Tel: 617–547–5552
Fax: 617–864–9405
Website: http://www.ucsusa.org/

UNITED FOR PEACE AND JUSTICE is a coalition of more than 1,400 local and national groups throughout the United States who have joined together to protest the immoral and disastrous Iraq War and oppose our government's policy of permanent warfare and empire building.

Contact: PO Box 607, Times Square Station, New York, NY 10108
Tel: 212–868–5545
Fax: 646–723–0996
Website: http://www.unitedforpeace.org/

The WAR RESISTERS LEAGUE is the United States' oldest secular pacifist organization, resisting war at home and war abroad since 1923. As one of the leading radical voices in the antiwar movement, it challenges military recruitment, organizes and trains for nonviolent direct action, and offers on-the-ground education. It organizes demonstrations, cooperates in coalition with other peace and justice groups, opposes military recruitment and all forms of militarism including war toys and ROTC, and supports men and women who resist the military at all levels. A major part of all its programs is to help people organize in their own communities, where real change begins. Its staff and members offer nonviolence and direct action training in civil disobedience, war tax resistance, and other ways to put revolutionary nonviolence into action.

The War Resisters League has strong international ties through its active membership in War Resisters' International, an organization with affiliates in over 80 countries.

Contact: War Resisters League, 339 Lafayette Street, New York, NY 10012
Tel: 212–228–0450
Fax: 212–228–6193
Email: wrl@warresisters.org
Website: www.warresisters.org

WOMEN IN BLACK (WiB) is a worldwide network of women committed to peace with justice and actively opposed to injustice, war, militarism, and other forms of violence. An important focus is challenging the militarist policies of their own governments. They are not an organization, but a means of communicating and a formula for action. Any group of women anywhere in the world at any time may organize a WiB vigil against any manifestation of violence, militarism, or war. WiB actions generally include women only. Actions often take the form of women wearing black, standing in a public place in silent, nonviolent vigils at regular times and intervals, carrying placards, and handing out leaflets.

Website: http://www.womeninblack.org

The WOMEN'S INTERNATIONAL LEAGUE FOR PEACE AND FREEDOM (WILPF) is an international NGO covering all continents with an international secretariat based in Geneva and a New York office focused on the work of the United Nations. Since its establishment in 1915, WILPF has brought together women from around the world to work for peace by nonviolent means, promoting political, economic, and social justice for all.

Contact: WILPF, 1, rue de Varembé, Case Postale 28, 1211 Geneva 20, Switzerland
Tel: +41–22–919–7080
Fax: +41–22–919–7081
Email: inforequest@wilpf.ch
Website: http://www.wilpf.int.ch/index.htm

WORLD CONFERENCE ON RELIGIONS AND PEACE (WCRP) is the largest international coalition of representatives from the world's great religions dedicated to promoting peace and addressing critical problems in areas such as conflict resolution, human rights, and development. Religions for Peace is active in more than 70 countries, working with national affiliates and regional organizations to find and implement local solutions to local challenges.

U.S. contact: 777 United Nations Plaza, New York, NY 10017
Tel: 212–687–2163
Fax: 212–983–0566
Email: info@wcrp.org
Website: http://www.wcrp.org/

THE WORLD FEDERALIST NATIONAL ASSOCIATION OF NEPAL (WOFNAN) is dedicated to the realization of global justice, peace, and sustainable prosperity through the development of democratic international institutions and the global application of international law. WOFNAN's vision is of a world in which people have a sense of citizenship beyond national borders, to include their region and the global community. Founded shortly after the creation of the United Nations in the Swiss city of Montreux as an international peace movement, WFM is an international nongovernmental organization with UN consultative status. A committed network of 28 member organizations and individual members in more than 80 countries is coordinated by WOFNAN's International Secretariat, co-located in The Hague and New York. WFM works with and helps to develop international civil society networks,and partners with like-minded governments and international organizations.

U.S. contact: 708 Third Avenue, 24th Floor, New York, NY 10017
Tel: 212-599-1320
Fax: 212-599-1332
Email: info@wfm-igp.org
Website: http://www.wfm-igp.org/site/

NOTES

CHAPTER 1   GIVING PEACE A CHANCE

1. Jonathan Sacks, *The Politics of Hope* (London: Vintage, 2000), 29–30.
2. Michael Apple, *Educating the 'Right Way'* (New York: Routledge, 2006).
3. Alfie Kohn, *What Does It Mean to Be Well Educated?* (Boston: Beacon, 2004).
4. Henry Giroux, *The University in Chains* (Boulder, CO: Paradigm, 2007).
5. Svi Shapiro, *Losing Heart* (Mahwah, NJ: Lawrence Erlbaum, 2006).
6. G. Salamon and B. Nevo (eds.), *Peace Education* (Mahwah, NJ: Lawrence Erlbaum, 2002).
7. Sacks, *The Politics of Hope*, 163.
8. Michael Sandel, *Democracy's Discontent* (Cambridge, MA: Harvard University Press, 1996), 25–26.
9. Michael Sandel, *Liberalism and the Limits of Justice* (Cambridge: Cambridge University Press, 1982), 179.
10. Abraham Joshua Heschel, *The Prophets* (New York: HarperCollins, 2001).
11. Sacks, *The Politics of Hope*, 64.
12. "Child Soldiers Around the World," *Council on Foreign Relations* (Dec. 2, 2005). (www.cfr.org/publication/9331).
13. "Stop Violence Against Women," *Advocates for Human Rights* (Feb. 1, 2006). (www.stopvaw.org).
14. "Death by Mass Unpleasantness: Estimated Totals for the Entire 20th Century," from *20th Century Atlas* (Sept. 2005). (www.erols.com/mwhite28/warstat8.htm).
15. Michael Walzer, *Exodus and Revolution* (New York: Basic Books, 1985).

CHAPTER 2   TRUTH AND VIOLENCE

1. Patrick O'Neil, "New Evangelicals Search for Faith, Not Lip Service," *Independent Weekly* (Aug. 6, 2008), 15.

2. Daniel Gilbert, *Stumbling on Happiness* (New York: Vintage Books, 2006), 98.
3. Olivia Johnson, "Optimism in Evolution," *New York Times* (Aug. 13, 2008), A23.
4. A good review of these philosophical outlooks can be found in Richard Bernstein, *Beyond Objectivism and Relativism: Science, Hermeneutics and Praxis.* (Philadelphia: University of Pennsylvania, 1983).
5. For an excellent and sympathetic account of these conflicting narratives see Michael Lerner, *Healing Israel/Palestine* (Berkeley, CA: North Atlantic Books, 2003).
6. Amin Maalouf, *In the Name of Identity.* (New York: Penguin Books, 2000), 75.
7. Grace Feuerverger, *Oasis of Dreams.* (New York: Routledge and Falmer, 2001).
8. Ibid., 138.
9. Thich Nhat Hanh, *Peace Begins Here* (Berkeley, CA: Parallax Press, 2004), 104.
10. Thich Nhat Hanh, *Anger* (New York: Riverhead Books, 2001), 35.

CHAPTER 3   UNDOING THE NARRATIVE OF COMPETITION

1. *The Corporation.* A film by Mark Achbar, Jennifer Abbott, and Joel Bakan (Big Picture Media Corporation, 2003).
2. Naomi Klein, *The Shock Doctrine: The Rise of Disaster Capitalism* (New York: Picador, 2008).
3. David Korten, *The Great Turning* (San Francisco: Berrett-Koehler, 2006), 181.
4. Riane Eisler, *The Real Wealth of Nations.* (San Francisco: Berret-Koehler, 2007), 131.
5. Korten, *The Great Turning*, 181.
6. Greg Smith, *Erving Goffman* (New York: Taylor and Francis, 2006).
7. Peter Gabel, *The Bank Teller* (San Francisco: Acada Books, 2000).
8. Svi Shapiro, *Losing Heart: The Moral and Spiritual Miseducation of America's Children* (New Jersey: Lawrence Erlbaum, 2005).
9. Elizabeth Dodson Grey, "The Culture of Separated Desks," Carol Pearson et al., eds., *Educating the Majority: Women Challenge Tradition in Higher Education* (Washington, DC: American Council on Education, 1989).
10. Zygmunt Bauman, *Postmodernity and Its Discontents* (New York: University Press, 1997).
11. Christopher Lasch, *Haven in a Heartless World* (New York: W.W. Norton, 1995).
12. Eisler, *The Real Wealth of Nations*, 188.
13. Ibid.

14. See, for example, Riane Eisler, *The Chalice and the Blade* (New York: HarperCollins, 1988).

CHAPTER 4   JUSTICE THEN PEACE

1. This information was found in the essay by Orlando Patterson, "The New Mainstream," *Newsweek* (Nov. 10, 2008), 41.
2. Karl Marx, *The Communist Manifesto* (London: Filiquarian Books, 2007), 21
3. In Abraham Heschel, *The Prophets* (New York: The Jewish Publication Society of America, 1962), 3.
4. This great account of the rise of modernity is found in Eric Hobsbawm, *The Age of Revolution 1789–1848* (New York: Vintage Books, 1996).
5. The list of those whose writing touches on the issue of the internalization of oppression is a long one and includes Paulo Freire, Bell Hooks, Franz Fanon, Michael Lerner, Eric Fromm, Richard Lichtman, Douglas Kellner, Henry Giroux, and Terry Eagleton, among many others.
6. R. Wilkinson and K. Pickett, *The Spirit Level* (London: Allen Lane, 2009).
7. Lesley Gill, *The School of the Americas: Military Training and Political Violence in the Americas* (Durham, NC: Duke University Press, 2004).
8. Peggy McIntosh, "White Privilege: Unpacking the Invisible Knapsack," H. Svi Shapiro, et al. eds. *The Institution of Education* (Boston; Pearson Publishing, 2006).
9. David E. Purpel and William McLaurin, *Reflections on the Moral and Spiritual Crisis in Education* (New York: Peter Lang, 2004).
10. See, for example, the work of Henry Giroux, Jean Anyon, Peter McLaren, Sonia Nieto, or Michael Apple.
11. Alison Lurie, "The Messsage of the Schoolroom," *The New York Review of Books* 4(2008) :31
12. Jonathan Kozol, *Savage Inequalities* (New York: Harper Perennial, 1991).
13. Joseph E. Stiglitz, *Globalization and Its Discontents* (New York: W.W. Norton, 2003).
14. In this section I draw on the excellent work by Amy Chua, *World on Fire* (New York: Anchor Books, 2004).
15. Ibid., 166.
16. Vandana Shiva, *Earth Democracy* (Cambridge MA: South End Press, 2008).
17. USDA Annual Report on Food Security (Washington, DC, Nov., 2008).
18. Letter from *Oxfam America* (Oct. 2005).
19. Jeff Faux, *The Global Class War* (Hoboken, NJ: John Wiley and Sons, 2006).
20. Mike Davis, *Planet of Slums* (London: Verso, 2007).

Chapter 5   The Violence of Invisibility

1. Allister Sparks, *Tomorrow Is Another Country* (South Africa: Struik Publishing, 1994), 47.
2. Ibid., 227.
3. Emmanuel Levinas, *Humanism of the Other* (Urbana: University of Illinois, 2006).
4. Terry Eagleton, *The Ideology of the Aesthetic* (Oxford: Blackwell, 2000).
5. Zygmunt Bauman, *Work, Consumerism, and the New Poor* (Buckingham, UK:Open University Press, 1998).
6. Edward Said, *Orientalism* (New York: Vintage, 1979).
7. Joe L. Kincheloe and Shirley Steinberg, *The Miseducation of the West* (Westport, CT: Praeger, 2004).
8. See, for example, Bernard Lewis, *The Crisis of Islam: Holy War and Unholy Terror* (New York: Random House, 2004).
9. For an interesting, if fictional, account depicting this history, see Geraldine Brooks, *People of the Book* (New York: Viking, 2008).
10. See, for example, Joel Spring, *American Education* (New York: McGraw-Hill, 2004).
11. For a powerful depiction of this, see *It's Free World*, a movie directed by Ken Loach (2007).
12. See, for example, Mike Davis, *Planet of Slums* (New York: Verso, 2006); also Arundhati Roy, *An Ordinary Person's Guide to Empire* (Cambridge, MA: South End Press, 2004).
13. Zygmunt Bauman, *Globalization* (New York: Columbia University Press, 1998).
14. United Nations Development Fund for Women website, 2009.
15. See, for example, Ariel Levy, *Female Chauvinist Pigs: Women and the Rise of Raunch Culture* (New York: Free Press, 2005); also Jean Kilbourne, *Can't Buy Me Love* (New York: Touchstone, 1999).
16. Barbara Ehrenreich and Arlie Hochschild, *Global Women: Nannies, Maids, and Sex Workers in the New Economy* (New York: Henry Holt, 2002).
17. Zygmunt Bauman, *Postmodernity and Its Discontents* (Cambridge: Polity Press, 1997); also Bauman, *Modernity and the Holocaust* (Ithaca, NY: Cornell University Press, 1998).
18. See Eugene Jarecki, *The American Way of War* (New York: Free Press, 2008).
19. See, for example, H. Svi Shapiro, *Losing Heart: The Moral and Spiritual Miseducation of America's Children* (Mahwah, NJ: Lawrence Erlbaum, 2006).
20. Jacob Hacker, *The Great Risk Shift: The New Economic Insecurity and the Decline of the American Dream* (New York: Oxford University Press, 2006).
21. David Korten, *The Great Turning* (San Francisco: BK Publishers, 2006); also Vandana Shiva, *Earth Democracy* (Boston, MA: South End Press, 2006).

NOTES   223

22. David Purpel and William McLaurin, *Reflections on the Moral and Spiritual Crisis in Education* (New York: Peter Lang, 2004).
23. Nel Noddings, *Caring: A Feminine Approach to Ethics and Moral Education* (Berkeley CA: University of California Press, 2003); also J. R. Martin, *Cultural Miseducation* (New York: Teachers College Press, 2002).

CHAPTER 6   VIOLENCE AND THE CRISIS OF MEANING

1. Maxine Greene, *Dialectic of Freedom* (New York: Teachers College Press, 1988).
2. Michael Lerner, *The Left Hand of God* (San Francisco: HarperCollins, 2006).
3. Ibid., 43.
4. Benedict Anderson, *Imagined Communities* (New York: W.W. Norton, 2006).
5. Jurgen Habermas, *Legitimation Crisis* (Boston: Beacon, 1975).
6. Benjamin R. Barber, *Jihad vs. McWorld* (New York: Ballantine Books, 1996).
7. Ibid., 78.
8. Ibid., 83.
9. Ibid., 85.
10. Ibid., 157.
11. Robert Jay Lifton, *Super Power Syndrome* (New York: Thunder's Mouth Press/Nation Books, 2003).
12. Ibid., 129.
13. Ibid., 125.
14. In the following pages I drew liberally from the wonderful book by John De Graaf, David Wann, and Thomas H. Naylor, *Affluenza* (San Francisco: BK Publishers, 2005).
15. Juliet Schor, *The Overspent American* (New York: Basic Books, 1998).
16. Schor, quoted in De Graaf et al., 29.
17. De Graaf, *Affluenza*, 36.
18. Erich Fromm, *To Have or To Be* (New York: Continuum, 2005).
19. De Graaf, *Affluenza*, 80.
20. Zygmunt Bauman, *Liquid Times* (Cambridge: Polity Press, 2007).
21. De Graaf, *Affluenza*, 55.
22. Chris Hedges, *War Is a Force That Gives Us Meaning* (New York: PublicAffairs, 2002).
23. Ibid., 15.
24. Ibid., 10.

CHAPTER 7   CRITICAL CITIZENSHIP

1. Eugene Jarecki, *The American Way of War* (New York: Free Press, 2008).

2. Dexter Filkins, *The Forever War* (New York: Alfred Knopf, 2008).
3. Jeremy Scahill, *Blackwater: The Rise of the World's Most Powerful Mercenary Army* (New York: Nation Books, 2007).
4. Linda J. Bilmes and Joseph E. Stiglitz, *The Three Trillion Dollar War* (New York: W.W. Norton, 2008); Rajiv Chandrasekaran, *Imperial Life in the Emerald City* (New York: Vintage, 2007); Farnaz Fassihi, *Waiting for an Ordinary Day: The Unraveling of Life in Iraq* (New York: Public Affairs, 2008); Peter W. Galbraith, *The End of Iraq* (New York: Simon and Schuster, 2006).
5. Michael Isikoff and David Corn, *Hubris: The Inside Story of Spin, Scandal, and the Selling of the Iraq War* (New York: Crown, 2006); Bob Woodward, *The War Within: A Secret White House History, 2002–2006* (New York: Simon and Schuster, 2008); M. Rai and N. Chomsky, *War Plan Iraq* (New York and London: Verso, 2002).
6. Chalmers Johnson, *The Sorrows of Empire* (New York: Henry Holt, 2005); also Chalmers Johnson, *Nemesis* (New York: Henry Holt, 2006).
7. Hannah Arendt and Amos Elon, *Eichmann in Jerusalem* (New York: Penguin Classics, 2006).
8. Andrew Bacevich, *The New American Militarism* (New York: Oxford University Press, 2005).
9. I mention here only a few of the individuals who have contributed to the development of a critical pedagogy. This field, and its allied feminist pedagogy, continues to be a rich and vibrant area of thought and practice with many creative minds continually adding theoretical and practical insights.
10. Critical analysis of popular culture has experienced an extraordinary growth since the early work of scholars like Raymond Williams, and later the pioneering work of the Centre for Contemporary Cultural Studies in the United Kingdom. In North America, some of the most well-known contributors include Bell Hooks, Henry Giroux, Lawrence Grossberg and Douglas Kellner, Stewart Ewans, Susan Bordo, Laura Kipnis, and Barbara Ehrenreich.
11. The concept of cultural hegemony is most associated with the Italian Marxist theorist Antonio Gramsci. It was he who elaborated the important distinction between societies in which class rule is maintained through direct coercion and those in which subordinate groups continue to support unequal and exploitative social relations through their being inculcated with beliefs that ensure a degree of conformity and consensus in the culture. In the latter process, popular culture and education play a crucial role in ensuring a broad consensus around social values and beliefs.
12. See, for example, Maxine Greene, *Dialectic of Freedom* (New York: Teachers College Press, 1988).
13. David E. Purpel, *Reflections on the Moral and Spiritual Crisis of Education* (New York: Peter Lang, 2004).

14. See the work of commentators like Angela McRobbie, Stuart Hall, Henry Giroux, and Dick Hebdige.
15. See Riane Eisler, *The Chalice and the Blade* (New York: Harper Collins, 1988).
16. Riane Eisler, *The Real Wealthy of Nations* (San Francisco: Berrett-Koehler, 2007).
17. Danny Schechter, *Embedded: Weapons of Mass Deception* (New York: Prometheus, 2003).
18. See the work of authors like Noam Chomsky, Rashid Khalidi, Chalmers Johnson, Gregg Grandin, Philip S. Foner, and John Bellamy Foster.
19. Howard Zinn, *A People's History of the United States, 1492-Present* (New York: Harper Perennial, 2005); James W. Loewen, *Lies My Teacher Told Me* (New York: Touchstone, 1995).
20. Richard Hofstadter, quoted in "Terror on the Streets of New York, Take One," *Newsweek* (Feb. 16, 2009): 40.
21. John Berger, *The Shape of a Pocket* (New York: Vintage, 2001), 210.
22. Report in the *Bulletin of the Atomic Scientists* (Chicago: Nov. 14, 2007).
23. National Priorities Project (Feb. 18, 2009) (http://www.nationalpriorities.org).
24. Robert Scheer, "Why Obama Doesn't Get Full Marks," *The Weekender* (Feb.28—Mar. 1, 2009): 10.
25. Johnson, *The Sorrows of Empire*, 154.
26. Ibid., 62.
27. Chalmers Johnson, *Nemesis* (New York: Henry Holt, 2006), 64.
28. Johnson, *Nemesis*, 45.
29. See, for example, John De Graaf, David Wann, and Thomas H. Naylor, *Affluenza* (San Francisco: Berrett-Koehler, 2002).

Chapter 8 A Pedagogy of Peace

1. See, for example, David Berliner, James Bell, and Bruce Biddle, *The Manufactured Crisis* (New York: Perseus, 1996); Gerald Bracey's notes on the distortions and inaccuracies of the current discussion on education can be found as a regular feature of *Kappan Magazine*. See also Gerald W. Bracey, *Setting the Record Straight* (Portsmouth, NH: W. W. Heinemann, 2004).
2. Svi Shapiro (ed.), *Education and Hope in Troubled Times* (New York: Routledge, 2009).
3. Others who have written powerfully about this, as well as myself, have found the following individuals to be influential: Michael Lerner, Cornel West, Henry Giroux, David Purpel, Alex Molnar, Jim Wallis, Riane Eisler, David Korten, Bell Hooks, Jean Kilbourne, and Douglas Kellner.
4. In the use of the term *Parhessia* I am indebted to Cornel West and his discussion of it in his book, *Democracy Matters* (New York: Penguin, 2005).

5. Maxine Greene, *The Dialectic of Freedom* (New York: Teachers College Press, 1988).
6. Herbert Marcuse, *Essay on Liberation* (Boston: Beacon Press, 1969).
7. Dan O'Meara, cited in Xolela Mangcu, *To the Brink: The State of Democracy in South Africa* (University of Kwa Zulu-Natal Press, 2008), 119.
8. Jeffrey Sachs, *The End of Poverty* (New York: Penguin, 2005).
9. Barack Obama, *The Audacity of Hope* (New York: Vintage, 2008).
10. Walter Benjamin, *Illuminations* (New York: Schocken Books, 1969).
11. Thich Nhat Hanh, *Peace Begins Here* (Berkeley, CA: Parallax, 2004), 116.
12. Ibid., 105; the word s*angha* is from the Sanskrit language and refers to a community or assembly with common vision.
13. Ibid., 98.

INDEX

9–11, 41, 157, 174, 196

Absolute monarchies, 136
Abu Ghraib, 159
Accountability, 7–8, 180
Adiaphorization, 119
Affirmation, 106
Affirmative Action, 89
Afghanistan, 120, 142, 155, 175
Africa, 51, 88, 90, 149
African-American, 19, 76, 77, 86, 126
Al Qaida, 157
Alienated, 105
America, 127
American, 113
American Christianity, 150
American Revolution, 78
Amin, Idi, 91
Amos (Hebrew Prophet), 77
Anderson, Benedict, 134
Anonymity, 104
Anti-semitism, 19, 35, 90, 107, 119, 122
Anxiety, 3, 7, 20, 21, 29, 42, 56, 60, 65, 68, 70, 83, 140, 145, 148, 184
Anyon, Jean, 59, 161
Anytown Program, 40
Apartheid, 2, 36, 46, 47, 85–86, 101–102, 105, 108, 159, 200
Apartheid divide, 85
The Apprentice, 63
Arab, 109, 113, 114
Arabic, 37

Arabs, 201
Arendt, Hannah, 158, 159, 164
Argentin (ian mothers), 126
Argentina, 159
Armageddon, 151
Asia, 90
Athlete/Athletics, 50–52, 65, 167
Atlantic, The (magazine), 104
Atwater, Ann, 25
Audacity of Hope, 197
Auschwitz, 103, 111, 127, 197
Auschwitz, Kingdom of, 104
Australia, 51
Axis of Evil, 149

Banality of Evil, 158, 159, 161
Barack Obama, 113
Barber, Benjamin, 137, 138
Baudrillard, Jean, 56
Bauman, Zygmunt, 110, 119, 140, 147
Beckton, Joe, 25
Bell Curve, 58, 70
Benjamin, Walter, 197
Berger, John, 173
Berliner, David, 180
Bible, 21, 68, 75
Birkenau, 103
Black, 117
Black (South Africans), 108
Blair, Tony, 156
Blowback, 170
Bolt, Usain, 50
Bordeaux, 103
Borlaug, Dr., 75

Bosnia, 11
Bowling for Columbine, 173
Bracey, Gerald, 180
Britain, 51, 91, 137, 156
British, 155, 156
British Foreign Secretary, 112
B'tselem Elohim, 195
Buddhist, 201
Buddhist teacher, 205
Bulletin of Atomic Scientists, 174
Bush, George W, 120, 133, 142, 149, 174
Bush Administration, 58, 120, 156, 157, 166, 175

Cambodia, 159, 169
Camus, Albert, 191
Cape Town, 1, 47, 107, 182, 191
Capitalism, 2, 4, 7, 14–15, 45, 52–53, 56, 63, 80, 82, 90, 112, 122, 124, 126, 136, 137, 138, 141, 170, 185
Carter, Jimmy, 46
Cash nexus, 122
Catholic, 25, 36, 37, 116
CBS, 172
Central America, 149, 156
Chain of being, 134, 196
Chambers, gas, 103
Cheat, 3, 5, 63, 64, 70
Chechnya, 120
Chile, 27, 81, 159, 169
China, 141
Chinese, 51, 172
Christian, 114, 196, 201
Christianity, 41, 138, 140
Christians, 139
Church, Catholic, 116
Civilized world, 113
Class inequality, 107
Clements, Howard, 25
CNN, 172, 173
Colbert, Stephen, 34
Cold War, 175
Collateral damage, 113
Colombia, 169

Color, skin, 107
Columbine, 173
Columbine, Bowling for, 173
Columbine, shootings, 173
Columbine High School, 62
Command, special, 103
Common sense, 164
Communism, 169
Conform/Conformity, 6–7, 30, 131, 159, 162, 164, 166, 186
Congo, 91
Congress, 176
Constitution, South African, 121
Constitution, U.S., 121
Consumer, 2, 4, 16, 52–53, 96, 126, 138, 139, 143, 146, 147, 148, 150, 151, 152, 182, 183, 188
Consumerism, 14, 136, 138, 139, 144, 146, 148, 150, 151, 203
Consumption, 2, 138, 144, 145, 152, 204
Contact hypothesis, 11
Cooperation, 71, 72, 203, 204, 208, 209, 211
Corporate, 8, 51, 92, 123, 137, 139, 140, 145, 157, 173, 174, 176, 214, 215
Corporation, 3, 53, 54, 64, 81, 155, 203
Correctness, political, 107
Covenant, 18–19
Crime, 1, 2, 20, 21, 86, 90, 177, 200
Critical pedagogy, 165
Critical social theory, 186
Critical utopianism, 186
Cronkite, Walter, 172
Crwys-Williams, Jennifer, 1
Cuba, 51
Culture, Western, 113
Curriculum, 6–8, 23, 31, 43, 58, 60, 83, 124, 125, 131, 148, 161, 173, 182, 187, 188, 191, 192

Index

Dalai Lama, 36
Damage, collateral, 113
Darwinian, 31
de Graaf, John, 144, 145, 146, 148
Defense, Department of, 174, 175
Democracy/Democratic, 1–2, 6, 7, 9–10, 13, 28, 37–38, 45, 78, 82, 84, 87, 90–92, 100–101, 107, 108, 113, 136, 137, 143, 149, 150, 153, 154, 156, 158, 160, 164, 167, 169, 170, 176, 187, 194, 195, 196
Democrat, 8, 107
Department of Defense, 174, 175
Depression, 14, 60, 65, 83, 130, 131, 145, 148
De-skill, 22
Despair, 14, 22, 46, 47, 91–92, 98, 184, 200
Destruction, Mutually Assured, 119
Dewey, John, 16
Dialogue, 8, 28, 32, 39–43, 47, 161
Dignity, 106
Discourse, democratic, 107
Discourse, liberal, 107
Dissent, 165

Eagleton, Terry, 110
East, backward, 113
Egypt, 137, 199
Eichmann, Adolf, 19, 158, 159, 164
Eichmann in Jerusalem, 158
Einstein, Albert, 31
Eisenhower, President, 153, 159
Eisler, Riane, 54, 70, 71, 99, 161, 168
El Salvador, 169
Ellis, Tim, 25
Empathy, 32, 37, 40–41, 45–48, 71, 96, 179
Engaged pedagogy, 105
England, Gordon, 175
English Premier League, 65
Enron, 175
Entertainment, 5, 53, 55, 138, 145, 148, 163, 176, 191

Eritreans, 90
Es muss sein, 187
Ethiopia, 90
Ethnic identity, 130
Ethnicity, 107, 117
Europe, schools in, 180
European reason, 114
European Union, 141
Evolution, 32–33, 70–71, 78
Exceptionalist, 150
Existential emptiness, 132
Existential purpose, 134
Existential value, 106
Existentialism, 129
Exodus, 21–22
Exploitation, 108

F-35, 175
Faith, 199
Farewell Address, 153
Fascism, 24
Fatalism, 98–99, 198–199
Fear, 2–6, 13, 17, 18–21, 34–36, 39, 41, 47, 49, 60, 64, 66–68, 72, 75, 87–91, 148, 154, 159, 165, 174, 181, 186, 190, 200, 201, 202
Federal Trade Commission, 148
Feminism, 79, 139
Feuerverger, Grace, 38–39
Final Solution, 103
Forgiveness, 46–48, 102, 200, 201
Foucault, Michel, 33
Fox, James Allen, 63
France, 91
Franti, Michael, 41
Freedom fighter, 113
Freire, Paulo, 16, 161, 189
French Revolution, 78
Friedrich, Otto, 104
Fromm, Erich, 146
Fundamentalism, militant, 137

Gabel, Peter, 56
Gandhi, Mahatma, 19, 24, 70–71, 75, 166, 205

Gas chambers, 103
Gaza, 108, 120
General Dynamics, 175
General Electric, 53
Genesis, 18
Genetic makeup, 106
Genocidal regime, 169
Genocidal treatment, 170
Genocide, Nazi, 111, 127
Genocide, Rwanda, 159
Germans, 172
Germany, 51, 91
Gilbert, Daniel, 28
Giroux, Henry, 16, 59, 100, 148, 161, 185
Givat Haviva Institute, 40
Global capitalism, 137, 138
Global citizens, 160
Global domination, 143
Globalization, 4, 14, 20, 140
God, 109
God-anointed role, 141
God-inspired purpose, 143
Goffman, Erving, 56
Goodman, Ellen, 145
Gordimer, Nadine, 105
Goyim, 35
Greene, Maxine, 59, 130, 131, 161, 164, 187
Grey, Elizabeth Dodson, 58
Guatemala, 169
Guns, 5, 20, 21, 35, 62

Habermas, Jurgen, 135, 136
Hamas, 109
Harrison, Beverley, 18
Hebrew, 17, 19, 37, 77–78, 182, 184
Hebrew bible, 195
Hedges, Chris, 129, 149
Hegel, 111
Hegemonic culture, 164
Hegemony, 17, 36, 79, 81, 164
Hermes, 189
Heschel, Abraham, 17, 165, 204
Hidden Curriculum, 58, 83, 191
Hinduism, 138

Hindus, 139
Hiroshima, 27
Hitler, Adolph, 27
Hoess, Rudolf, 103
Hofstadter, Richard, 171
Holland, 91
Holocaust, 19, 39
Homophobia/Homophobic, 20, 41–42, 79, 82, 94, 107, 108, 185
Honduras, 169
hooks, bell, 161
Hope, 197
Hopi, 191
Human dignity, 165
Human Relations Commission, 25
Human rights, 107
Hundred-year war, 108
Hurricane Katrina, 142
Hussar, Bruno, 37–38
Hutus, 90

Ibo, 90
Identity, ethnic, 130
Identity, national, 130
Identity, politics of, 107
Ideology, 7, 59, 61, 64, 67–69, 84, 86
Ideology, power of, 166
Idi Amin, 91
Imaginary communities, 134
India, 141
Indian wars, 170
Individualism, 4, 14, 94
Indonesia, 90, 81, 169
Institute of Economics and Peace, 181
Internalization/Internalize, 18, 22, 79, 93, 130
Internet, 116, 119, 120, 163, 166, 177
Invisibility, 12–13, 15, 62, 94, 105, 106
Iran, 27, 81, 137, 149, 169
Iran-Iraq war, 157
Iraq, 81, 116, 120, 137, 142, 153, 155, 157, 169, 175

Iraq War, 68, 176
Iraqi oil fields, 157
Iraqis, 157
Ireland, 11, 189
Irish, 172
Isaiah, 204
Islam, 27, 91, 92, 137
Islamic, 91, 109
Islamic Revolution, 149
Israel, 11, 137, 169, 189, 201
Israeli Jews, 109
Israeli settlers, 169
Israelis, 179, 201
Israelites, 199

Jackson, Michael, 177
Japan, schools in, 180
Japanese, 172
Jerusalem, 158
Jesus, 68, 199
Jew, 158, 201
Jewish, 91, 114, 196
Jewish prisoners, 103
Jews, 11, 65, 108, 111, 117, 139, 142, 189, 197
Jews, Israeli, 109
Jews of Nigeria, 90
Jihad, 138, 139
Jihad vs. McWorld, 137
Jim Crow, 46, 76
Joe the Plumber, 88
Johnson, Chalmers, 170, 174, 175
Johnson, Shaun, 1
Jordan, River, 197
Josephson Institute of Ethics, 63
Judaism, 138
Justice, social, 160, 161

Kashmir, 189
Katrina, Hurricane, 142
Keillor, Garrison, 58
Kenya, 90
Khmer Rouge, 169
Kikuyu, 90
King, Martin Luther, 199
Kingdom of Auschwitz, 104

Kohn, Alfie, 59
Korea, 51
Korten, David, 54–55, 140
Koyaanissqatsy, 191
Kozol, Jonathan, 85–86
Kuhn, Thomas, 33

Laos, 90
Lasch, Christopher, 66
Latin America, 81
Lebanon, 81
The Left Hand of God, 133
Lerner, Michael, 39, 133, 140, 142
Levinas, Emmanuel, 96, 109
Liberal democracy, 136
Liberal discourse, 107
Liberation, 2, 21–22, 88, 93, 102
Lifton, Robert Jay, 141
Lockheed Martin Corporation, 175
Loewen, James, 170
Lurie, Alison, 83
Lyotard, Jean-Francois, 33

Maalouf, Amin, 36
Macedo, Donaldo, 161
MAD (Mutually Assured Destruction), 119
Makeup, genetic, 106
Malaysia, 90
Mandela, Nelson, 105
Manichean world view, 12, 26, 27, 49, 132, 139, 142
Marcuse, Herbert, 135, 188
Marx, Karl, 77, 122, 136
Marxist, 106, 129
Material injustice, 106
Matriarchal values, 168
McIntosh, Peggy, 81–83
McLaren, Peter, 161
McWorld, 138
Media, 11, 14, 41, 50–51, 53, 62, 76
Mega-churches, 133
Meritocracy/Meritocratic, 82, 84, 85
Messenger of the Gods, 189
Middle East, 137, 140

Miliband, David, 112
Militant fundamentalism, 137
Militarism, *see* War/Military/
    Militarism
Military-industrial complex, 159
Molnar, Alex, 148
Monarchies, absolute, 136
Monbiot, George, 153
Moore, Michael, 55, 173–174
Moral relativism, 140
Mosaddeg, Mohammed, 137
Muslim, 113, 114, 137, 140, 172, 196, 201
Muslims, 91, 117, 139, 142
Mutually Assured Destruction, 119
My Lai, 159

NAFTA, 95
National identity, 130
National Priorities Project, 174
National purpose, 143
National security state, 176
Nationalism, 149
Natural rights, 107
Nazi, 111, 159, 164
Nazi Europe, 158
Nazi genocide, 91, 111, 127
Nazi/Nazism, 19, 24, 35, 36, 91
NBC, 50
Nemesis, 175
The New Yorker, 158
Newlands, 1
NGO, 198
Nicaragua, 27, 81, 169
Nieto, Sonia, 161
Nietzsche, Friedrich, 34
Nigeria, 90
No Child Left Behind, 57
Nobel literature laureate, 105
Nobel Prize, 38, 47, 75, 105, 155
North Carolina, 10, 40, 58, 174
Northrup Grumman, 175
Norway, 11

Obama, Barack, 75, 113, 176, 177, 179, 197
Obama, Michelle, 76
Obama, President, 137
Olympic, 49–52
O'Meara, Dan, 189
Organisation for Economic Cooperation and Development, 89
Orwell, George, 121

Pahlavi, Shah, 137
Pakistanis, 91
Palestine, 201
Palestinian people, 169
Palestinian problem, 137
Palestinians, 11, 108, 179, 189
Palmer, Parker, 161
Panama, 81, 169
Parrhesia, 185, 186, 187
Passover, 197, 199
Patch, Harry, 49
Peace Begins Here, 179
Peace education, 8, 10–11, 23–25, 47, 93
Pedagogy, 12, 15, 22, 40, 43, 70, 102
Pentagon, 174
Pharaoh, 93, 197
Phelps, Michael, 50
Philippines, 90, 169
Pickett, Kate, 80
Poland, 103
Political correctness, 107
Politics of identity, 107
Popular culture, 163
Positivist, 124
Post-positivist, 162
President Eisenhower, 159
President Franklin Roosevelt, 193
President Obama, 137
Prime Minister, 156
Prisoners, Jewish, 103
Profit, 3, 51, 53, 122–124, 147, 155, 170, 203–204

Protestant, 36, 37
Public Relations, 56
Purpel, David, 59, 82, 161, 165

Rage, 2–3, 5, 12–14, 41, 47, 62, 65, 78, 80, 83, 89, 92, 109, 110, 130, 136, 137, 139, 190, 200, 203
Raleigh, 174
Reagan, 133
Reality TV, 55, 56, 188
Recession, 76, 143, 193
Religious right, 133
Religious traditions, 106
Republican, 8
Right Hand of God, 142
Rights, human, 107
Rights, natural, 107
Rituals, 51
Rizek, Rayek, 39
Roche, James, 175
Rome, 103
Roosevelt, Franklin, 193
Rorty, Richard, 33
Russia, 51, 90
Russians, 172
Rwanda, 11, 90, 159
Ryan, William, 87

Sachs, Jeffrey, 193
Sacks, Jonathan, 4, 5, 16, 18
Saddam Hussein, 113, 149, 157
Said, Edward, 113
Salaam, 185
Salonika, 103
Sandel, Michael, 16
Sangha, 199, 201, 202
Sartre, Jean-Paul, 129
SAT, 59, 84, 184
Saudi Arabia, 137
Scarcity, 13, 68, 69, 87, 130, 191
School of the Americas, 81
Schor, Juliet, 144, 145
Security, 1, 3, 5, 9, 14, 29, 89, 92
Seeds of Peace, 40

Segregation, 20, 46, 102, 108
Senate, U.S., 157
September 11, 2001, 112, 141, 170
Shah (of Iran), 169
Shah of Iran, 149
Shah Pahlavi, 137
Shalom/shalem, 19, 182, 185
Shiva, Vandana, 92
Sierra Leone, 91
Socialism, 88
Socratic, 32
Sonderkommando, 103
South Africa, 1, 2, 3, 11, 36, 37, 46, 47, 101, 105, 107, 108, 159, 189, 200
South African Constitution, 121
South America, 149
Southern New Hampshire University, 179
Soviet Union, 51, 141
Soweto, 105
Spain, 11
Sparks, Allister, 105
Special Command, 103
Sport/Sports/Sporting, 5, 50–52, 63, 65, 67, 72, 83, 107, 148, 164, 177, 191
Springer, Jerry, 5
Sri Lanka, 189
Standardization/Standardized, 9, 31, 58
Stiglitz, Joseph, 155
Stockholm International Peace Research Institute, 175
Stress, 7, 60, 124, 136, 139, 144, 146, 148, 154
Students of color, 104
Superpower syndrome, 141
Survivor, 63

Table Mountain, 1
Talmud, 15, 18, 126
Talmudic study, 165
Tarfon, Rabbi, 24

Index

Technology, 4, 10, 48, 52, 53, 92, 99, 119, 125, 131, 152, 181, 203
Teets, Peter B., 174
Terkel, Studs, 26
Terror, War on, 112, 113
Terrorism, 155
Terrorists, 112
Tests/Testing/Standardized Testing, 6–9, 30–31, 58–60, 63, 65, 67, 83, 124, 131, 132, 162, 163, 180, 181, 186, 192, 202
Thailand, 90
Thich Nhat Hanh, 46–47, 179, 200, 201
Tikkun, 185
Tikkun Olam, 18, 184, 185
Tolle, Eckhart, 49
Torah, 35
Torres, Dara, 50
Traditions, religious, 106
Transitional justice, 101
Transkei, 105
TRC, 101
Trotsky, Leon, 153
Truman, Harry, 27
Truth and Reconciliation, 159
Truth and Reconciliation Commission, 46, 200
Truth-telling, 40
Turks, 91
Tutsi, 90
Tutu, Desmond, 47–48, 101, 182

U.S. Constitution, 121
U.S. Senate, 157
U.S. support for..., 137
Ubuntu, 182, 183, 185
Uganda, 91
Unbearable Lightness of Seeing, 191
UNICEF, 55, 212
Unilateral power, 143
Unipolar world, 140

United Nations, 21, 89, 156
United Nations Declaration of Human Rights, 121

Vietnam, 90, 169
Vietnam War, 156, 159
Virginia Tech shootings, 62–63

Walker, Alice, 75
Wall Street, 140, 180
Walzer, Michael, 21–22
War, hundred-year, 108
War, Iran-Iraq, 157
War, Vietnam, 156, 159
War is a Force that Gives us Meaning, 129
War/Military/Militarism, 6, 7, 10–11, 14–15, 17, 19–24, 27, 36–38, 44–45, 49–51, 53, 64, 68, 81, 87–88, 90, 92, 108–109, 112–114, 116, 119–121, 126, 129–130, 132, 141–143, 145, 149–152, 153–158, 159–160, 164, 166–177, 185–186, 188, 189, 194, 197–198, 203–204
War on Terror, 112, 113
Wars, Indian, 170
Welch, Sharon, 140
West, Cornel, 16, 96, 161
White, Thomas E., 175
Wilde, Oscar, 123
Wilkinson, Richard, 80
Williams, Raymond, 22, 61
Woods, Tiger, 177
World Bank, 193
World Institute for Development Economics Research, 193
World Trade Center, 196
World War I, 49
World War II, 27, 145

Zinn, Howard, 170

GPSR Compliance

The European Union's (EU) General Product Safety Regulation (GPSR) is a set of rules that requires consumer products to be safe and our obligations to ensure this.

If you have any concerns about our products, you can contact us on

ProductSafety@springernature.com

In case Publisher is established outside the EU, the EU authorized representative is:

Springer Nature Customer Service Center GmbH
Europaplatz 3
69115 Heidelberg, Germany

www.ingramcontent.com/pod-product-compliance
Lightning Source LLC
LaVergne TN
LVHW051913060526
838200LV00004B/123